CHRISTIAN ETHICS

CHRISTIAN ETHICS

A Case Method Approach

Robert L. Stivers
Christine E. Gudorf
Alice Frazer Evans
Robert A. Evans

ORBIS BOOKS
Maryknoll, New York 10545

The Catholic Foreign Mission Society of America (Maryknoll) recruits and trains people for overseas missionary service. Through Orbis Books, Maryknoll aims to foster the international dialogue that is essential to mission. The books published, however, reflect the opinions of their authors and are not meant to represent the official position of the society.

Published by Orbis Books, Maryknoll, NY 10545

Manufactured in the United States of America

Library of Congress Cataloging-in-Publication Data

Christian ethics: a case method approach/Robert L. Stivers ... [et al.].
    p. cm.
   Includes bibliographies.
   ISBN 0-88344-424-0
   1. Christian ethics—Case studies. I. Stivers, Robert L., 1940-
BJ1251.C49 1989
241—dc19   89-30543
                                       CIP

Contents

for Friday

10/13

PART VII
SEXUALITY

10/15

PART VIII
LIFE AND DEATH

Introduction

Christian Ethics and the Case Method

The student pensively approached the case teacher after class and finally mustered some words: "That case really hit home. The characters were different, but they could just as well have been my family. Not long ago we went through exactly the same thing." Another student, laying back for the first to finish, finally edged up and joined in: "And the question that woman in the front row asked about euthanasia, that's the precise question I wanted to ask but couldn't find the right words."

These two statements, often encountered in one form or another by case teachers, reflect something enduring in human behavior: while every individual is unique, ethical problems and questions about what is right or good tend to recur. These recurrences and the dilemmas they represent can be recorded and replayed to help others learn to make better ethical choices. Case studies are one way to capture past occurrences, and case teaching is a method to enable individuals and groups to make better choices.

This book is about making ethical choices and forming Christian character. It contains sixteen cases arranged under eight part titles. Accompanying each case study is a commentary by one of the authors that is intended to aid understanding of the case from a Christian ethical perspective. The purpose of the book is to offer an approach to contemporary social issues and to underscore the importance of the Christian ethical dimension in these issues and in character formation. The authors are enthusiastic about the case approach as one way to aid in the process of making ethical decisions and forming character.

THE PAPER CHASE

Some readers may wonder whether the authors' enthusiasm for cases is warranted. Several years ago the movie and television series *The Paper Chase* stamped the case method with a popular but mistaken image. The setting in the Harvard Law School was establishment, hierarchical, and formal. The teacher was dour, crusty, and demanding. The students were overworked, underrewarded, and overambitious.

The task of recommending such an abrasive approach to those who teach Christian ethics would be imposing. Few colleges, seminaries, or churches fit the mold of the Harvard Law School. By comparison most teachers of Christian ethics are soft touches. Few theological students are as ambitious or crafty as those in the drama. The title of the movie and series underscores that contrast. It conjures up the image of overburdened students questing after reams of detailed irrelevance disgorged by a paper-drunk photocopy machine.

But this book does not recommend the abrasive version of the case method employed in *The Paper Chase*. Rather it offers the method itself, and the potential of the method for teaching and learning about Christian ethics. The authors are confident this potential can be realized. Since the method was first developed at the Harvard Business School, it has moved far beyond Harvard, receiving wide acceptance nationally in business and law schools. In the past two decades it has also been successfully adapted to religious studies. This proven track record and personal experience with the case approach are the basis of the authors' enthusiasm.

MAKING ETHICAL DECISIONS

Ethical decisions are made on a number of levels. On one level decision making seems to flow easily. Individuals follow their gut-level intuitions and muddle through situations reactively. This approach can be effective if the individual is caring and the situation is uncomplicated and more or less personal. It is less effective in complex social situations and can be disastrous when the individual is uncaring, ethically immature, or shut up in a small social world.

On another level making ethical choices is both difficult and complex. Logical and abstract reasoning comes hard to some. In certain situations the chooser is bombarded by a bewildering array of conflicting and complex facts. Finding relevant ethical norms from the tradition to apply to particular situations is difficult at best and can easily be shortcut or sidetracked with simplistic proof texting.

Once relevant norms are discovered, their application is tricky. The norms frequently offer conflicting counsel. Indeed, this is the primary reason that ethical decisions are problems. There is seldom a straight path from a single norm to an easy decision. If there were, no problem would exist. The decision maker is most often caught between equally attractive or unattractive alternatives. Worse, the path is usually made treacherous by intersecting problems and relationships which complicate situations and suggest "exceptions" to rules. Lastly, and hardly necessary to point out, relationships themselves are tricky. The chooser possesses a limited freedom and is quite capable of being arbitrary in its use.

The case method of instruction recounts past occurrences in order to assist individuals and groups through complexity to good or at least better choices. Cases help sort out the choices and give the student an opportunity to move down the path from the identification of norms through the maze of intersecting facts and exceptions to the selection of the best alternative.

CASES AND THE ELEMENTS OF AN ETHICAL DECISION

There are many types of case studies. They range from imagined dilemmas, to in-depth histories of organizations, to one-page "verbatims" which report a single incident. The cases in this volume are descriptions of actual situations as seen by a writer usually through the eyes of a participant. The situations normally entail a decision to be made which is left sufficiently open to allow students to enter the process of decision making.

Such a method is well-suited to the study of Christian ethics, for it drives the student to take the insights of tradition and theory, apply them to an actual situation, and then reconsider the adequacy of theory and tradition. Involved in this movement from theory to practice and back to theory are all the elements which go into an ethical decision.

The Normative Tradition

The first of these elements is the tradition, including insights from the Bible, historical and constructive theology, church positions, and one's own community of believers. The Christian tradition is the main source of norms in Christian ethics, although secular and other religious sources may inform those ethics.

The process of deriving norms from the tradition is complex and frequently abused. In actuality the tradition is many different traditions, each with its special nuances. Finding in these various historical traditions consistent ethical guidelines which also apply to the twentieth century is not as simple as it may first appear.

The appropriate way to go about finding out what the Bible or any other authoritative text has to offer is first to study the text prayerfully with consciously chosen interpretive schemes. Further, the text must be understood within its own context. Once these steps have been taken the text must be compared with similar texts in order to establish dominant themes, and those themes must be checked against more encompassing theological understandings of the community of faith. The themes then become guiding norms to be applied to present situations, which always exist in a time and culture alien to those in which the text was produced. None of these steps is either neat or clean.

Among abuses, especially with the Bible, proof texting is one of the most troublesome. Proof texting is understood here as using an unexamined text to support what is believed on other grounds. The method is simple and convenient: find an isolated verse or two which somehow relate to the decision, make a quick interpretive guess, and let those addressed assume you have authority for your point. Neat and clean, except that it often twists the texts and leads to poor decisions.

The teachings of the traditions on nonviolence are a good illustration of the complexity of deriving and applying norms. The many texts having to do with peacemaking in the life of Jesus, when studied carefully, establish a consistent picture of a man in whose life nonviolence was a dominant approach. Some texts suggest he might have been willing to make exceptions, but none are conclusive. Nonviolence is thus normative in the Gospels, and when that is coupled with the Old Testament understanding of *shalom* and the theological understanding of God's love, the result is sound authority for the pacifist who applies the norm without exception.

To some, however, the texts in Deuteronomy, Joshua, and Judges that picture God as demanding violence during the conquest of the land give authority for crusades to stamp out evil. Nonviolence is normative except when evil is obvious and threatening. To others, Jesus' equally consistent support for the poor and social justice means violence is permissible if certain strict criteria of justifiability are met. Thus while all agree that nonviolence is normative, in fact the various traditions stress different elements in the Bible and apply the norm in quite different ways. The case "Vietnam's Children" is a good illustration of this.

All this attention to complexity is not to suggest that finding a normative basis and applying it consistently are impossible. Were this so, there would be no Christian ethics, and the Bible would be irrelevant for Christian life. Rather it is intended to help avoid oversimplification, to indicate that a range of positions have authority, and to counsel integrity and toleration in ethical debate.

Theory and Fact

A normative basis is not sufficient unto itself, since the tradition does not address all aspects of reality. Scientific theories which attempt to interpret empirical facts must be added. Both theories and facts are essential in ethics because they give understanding and empirical grounding to those in situations in which ethical decisions must be made. Without theories and facts, norms wander around in confusion, unable to inform the situation.

To illustrate the relation of norms, theories, and facts, consider poverty in the Third World. Approximately five hundred million people are seriously malnourished in a world with more than enough food to go around. This is a fact. The numbers, however, only indicate magnitude. Economic and political theories are necessary to give meaning to the numbers and suggest alternative courses of action. Norms, such as Christianity's concern for the poor, make these numbers a scandal and are the basis for selecting among competing economic theories and alternative courses of action.

Or consider the role of biological theory in the case "Snake in the Grass." Theories of evolution, genetic structure, and ecological balance give meaning to raw data about species extinction and alert communities to the consequences of reducing the gene pool and disturbing biotic communities. The norms of stewardship and care for the earth turn the realities of species extinction and biological equilibrium into moral problems.

In all this cases provide a point of contact between empirical fact on the one hand and tradition and theory on the other. In addition, the insights of tradition and theory need actual cases to mark their limitations and test their validity. Actual cases, in turn, need tradition, theory, and empirically established facts to provide understanding and direction.

Cases encourage students to give moral principles, facts, and theories a work out, so to speak. Not quite the same as being in an ethical dilemma oneself, cases are a good substitute and as close as teachers and students can sometimes get to a particular problem. They also offer the critical distance which is often missing when a dilemma is one's own. Such critical distance keeps the dialogue between theory and practice alive.

Contexts and Relationships

The immediate situation of a case, the larger context, and the relationships found in it provide the setting for a particular ethical decision. The cases in this volume present actual moral dilemmas in the lives of real people. They are not fabricated.

A well-written case seldom presents a neat situation where decisions flow easily from norms. Theory does not always apply. Norms conflict. Individuals display a normal range of cantankerous behavior. In other words, there are no right answers, and students are faced with both the possibilities and the problems of being ethical as they are forced into the vortex between ideal and real in considering actual human problems.

Once in this vortex students and teachers discover the importance of additional factors found in situations. The individuals in a case often seem to have conflicting motives and goals. The means used to strive toward and attain goals sometimes seem questionable or not justified by the ends sought. The consequences of different courses of action must be weighed against each other and put into relation with motives, means, and ends. A choice between following principles and seeking effective compromises is often inherent in decisions.

Also in this vortex students and teachers encounter the vagaries of personal relationships and further problems with the exclusive use of norms to guide action. In recent years relationships and what is being called "embodied reason" have come into prominence in the study of ethics. Accompanying this newfound importance has been criticism of abstract dualisms, such as mind and matter or spirit and flesh, which tend in the tradition to devalue women and minorities. Also criticized has been the heavy stress on abstract norms and their deductive application in decisions to the exclusion of relationships.

While those who offer this criticism do not reject abstract distinctions and norms, they are urging decision makers also to consider the way many have traditionally made choices, that is, through reason linked to experience.

To make these distinctions clearer an illustration from the actual teaching of the case "Rigor and Responsibility" is useful. The teacher on one occasion used this case to demonstrate different modes of thinking. After some preliminaries, he asked the group what norms from the Christian tradition applied to the case. The teacher found the responses, mostly from men, to be predictable, logical, and concise. Stewardship of resources, care for the poor, and the seductive nature of possessions were each developed with precision.

The teacher then asked two women to sit in front of the class and discuss with each other the dilemma of building a vacation cabin which faces the couple in the case. No instructions were given except to say they were to reflect on the case. There was little if any mention of norms. What dominated was the relationship between husband and wife and how their decision would affect others in their lives.

The class did not immediately recognize the differences in the two approaches. When the teacher pointed out what he had intended and in fact had seen, there was general recognition and agreement that both deductively applied norms and inductively embodied reason are valid and contribute to making decisions.

But each has dangers as well. The exclusive use of deductively applied norms runs the danger of rigidity and legalism. Changed contexts and new relationships are ignored. Love between persons and the abnormal aspects of actual situations tend to get lost as traditional norms become the exclusive guide to decisions. The much used example of truth telling which leads to loss of innocent life is an obvious example.

The opposite is true of pursuing experience-based reason to the exclusion of larger contexts and norms. Students and teachers tend to lose themselves in relationships and the processes of everyday living. When they do, they lose sight of the larger context in which they exist and the wisdom of the ages embodied in traditional norms.

A vortex in nature, although more noticeable because of its swirling action, is always part of a larger air mass or body of liquid, as in a cyclone or a whirlpool. So also relationships have contexts, and the context is not always obvious. "Mary Gardner's Fourth Pregnancy" presents a woman faced with the decision of whether or not to terminate a pregnancy. The case does not, however, make reference to the heated national debate over elective abortion and its relevance for the freedom of women. In this instance students may be left to discover the larger context. In other cases the teacher may want to point it out. Whichever, both students and teachers should recognize that relationships always have larger contexts.

Much the same can be said for norms. As with cyclones in nature, the human conditions which produce ethical problems tend to recur. No ethical problem is entirely novel. And as meteorologists are able to forecast the paths of cyclones with a fair degree of accuracy, so traditional norms predict, so to speak, the ethical path in most situations and contexts.

Method

This leads to the fourth element in making an ethical decision. Method is the way the elements of making an ethical decision are pulled together to reach a conclusion. No single method of relating norms, facts, theories, contexts, and relationships to each other and to specific situations can be called Christian. There are a number of methods, each with advantages. The authors have not tried to impose a particular method in either their approach to the cases or the commentaries which follow them. They are convinced that method is important, however, and that an adequate method touches base with each of the elements.

The case approach is conducive to the teaching of method. A specific case can be used to focus on method. Over the course of a semester or study series the teacher can use and ask students to use a single method so that they will acquire skill in employing that particular methodology. Alternatively, the teacher can employ several methods and request that students experiment with and evaluate each. Or finally, consciousness of method may be left to emerge from the process of doing ethical reflection.

The commentaries which follow each case are organized around the elements of making an ethical decision. The commentaries do not spell out how these elements are to be put together to reach a decision. The authors would be remiss, however, if they did not indicate a few typical approaches. Students can, of course, start with any of the elements, but the usual approach is to begin with and emphasize either norms or situations.

The approach which starts with and stresses norms is called the deontological approach. The word "deontological" comes from the Greek word *deon,* which means "binding," and refers to the study of duty and moral obligation. For the sake of simplicity it will be referred to as the normative approach.

The tendency in this approach is to let norms, rules, principles, standards, and ideals be decisive or binding in making choices. The degree of decisiveness that should be afforded to norms has been a matter of contention in Christian ethics. To call an approach normative means that it has a fairly high degree of decisiveness. Most of those who take a normative approach, however, are willing to admit some exceptions to norms occasioned by contextual and relational variations. Used in a flexible way, the normative approach is appropriate. Indeed, the authors are of a common mind that considerable attention should be given to norms in all situations.

The extreme, legalism, presents difficulties, however. Following rules to the exclusion of contextual and relational factors is a problem for Christians because of its rigidity, frequent heartlessness, and the obvious polemic against it in the sayings of Jesus and the epistles of Paul.

If legalism is one extreme at the end of a spectrum, and the normative approach is its valuable cousin, then making decisions solely on the basis of one's own experience and desires lies at the other end, and the situational approach is its cousin. The approach which starts with and emphasizes situational factors and consequences of acts goes under the names "situational," "consequentialist," or, in extreme form, "antinomian," from the Greek word *nomos,* which means "law." Antinomians are opposed to legal approaches to ethics.

For simplicity the term "situational" will be used to describe this approach. In it the decision maker looks to goals and seeks the best possible outcome. The contextual and relational elements which make situations different are taken very seriously. The situationalist is much more willing to admit exceptions and to grant greater weight to good results as opposed to consistency with norms.

Again the extreme is a problem. An approach which excludes norms, sees only the exceptions in situations, and relies on a "will it work" attitude denies the Bible, theology, and historical norms as guides in the Christian life. The extreme is hardly ever encountered and is bedeviled by sin. Its effective use requires very good people with very well developed moral habits, which is really to say people with ingrained norms.

That the extreme is a problem does not make a starting point in situations and an emphasis on special circumstances and consequences invalid. The authors are also in agreement that these elements must be factored into decisions.

What this leaves is a mixed approach which includes attention to norms and situations as well as the other elements of an ethical decision. Where the student starts may produce a distinctive emphasis, but as long as the other elements are factored in, ethical decision making can avoid the problems associated with the extremes.

The authors offer no magical formula for plugging in the elements. It would be helpful if they could. Unfortunately, differences in problems — each requiring its special analysis and weighting of elements — the guidance of the Holy Spirit, human freedom, and the unpredictability of situations rule out formulas. The authors can only urge that all of the elements be consistently considered in situations. Students and teachers must finally develop their own methods and make their own decisions.

Character Formation

Character formation is distinct from the elements which go into ethical decisions, but is important nonetheless to the ethics of decision making.

Character is formed in a complex interaction of self and society. Many elements contribute to this interaction: gender, social class, race, religion, ethnic background, family and institutional influences, specific experiences, worldviews, and loyalties. The interaction produces a distinct set of perceptions, habits, and intentions which dispose an individual or group to act in certain ways. The task of Christian character formation is to predispose individuals to act in situations in ways which are appropriate to Christian norms.

Central to any Christian understanding of character are the loving relationships between God and persons and among persons involved in faith. In ethical decisions no element is as important as faith. Rationality, the core of the preceding elements, keeps faith and love from wandering aimlessly down the path of good intentions. But reason easily degenerates into duplicity and hard heartedness without faith and love. As the saying goes, "Even the devil can quote scripture."

In doing ethics faith is the heart, reason the head, and Christian character the mature union of the two in love. Insofar as faith is a gift of grace, character cannot be taught. Insofar as character is a product of reason, it can be both taught and developed. Faith can change perceptions, habits, and intentions; good teaching and practice can develop them.

Few teachers have consciously used the case approach to form character. Case discussions are a good resource for character formation, however, and in the process of repeatedly making moral judgments, moral maturity does increase, or at least that has been the experience of case teachers. Character development may therefore be an unintended positive side-effect of the case method. Many teachers may prefer leaving it that way, but there is no reason why character development cannot be made more explicit.

The case approach is particularly conducive to what Paulo Freire calls education as liberation. For Freire a liberating education relies less on the transference of information than on the development of a critical consciousness which leads to the transformation of the learner's world. The transference of information is important to the communication of a collective memory; but if its goal and effect are only the "banking" of knowledge and the deposit of static, completed projects, character formation is seldom furthered.

Character formation in a Christian context is a process in which information becomes grist for liberation in Christ. Liberating education involves genuine dialogue between teacher and student. They are partners in education, teaching each other. The case approach promotes dialogue and in so doing encourages students and teachers to take what has been "banked" with other methods and appropriately "spend" it on critical consciousness.

FLEXIBILITY

Cases can be used to form character, to analyze problems, to teach method, to understand human relationships, to test theory, and so on. The case approach is flexible, and this flexibility makes the purpose of the teacher in using the method of great importance. Cases lend themselves to one or a multiplicity of purposes, and teachers need to be clear what they are trying to accomplish. Purpose should govern the selection of cases, how they are taught, and the outcome. This cannot be emphasized enough. Purpose governs use.

What the authors have not done and in fact cannot do is set the purpose for students and teachers. They can suggest a range of options, for example, introducing students to complex social issues, using cases as an entry into the tradition, the teaching of method, and the development of character; but selection must remain with the user. This also means that cases can be misused for the purpose of indoctrination and manipulation. Teachers and students should be aware of this, although misuse of method is not peculiar to the use of cases.

Flexibility has still another dimension. The case method is appropriate to a variety of learning situations from the classroom to church groups, to the small rump sessions found in coffee shops, dorms, and living rooms. Those who use the method regularly find that it stimulates discussion, breaks up the one-way flow of lectures, and eliminates the silence which often permeates abstract discussions. The method is dialogic and thus meets the needs of instructors and learners who prefer more dialogic approaches. But discussion is only the most frequent way cases are used, and discussion can be more or less structured by teachers depending on their purposes.

The method also has internal flexibility. Role plays, small groups, voting, and mini-lectures, a fuller description of which can be found in the Appendix, are only a few of the ways cases can be presented. Cases are not particularly good for presenting normative material and scientific theories. Experienced case teachers have found that lectures and outside reading are more appropriate for introducing this kind of material. Thus where significant background information is required for intelligent choices, the authors recommend using cases for the purposes of opening discussion of complex problems, of applying theory and the insights of tradition, of bringing closure and decision, and of encouraging the development of a critical consciousness.

ISSUES AND COMMENTARIES

The issues which the cases raise were given careful thought. The obvious issues are those designated by the part titles. A characteristic of a good case, however, is that it raises more than one issue. Some cases raise numerous issues. Thus besides the issues highlighted by the part titles there are what might be called connecting issues. There is no part that is explicitly about women and men, for example, yet at least six of the cases address problems associated with the changing relationships of contemporary women and men. No part is entitled "racism," but it is a central issue in at least three cases and a related one in several others.

The issues highlighted by the part titles were selected on the basis of current importance, lasting significance, availability of case material, and variety. Subjectivity, stemming from the authors' interests, no doubt also crept in.

The connecting issues are not so obvious and should be identified. In some instances these issues are as important as the highlighted issues. Women and men and racism are again examples. Other connecting issues are not as central and yet recur in a number of cases.

These connecting issues were selected on the basis of the same criteria as those highlighted in the part titles. A partial list includes: women and men; racism; land and resource use, including sustainability; national and global dimensions of poverty, wealth, consumption, and social justice; value consistency; the use of the Bible and the tradition in ethics; economic systems; corporate and government social responsibility; method; vocation; and character. Other issues could no doubt be identified and all of them could be developed with greater specificity. This list is merely to indicate that cases have multiple issues, and the rubric under which a case appears may not be the issue the teacher or student chooses to highlight.

There is still a third type of issue. Some of the commentaries speak, for example, of the coming reign of God. General criteria for decision making such as "the loving thing to do," "appropriateness," "the fitting," "following the way of the cross," or even the utilitarian theme "the greatest good for the greatest number" are common in ethical discussions. The commentaries are not organized around any such themes. To so organize the commentaries would in some cases have meant forcing a method on a case. There is no objection to organizing around such themes, and the authors occasionally use them, but teachers and students should make this choice.

The commentaries themselves are provided because past experience shows that interpretive summaries help students and teachers by providing leads into cases and avenues of analysis. These commentaries are not definitive interpretations. They are the observations of individuals trained in Christian theology, ethics, and the case method. They are not out of the same mold, although they do attempt to use the elements which go into an ethical decision as their starting point. There are stylistic differences and variations in emphasis resulting from their multiple authorship. They are intended as aids, not as substitutes for creative thinking, analysis, and decision making.

As mentioned before, the content of the interpretive summaries is not arbitrary. It is organized around the elements which go into making an ethical decision; however, for the sake of variety and flexibility it was decided that each commentary did not have to discuss elements in the same order. The commentaries are designed to touch base with these elements, although for a given case each element may not be covered with the same thoroughness and on occasion one may be omitted. Brevity has also governed design. In some of the cases analysis of one or more of the elements does not add significant insight. However, consistent consideration of the basic elements in ethical decision making is a commitment of the authors which has emerged from personal and teaching experience.

No doubt in these commentaries there are things omitted which teachers will want to add and points made which teachers will disagree with and want to comment upon critically.

THE NEW EMPHASIS ON ETHICS

This is the appropriate time for a vigorous new emphasis on ethics. Rapid social change and high mobility continue to tear people loose from their moorings in the extended family, settled communities, and traditional authority. The ethic of individualism, which in an effort to find new moorings in a sea of relativity made the self the center of moral deliberation and substituted feeling good for being good, has failed to deliver. This failure was predictable because the individual can neither feel good nor be moral apart from community, or at least that has been a key insight of Christianity from its beginnings.

There is no return to the simple past of extended families, settled communities, and traditional authority. This does not mean, however, that a new emphasis on ethics is doomed. New forms of community are emerging, and with the failure of individualism comes the need to find a center other than the self. For Christians that center is found in faith, the dynamic relationship to God and to others which is the foundation of both good feeling and good acts.

The case approach to teaching is dialogic and fosters interpersonal relationships. It is an approach which can be effectively used to teach the rudiments of ethical decision making, to form character, and to foster a philosophy of education as liberation. It is no panacea, just a very good tool to help invigorate a new and necessary emphasis upon ethics.

PART I

FAMILY

Case

Rigor and Responsibility

David Trapp hung up the phone and paused to reflect. He had just spoken with his good friend Al Messer. Al had offered to build the cabin. For several months David and his wife, Nancy, had considered building on the two acres of Clark Lake property left to them the year before by David's uncle. The nagging question returned to David. Now that the means were there, was it right to build?

David lived with his wife and two children on a quiet residential street on the outskirts of Toledo, Ohio. David was a lawyer with a downtown law firm which encouraged him to spend up to 15 percent of his time with clients who could not afford to pay. David always used the full allotment, considering it one way in which he could respond in faith to a pressing human need. David was also active in community affairs. He was vice-president of a statewide citizens' action lobby for more progressive taxation. Locally he was on the planning committee for the new community center and led adult education classes at his church. What troubled David the most was relating his sense of outrage at injustice to his enjoyment of good food, travel, and water sports.

Nancy Trapp was a buyer for an office furniture supplier. Her work involved increasing responsibility, and she found it difficult to leave unfinished business in the office. Recently she had been elected to a two-year term as president of the P.T.A. at the children's school. She had not foreseen the constant interruptions such a position would bring. The telephone never seemed to stop ringing, especially on the weekends when people knew they could find her at home.

Decision making was more or less a family affair with the Trapps. David and Nancy seldom disagreed on family matters and to David's recollection never on a major one. The children, Darcy and Ben, ages ten and eight, were consulted on major decisions and their voices taken into account.

Nathan Ferguson was the pastor of the local congregation in which the Trapps were active participants. Nathan had recently sold a piece of property he once had intended for recreational purposes. The proceeds from the sale had been donated to a church-sponsored halfway house for drug addicts in downtown Toledo. Shortly after Nathan had sold the property, he had begun to preach and teach in a low-key way on the subjects of possessions, overconsumption, and the materialism of American society. His eventual aim was to have his parishioners understand and consider forming a community based on the community in Jerusalem described in the opening chapters of the Book of Acts. He envisioned this community as one in which possessions would be held in common, consumption limited to basic necessities, and time and money given to programs among the poor that were based on a principle of self-reliance.

Clea Parks was David's colleague and an active participant in the church's adult education classes. What amazed David was how she could combine a concern for the poor with a way of living which allowed for occasional extravagances. Like David, Clea made full use of the firm's 15 percent allotment of time to work with poor clients. She was also on the board of the halfway house for drug addicts. In contrast she and her husband traveled to Bermuda for tennis and golf and to Sun Valley for skiing. This fall they were headed to the Holy Land for three weeks.

Shortly after the settlement of his uncle's will, which in addition to the two acres included enough cash to construct a modest cabin, David and Nancy discussed the matter of building. David expressed his ambivalence. He wondered about limits to self-indulgence. His desire for the cabin seemed to be locked in a struggle with his conscience. "How can we build a second place," he asked Nancy, "when so many people are living in houses without roofs or simply do not have a home at all? Can we in good conscience consume as heavily as we do while others are crying out for the very things we take for granted and consume almost at will?"

He also considered the matter of energy consumption. Again directing his reflections to Nancy, he said, "Think about the amount of energy used in construction and the going to and fro which will follow. Is this good stewardship of resources? Does it reflect our responsibility as American citizens to conserve fuel? And what sort of legacy are we leaving to our grandchildren, not to mention the lessons we are teaching our own children?"

He then rehearsed once again a pet theme: the excessive materialism of American society. "The Bible is quite explicit about possessions," he insisted. "Possessions can easily plug our ears to the hearing of God's word. A person cannot have two masters. The rich young ruler went away empty because he was unwilling to give up his possessions. The tax collector Zacchaeus is commended by Jesus for his willingness to give one-half of his possessions to the poor. And Jesus himself lived without possessions, commanding his disciples to do likewise."

He paused to think about this further. "Is it possible," he asked, "to avoid the spirit-numbing nature of possessions short of self-denial? And if I'm not going to opt for self-denial, then I at least have to ask in what way my consumption helps to perpetuate a system which is getting further and further away from the simplicity of Jesus." Again he paused, adding, "I guess it all boils down to the ethics of the Sermon on the Mount which Pastor Ferguson keeps talking about. Does the rigor of the sermon's ethic represent the only valid Christian option? Is it possible to live much in excess of basic needs if this ethic is taken seriously? And if we conclude that the sermon is not a new set of laws, what is its relevance anyway?"

Nancy's response was slow in coming both because she was sensitive to David's imaginative conscience, and because she wanted a place to separate herself from work and to teach the children the water sports she and David both enjoyed. "I can understand your commitment," she told him. "It's not a matter of guilt for you. But I just don't feel quite as strongly about those things as you do. The pressure has been getting worse lately, and I feel the need to share with you and the children in a more relaxed setting. The kids are getting older fast, and in a few years they'll be beyond the age where they'll be around to learn water sports."

"The materialism you are so concerned about," she went on to say, "has also made for creative new possibilities. It's not possessions themselves, but how we use them that makes a difference. It's the willingness to give, and we give enough what with 15 percent of your time and the giving of more than 10 percent of our incomes to church and charity. And think about what giving up our possessions will do. Without programs to transfer our abundance to the poor, giving things up will go for naught or perhaps contribute to the loss of someone's job. That is just the way things are. Think about Al Messer."

David had not been quite sure what to make of Nancy's comments. The old nagging questions kept coming back. His conscience just would not let him off easily.

Then Nathan Ferguson had begun his sermons and more recently had conducted a series of six sessions in the adult education class which David led. Nathan returned time and again to the teachings of Jesus: to the Sermon on the Mount, to the rich young ruler, to Zacchaeus, to the love communism of the early Christian community, and to the call of the prophets to justice and care for the poor. Nathan had not talked in a demanding or accusatory fashion, but neither had he let his parishioners off the hook. To David it seemed that Nathan's every thought had been directed straight at him.

At the office Clea hit him from the other side. At first she had merely commented on Nathan's sermons and classes. She thought Nathan was too perfectionistic. She appreciated his concern for the poor and his awareness of how possessions can close one's ears to the word of God. But she did not see how individual sacrifices produced the social change they all wanted.

She also had a contrasting view of the Sermon on the Mount. "We cannot live the sermon," she explained. "It's impossible, and anyway wasn't intended for everyone. Ethical rigor is right for folks like Nathan, but what most of us are called to is responsibility: to the right use of possessions, to a willingness to give, and to advocacy of justice in word and deed. The choice is not between self-indulgence and self-denial. There is a third option which is living responsibly with concern for all those issues Nathan talks about and still appreciating the finer things in life."

When David told her about the lake property and Nancy's needs, she had begun to push him a bit harder. "Come on, David," she would say, "it's all right with Jesus if you build. Jesus enjoyed life and participated in it fully. The church tradition is quite ambiguous on possessions and wealth." Another time she put it bluntly: "What right do you have to force your values and views on Nancy and the children?" Lately she had been twitting him. Just the other day with a big grin on her face she had called him "the monk."

Al Messer's call had jolted David and increased his sense that something had to give. Al had told David he could build the cabin out of used lumber and had found a place where he could get insulation and thermopane window glass at reduced prices. Al had also indicated he needed the work because business had been a bit slow lately.

Nancy entered the room and guessed what was troubling David. "I know what's bothering you," she said. "If we build, those old questions about the poor, materialism, and limits to consumption will nag at you. You might not even stick to a decision to build. If we don't build, you'll feel you have let the kids and me down and you'll miss your favorite sports. How can we decide this thing?"

Commentary

Rigor and Responsibility

Taken at face value this case is about Nancy and David Trapp struggling to decide whether or not to build a vacation cabin. But at a deeper and more comprehensive level the case is addressed to all non-poor Christians, and the issue is how to live as Christians in a materialistic world where ostentatious luxury and grinding poverty exist side by side. That the focus is us should not be lost as this commentary threads its way through David and Nancy's dilemma.

THE ISSUES

The superficial problem of putting a considerable inheritance to use in a second home quickly gives way in this case to an underlying central issue and a number of important related issues. The central issue stated in very general terms is this: How is a family which calls itself Christian to live? This general question can be given greater specificity by considering the title of the case. Should an affluent family give up what it has and follow the rigorous "holy poverty" of Jesus or is there an alternative called "responsible consumption," which stresses right use and good stewardship of material resources? Realizing that a continuum of options is possible between the "either" of rigor and the "or" of responsibility, these two options may be contrasted for the purpose of analyzing the decision the Trapps must make.

Before getting into this contrast, however, note should be taken of the important related issues, since for some they may well be more significant. First are the issues raised by the context of the case. David and Nancy's decision does not sit in a vacuum. It stands tall in a world where over five hundred million people are seriously malnourished and live in miserable poverty, some without even a single roof over their heads.

It stands in a country where unemployment, symbolized in the case by Al Messer, has consistently run above 7 percent in recent years, and the distribution of income and wealth has shifted significantly in favor of the wealthy.

It stands within pockets of environmental awareness in which concern about the sustainability of natural resources and the capacity to absorb pollution is very real. Included in this is the problem of how to relate to the rest of nature given the injunction to subdue and have dominion in Genesis 1:26–28.

It stands finally in an historical situation where women and men are experiencing new freedoms, and the patriarchal domination of family decisions is fading.

A second set of issues arises from the family context. One is the problem of overwork represented by David and Nancy's need to "get away." Related too is the experience of their children, Ben and Darcy, who must now find their way in a family of overworked parents and the luxurious options presented by a considerable inheritance. What sort of character are David and Nancy trying to build in their children?

Still another contextual issue is that of individual action in a world with a human population over five billion. How do people like David and Nancy influence others to do justice and exercise Christianity's so-called preferential option for the poor? Will individual acts of self-sacrifice make a difference? Should they spend their time and money in church and political action groups as Clea and David now do? Should they stop consuming so much even though they know market economies need consumption to sustain high levels of employment?

Something also needs to be said about the guilt which is felt by Nancy and especially by David. What is the function of guilt in the Christian life? What resources are available to understand and come to terms with guilt?

Finally, there are a number of issues raised by the Christian tradition. What do the Bible and subsequently the tradition have to say about poverty, wealth, and consumption? What is the vocation of a Christian with regard to these matters?

THE MAIN QUESTION

So how are we to live? Over a recent six-year period this case was taught thirty-five times, and each time the participants were asked to indicate whether they thought David and Nancy should build the cabin. The sampling was not scientific, the question lacked nuance, and the teacher might have influenced the vote in subtle ways, but the results are interesting nonetheless. Of the 872 who indicated their preference, 629 or 72 percent said "yes." Undergraduate students were even more emphatic, weighing in at 80 percent.

What was more striking than the numbers was the tendency of those who voted "yes" to assume that consuming goods and services in quantity is the natural thing to do. This is not surprising given the daily barrage of commercial propaganda whose purpose is to sell a way of life which encourages heavy consumption. In spite of this assumption, the problems of poverty and materialism troubled many of them as indicated by their interest in the case, expressions of guilt, and apparent needs to dismiss Nathan Ferguson and to justify their own decision.

That North Americans consume more goods and services than any people in history is a fact. That they are more materialistic is a value judgment which would seem to be supported by the number and actions of those who voted "yes." In contrast it is instructive to probe biblical and historical Christian understandings.

The first thing to consider is the Bible's consistent call to justice. According to Christian tradition, justice is rooted in the very being of God. It is an essential part of God's community of love and calls followers of Jesus Christ to make fairness the touchstone of their social response to other persons and to the rest of creation. Included in the biblical understanding of justice is a special concern for the poor.

The biblical basis of justice and a special concern for the poor start with God's liberation of the poor and oppressed Hebrew slaves in Egypt and the establishment of a covenant. This theme continues in the prophetic reinterpretation of the covenant. Micah summarized the law: "to do justice, and to love kindness, and to walk humbly with your God." Amos was adamant that God's wrath would befall Israel for its injustice and failure to care for the poor. Isaiah and Jeremiah were equally adamant.

In the New Testament the emphasis on social justice is somewhat muted in comparison to the prophets, but the concern for the poor may be even stronger. Jesus himself was a poor man from a poor part of Israel. His mission was among the poor and his message was directed to them. He blessed the poor and spoke God's judgment on the rich. On the cross he made himself one of the dispossessed. In the early Jerusalem community, as recorded in Acts 1–5, the basic economic needs of all members were taken care of as the wealthier shared their possessions so none would be deprived.

There can be little doubt that justice, which involves a passion for fairness and a special concern for the poor, is one of the strongest and most consistent ethical themes of the Bible. The ethical aim of justice in the absence of other considerations should be to relieve the worst conditions of poverty, powerlessness, and exploitation, and to support programs which help the poor and malnourished to achieve productive, useful, and sharing lives.

With regard to wealth, poverty, and consumption, two general and not altogether compatible attitudes dominate biblical writings. On the one side there is a qualified appreciation of wealth, on the other a call to freedom from possessions which sometimes borders on deep suspicion of them.

The Hebrew scriptures take the former side, praising the rich man who is just and placing a high estimate on riches gained through honest work. Alongside this praise is the obligation to care for the weaker members of society. Nowhere do the Hebrew scriptures praise self-imposed poverty or beggars.

Both sides are found in the teachings of Jesus. His announcement of the coming community of God carries with it a call for unparalleled freedom from possessions, and complete trust in God. The service of God and the service of riches are incompatible. Jesus himself had no possessions and prodded his disciples into what has been called "holy poverty," which includes the renunciation of possessions.

Nevertheless, Jesus took for granted the owning of property. He was apparently supported by women of means and urged that possessions be used to help those in need. Jesus did not ask Zacchaeus to give up all his possessions. He dined with hated tax collectors and was fond of celebrations, especially meals of fellowship. These examples echo the Hebrew scriptures' stress upon the right use of wealth.

This mixed mind continued in the early church. On the one side was the Jerusalem community where goods were shared in common. This seems to follow Jesus' preachings about radical freedom from possessions. On the other side stands Paul, who did not address the problem of wealth, although he himself had few possessions and was self-supporting as a tentmaker. He did, however, stress right use, made clear his center in Jesus Christ, and called on his congregations to support the poor in Jerusalem.

The later tradition continued this mixed mind. One statement by Martin Luther recorded in the winter of 1542–43 during his "table talk" catches the mind which is suspicious of wealth.

> Riches are the most insignificant things on earth, the smallest gift that God can give a person. What are they in comparison with the word of God? In fact, what are they in comparison even with physical endowments and beauty? What are they in comparison with gifts of the mind? And yet we act as if this were not so! The matter, form, effect, and goal of riches are worthless. That is why our Lord God generally gives riches to crude asses to whom nothing else is given.

The biblical witness on consumption follows much the same twofold pattern. The basic issue in the New Testament and later in the early Christian community was that of self-denial versus contentment with a moderate level of consumption. On the one side were those who translated Jesus' radical teachings about wealth and possessions and his own way of living into a full-blown asceticism. This movement eventually evolved into monasticism. On the other side were those who took Jesus' fondness for celebrations and meals of fellowship as a reason to reject asceticism. Along this line Paul preached an inner freedom which stressed contentment with self-sufficiency.

The tradition thus has been of two minds, and if it has not finally been able to make these minds up, it is clear on at least one guiding norm. This norm is best called "sufficiency" and emerges when justice is added to the teachings on wealth and consumption.

Sufficiency is the timely supply to all persons of the basic material necessities, defined as the minimum amount of food, clothing, shelter, transportation, and health care needed to live some margin above subsistence. This norm does not resolve the divided mind of the tradition, but it does establish a floor below which a just community does not let its members fall.

Sufficiency alone, however, is not complete. Future generations need to be factored into present calculations of sufficiency. Sufficiency must be sustained, a task not as easy as well-stocked supermarkets and department stores would suggest.

The issue with sustainability is whether there are limits to some forms of economic growth, in particular those forms which use large amounts of finite mineral resources and cause pollution. The food to supply a world population growing at a rate of 1.7 percent is also a key factor in the issue of sustainability. Many are optimistic about the capacities of new technologies and the free-market price system to circumvent limits to growth. Others reject this optimism or are deeply concerned about the technological mindset which would result from "success." For David and Nancy this issue hits home when they stop to consider the resources they are using to build the cabin. The issue also surfaces in Al Messer's offer to used recycled materials and to make the cabin energy efficient.

One important biblical contribution to the discussion of sustainable sufficiency comes from the norm of stewardship. In the Bible stewardship is care for the earth and care for persons. The present generation takes in trust a gift from the past with the responsibility of passing it on in no worse condition.

The writers of Genesis introduced the concept in the very first chapter of the Bible when humans are given dominion and ordered to subdue the earth. In spite of the harshness of the words "dominion" and "subdue," their meaning in the larger view of the Hebrew scriptures is clear. Men and women are seen as God's viceroys. It is God who owns the earth as a monarch. The viceroys have complete authority as commissioned by the monarch, but their authority does not include despotism or despoliation. They are to pattern their rule on that of God. For the Hebrews this pattern was set by the God who delivered them from Egypt and entered into covenantal relationship with them. For Christians it is set by Jesus Christ. Neither of these patterns sanctions injustice toward people or misuse of nature.

To summarize, justice and sustainable sufficiency are guiding norms. What they do is give permission to people to put into practice the two minds of the tradition, which, for lack of commonly accepted names, have been called rigorous discipleship and responsible consumption. What they do not do is give people free reign to engage in heavy consumption, materialism, and selfish individualism. Nor do they come down on the side of either rigorous discipleship or responsible consumption, although proponents will argue for one or the other.

The option of rigorous discipleship counsels the Christian to live a life of simplicity, to satisfy only the most basic needs, and to give all that she or he has to the poor. It is a life of surrender to the community of God. And even if the ethics of Jesus as exemplified by holy poverty cannot be lived perfectly, at least the disciple of Jesus should aim in that direction. Living in the grace of God through faith, the Christian has resources to respond with total commitment.

The option of rigorous discipleship emphasizes the new age introduced by Jesus Christ almost to the exclusion of the old age of sin and death. Christians see the sin of the old age, and are freed from it through the power of God. Hence radical changes in ways of living are demanded, and followers make these changes with enthusiasm.

The option of rigorous discipleship is attractive. It does not bog down in the inevitable relativities of the old age. It is simple, direct, and often accompanied by communities approximating the sharing found in the early Christian community in Jerusalem recorded in Acts 1–5.

Unlike the option of rigorous discipleship, the option of responsible consumption does not take its main cues directly from the teachings of Jesus. This does not mean it is less biblical, but that it rests more heavily on the main themes of the Bible, in particular on the tension between the old and new ages and the persistence of sin. Like those taking the option of rigorous discipleship, Christians with this option are concerned for the poor and aware of the problem of being tied to possessions. They do not, however, take the asceticism of Jesus literally or urge the surrender of all possessions.

Reduced to basics, those who follow this option wrestle with what it means to live between the ages, taking both ages seriously. In contrast to a heavy stress on the new age, they point to the realities of the old age or to the ambiguity of life between the ages. The problem for them is not radical discipleship but how to act responsibly and to begin processes of change which will lead to sustainable consumption and greater justice. Their mood is sober, their program moderate and reformist in nature. They also have a greater appreciation of material consumption.

This option is attractive to less ascetic Christians. It avoids the temptation of appeals to feelings of guilt. It accounts for the complexities of living in the world as it is. It does not seek to achieve an impossible ideal and thus avoids illusion and fanaticism.

Rigorous discipleship and responsible consumption represent two options for Christian living. Stated in extreme form they offer a radical choice and are opposed to each other. While stating the options in this way highlights their distinctiveness, it also exaggerates their opposition and results in stereotyping.

In actual fact most North American Christians live beyond the option of responsible consumption. On them both options act as a moral brake. Of those who would call themselves rigorous disciples many live somewhere in between the two options. This gives room to find what the two options have in common.

They both put trust where trust belongs, that is, in God's community in Jesus Christ, not in material possessions or ways of life. Both seek to avoid a self-centered individualism and to be concerned with the affairs of the community. Both are sensitive to the plight of the poor. Both seek a greater approximation of justice in existing structures. Both are valid Christian options which should inform each other.

THE RELATIONSHIPS

While the task of finding guidance in the tradition is essential to making an ethical decision, once done conflicts still remain. In this instance the tradition offers two contrasting and persuasive options, and the Trapps are faced with trying to orient themselves in relation to these two options. Perhaps the relationships in David and Nancy's lives can help them decide how to act.

David and Nancy are like the hub of a six-spoke wheel with each spoke a link to persons on the rim of their lives. David and Nancy are the hub because they are the ones with the decision. The main burden rests with David since Nancy has already indicated that she wants to build and thinks building is a responsible use of their inheritance.

David's relationship to himself is important in this context. Some observers might characterize David as guilt-ridden. This may be true, and if so, David needs to consider further that his sense of guilt may be a warning signal to his own inner alienation.

Alternatively, what these observers characterize as David's guilt may be a projection of their own. It may be that when they see David wrestling with the two minds of the tradition, they become aware of their own avoidance of the issue. Further, this is not simply an interior matter for David. An important source of ethical guidance for David, as for anyone, is the counsel of close friends. David has been seeking their guidance and taking time to mull it over before he decides. This is healthy.

Ultimately he and Nancy must decide because not to decide is the decision not to build. David is drawn to both rigor and responsibility. He cannot have it both ways with the cabin, at least in his own mind. To see the cabin as a reward for David's considerable professional rigor and church work might be an out. Many will want to take this line and see David as deserving God's special favor for being such a good Christian. This out smacks of works righteousness, however. Worse, it assumes a god who plays with human freedom and acts arbitrarily with rewards and punishments. Since the holocaust, this god is dead.

So David and Nancy must decide and something will be lost in the process, either the joys of a cabin or the joys of living simply. Dealing with such losses is one reason that forgiveness is so crucial in Christianity. Choices must be made, and sometimes bad choices are elected. The tradition says that with repentance, sin is forgiven.

David's relation to Nancy is not imperiled either way. She seems to understand his qualms and is willing to accept them as long as David does not impose them. The problem in the hub does not appear to be their relationship. Rather it seems to be their failure to recognize the sources of their felt needs for a cabin.

Is the real problem not one of overwork and an unwitting acceptance of materialism? And to think that a cabin will relieve work pressures is utopian in the extreme. Cabins are in fact a lot of work. Perhaps what David and Nancy ought to consider is slowing down. Self-sacrifice is not a virtue in itself, and when it becomes something which must be done, the saving power of the cross is lost.

Nancy may be trapped by many of the forces which enslave women today. Liberation for women produces the opportunity for satisfying jobs outside the home, yet at the same time the duties of homemaker, mother, and wife often remain as demanding as before. Life becomes a daily round of serving others, but without the joy and wholeness that comes with a freely given self. The self gets submerged in the processes of existence. Joy goes, and wholeness is lost. Before she adds a cabin to her list of things to do, perhaps she ought to sit down and find the self which she thinks she is giving, but in actuality may be losing in all her activity. The same thing probably applies to David.

The spoke to the children is particularly important. Children learn in myriad ways, consciously and unconsciously. While David and Nancy want Ben and Darcy to acquire skills in certain sports and to relate to their children more, building a cabin may have unintended side-effects, such as encouraging materialism and social apathy. Again, slowing down is probably the best antidote for insufficient time with children. Also, it is probably incorrect to assume the children will want to be at the cabin as they grow older and the action shifts to the high school scene in Toledo. A cabin can lead to less time with the children as their interests shift.

The spoke to their pastor is their bridge to rigorous discipleship. Nathan is the living example which has pricked David's conscience. Clea seems impervious to Nathan's soft sell. The rest of the congregation is probably divided and will become increasingly so the harder Nathan pushes. Given the great numbers for whom rigorous discipleship is foreign, Nathan will be ignored on this issue, however, unless he does push harder.

For Nathan to be ignored would be a shame because the satisfactions of simple living need articulation and modeling. David and Nancy's dilemma is intensified because Nathan offers an alternative and the occasion to be a light to others. To go in the opposite direction and build the cabin might even be a blow to Nathan. Whatever they decide, Nathan should be apprised early, and the lines of communication kept open. Too little is known about Nathan to gauge his reaction.

Much the same goes for the spoke to Clea. She obviously has not elected Nathan's option. In fact there are some indications she may even be exceeding the bounds of responsibility. In any case she represents a side of David and Nancy as well as the views of many in the church. What needs to be done is to avoid a division into factions. That could pull the community apart, which would be a tragedy given that both options are viable.

The relation to Al Messer is tricky. David and Nancy feel responsible to Al as a friend, but Al represents something far larger. Jobs are determined in a market economy by supply and demand. Al's services are not in demand, and David and Nancy have the opportunity to relieve his unemployment temporarily. The irony, even tragedy, of this situation is that the more materialistic North Americans become, the more people have jobs. And if they do not consume, good people are thrown into poverty. It is a "catch 22" for rigor, at least in the short run.

David and Nancy alone cannot make up for the shortcomings of an economic system. Thus their responsibility to Al is limited. If they do not give him the work, he should be in their prayers and conversations. His plight should be considered in their political action.

The fifth spoke runs to David and Nancy's larger family. It involves the inheritance. In some families close relatives would be horror struck if the inheritance were "given away." Family fortunes are heirlooms which the current possessors really do not own. The sole function of the inheriting generation is to steward for future generations. However much this family attitude reflects selfish attachment to material goods, and however much Jesus prepared his disciples for this in his warnings about divisions over the gospel, the potential for family conflict is present.

The final spoke leads to the global village. David and Nancy do not live in a cocoon of only close relationships. They are citizens of the world, and this world has far too many malnourished and poor people who experience poverty as an unholy necessity. David and Nancy have the luxury of choosing or not choosing holy poverty. They also have a developed sense of responsibility to the larger world. These two things go hand-in-hand. What is given up may be transferred to others. This will not change the world overnight, but if wisely given, it may help improve a few lives.

DIRECTIONS

Since there are so many issues raised by this case, selection is necessary. The family decision with its normative bases in rigorous discipleship and responsible consumption is the most important of these issues. High levels of consumption are in tension with the norms of earlier Christians who never knew abundance and were suspicious of the pockets of overconsumption they saw. The other side of the coin, poverty, has always been rejected unless it is freely chosen as a vocation.

Ironically, many economists argue that the only way out of poverty is the increased consumption which is part of economic growth. In this view "holy poverty" and the virtues of simple living are in opposition with Christianity's preferential option for the poor. It is important to be cognizant of this view, but it is also likely that the view is propounded largely as a means of avoiding serious confrontation with the option of rigorous discipleship.

This case is located under family issues. This location was intentional and was meant to focus on the process of this man and this woman coming to a decision. Family decisions are fraught with snares. Little things are hidden away over the course of a marriage and sometimes trip up the partners. There is always the context of relationships, and today there is the added tension of changing male/female relationships. Steering the family between these snares and booby traps is no easy task.

ADDITIONAL RESOURCES

Abrecht, Paul, ed. *Faith and Science in an Unjust World.* Vol. 2. Geneva: World Council of Churches, 1980.

Birch, Bruce C., and Larry L. Rasmussen, *The Predicament of the Prosperous.* Philadelphia: The Westminster Press, 1978.

Hengel, Martin. *Property and Riches in the Early Church.* Trans. John Bowden. Philadelphia: Fortress, 1974.

Shinn, Roger L., ed. *Faith and Science in an Unjust World.* Vol. 1. Geneva: World Council of Churches, 1980.

Stivers, Robert L. *The Sustainable Society.* Philadelphia: Westminster, 1976.

———. *Hunger, Technology, and Limits to Growth.* Minneapolis: Augsburg, 1984.

Yoder, John Howard. *The Politics of Jesus.* Grand Rapids: William B. Eerdmans, 1972.

Case

The Fortunate Illness

Sam Evers sat behind his desk in the Lakeview Family Services Center, his right hand on the telephone and his left marking Alan Thompson's office phone number. It was now the end of August. In July Suzanne Thompson had requested joint marriage counseling for herself and Alan as soon as their family returned from vacation. Sam had told Suzanne he was pleased to hear this and would call to make an appointment. At the time, however, Sam noted on Alan's record that the crucial factor would be whether or not Alan had been sober during the intervening month.

Before making the call, Sam Evers stopped and reread his notes in the Thompson files. Alan and Suzanne Thompson's counseling history over the past eighteen months was complex. Although they had first come to the center for joint marriage counseling, it became evident that neither one was ready to work on the marriage. In Sam's opinion Alan's drinking made it virtually impossible for him to deal meaningfully with issues in the marriage. At the same time it was evident that Suzanne had work of her own to do in therapy and needed greater distance from the marriage. They both began individual therapy with separate counselors, Alan with Sam and Suzanne with a woman counselor, Marion Ackridge. At several points during the past year Sam and Marion had shared notes and discussed the Thompson case.

Alan Thompson, forty-two years old, and Suzanne, thirty-nine, had been married for seventeen years. They had six children. Alan, a college graduate, had worked with Allworth Advertising Agency for more than twelve years. On a salary of $45,000 a year, they owned a home in what was generally considered one of the city's more affluent suburbs. Sam described Alan as a handsome man, a "snappy dresser," who in contrast to the casual atmosphere of the Lakeview Center, always came to his appointments in suit and tie. Other descriptive terms came to Sam's mind: charming, de-

---

bonair, fast-talker. Sam checked his notes: "Very articulate man with large vocabulary, subtle nuances of expression. Intellectualizes. Avoids deep feelings; a well developed defense system." Alan had said that he usually gave people the impression of being a very outgoing person, but he described himself as "a loner."

Sam considered both Alan and Suzanne conventional people, politically and socially conservative. They were raised as Roman Catholics, and though they indicated they were not regular in church attendance, each indicated a strong orientation to the values and moral standards taught by the church. They had often discussed their roles as husband and wife in terms of "duty" and "Christian responsibility."

Sam turned his thoughts to Suzanne, who had spent fifteen of the past seventeen years being a full-time wife and mother. She had completed two years of college and had some training in nursing before marriage. In the first interview she described herself as an "obedient wife," geared to meet Alan's expectations. As Suzanne had worked with Marion, she came to see how much of her life was in response to Alan ever since the beginning of their marriage when she had quit her training as a nurse. In rereading the notes made by Marion Ackridge, Sam was aware of how much Suzanne had changed in the past eighteen months. Sam recalled the terminology, "the fortunate illness," as applied to alcoholism by counselors, who often found that therapy precipitated by an alcoholic crisis led to personal growth for other family members. Sam was troubled, however, as he thought over one of Marion's notes, "The changes in Suzanne, as she has developed more self-confidence and clear self-identity, may be more than Alan can deal with."

Sam moved back to Alan's file and traced the chronology of his treatment, particularly the situation prior to Alan's coming to Lakeview Center. A heavy drinker since college, Alan had reached the point in his work two and a half years ago when he would take two drinks, usually martinis, before a client presentation. Although Alan was "functional" on the job, Alan's supervisor had confronted him about his slurred speech and affected performance. Out of fear of losing even more control on the job, Alan admitted himself to a twenty-three-day hospitalization treatment for alcoholism. In later recalling his impressions of this experience, Alan expressed it as "ego shattering." When he had been drinking, he was convinced of his importance to the company and of his great capabilities. Only when his body was rid of the chemical, and after the therapy which followed, was Alan able to recall any incidents when alcohol had negatively affected his work. He joined Alcoholics Anonymous and was sober for almost nine months.

Alan returned to drinking and was then rehospitalized, this time for a ten-day period. Through hospital counselors, he and Suzanne discussed their marriage as a factor in his drinking. It was at this point that the couple had come to Lakeview Family Services Center for marriage counseling.

They had two sessions as a couple and then began individualized counseling with Sam and Marion.

Sam turned back to Suzanne's file. During the period of individualized counseling, which centered for Suzanne on how she could cope with Alan's alcoholism, Suzanne began to express her feelings about Alan:

He has always been an arrogant man, very proud of his self-discipline. But when he drinks, he is not in control of himself. I think this must frighten him. Then he needs to control me and the children even more. This is what we fight over. Alan says I'm too easy on the kids, that I'm a poor excuse for a mother because I give them too much freedom. He controls all the finances and cuts back on my household allowance when I buy anything frivolous for the kids. I get angry and tell him that if he were better in that crummy job, he would have advanced much further, and we would not have to pinch pennies so much. I worry about the effect on the kids. Andrew at four is a chronic bed wetter, and two of the older girls are having serious problems at school. They all suffer from constant tension.

During this period of counseling, last September through November, Suzanne became more involved in community activities and took several classes in handicrafts. All but one of her children, now ages four to fifteen, were in school, and Suzanne was considering returning to her career in nursing. Alan began to drink heavily, and Suzanne packed his suitcase and put him out of the house. Alan lived in a rooming house for six days and returned home sober. This had been just prior to Christmas.

Sam Evers then scanned the next few pages of notes and remembered the events of that past spring with some discomfort. In his counseling with Alan, Sam began to suspect that Alan was drinking again, not a great deal, but just enough to "test" his own self-discipline. During this period Alan avoided all discussion of his home life. Sam called on Marion Ackridge for a conference.

Marion indicated that Suzanne Thompson had begun to express her new freedom in ways Marion had not really expected. For the first time in her life, Suzanne had formed a relationship with another man and was experiencing what Marion termed "teenage romance." The man, Bob Edwards, was single, described by Suzanne as "very romantic," a close mutual friend of the Thompsons, and an alcoholic. Suzanne was sure Alan did not know about the affair.

Two weeks later Alan called Sam Evers in a rage and demanded an immediate appointment. The night before in an argument Suzanne had shouted out the truth about her affair. Alan said he was seriously considering divorce but "held back because the man would not be able to support the family. He lives in the YMCA and can barely support himself."

The following week Alan and Suzanne came for joint counseling with

Sam and Marion. Alan began this session by indicating that he doubted if their marriage should continue. However, as the conversation progressed, Alan said to his wife, "I don't know if I can trust you. Can I risk more pain?" And finally, "Yes, I'll give it one more try." Sam had starred these statements in his notes as the first time he had ever heard Alan Thompson express personal feelings to his wife.

As the conversation continued, Marion Ackridge turned to Suzanne: "If you and Alan are going to work with us on your relationship, one basic condition must be that you no longer see your friend." Suzanne cancelled the following joint interview.

During the month of May, Alan continued his sessions with Sam. He invariably arrived angry. Suzanne was continuing to see Bob Edwards. Sam noted that Alan had developed an obsession about his wife's comings and goings and her daily contacts with Edwards. Alan began to follow them. He told Sam that he had seen them in the grocery. It was raining and Suzanne asked Alan to give Bob a ride back to his room. Then the following night Suzanne said Bob was ill, and Alan drove to the drugstore for medication. Although Alan seemed unruffled and expressed his concern for Suzanne's "best interests," his depression deepened. His drinking continued. He admitted to Sam that when he left the house the night before, he did not know until he reached the corner whether he would go to the bar or the drugstore. Later that night he drank until he vomited and fell asleep. Although he made his rage known to Sam, Alan indicated that he refused to give Suzanne the satisfaction of seeing him angry. Sam considered how voluntary Alan's retention of anger actually was. During the following appointment Alan told Sam he had taken an office girl to bed, and that he had to drink to do it. There was no conversation at all between himself and Suzanne.

The last week in May Alan told Sam he had worked out an arrangement to spend his evenings at a local halfway house. This would serve the dual purpose of giving him added AA exposure and take him out of the crisis environment of his family. He would go there directly from work and return home only at bedtime.

The first two weeks of June passed. Alan missed both counseling appointments. Worried, Sam called and arranged for a special session with Alan. When Alan came in, he said he had not had anything to drink for four days. Sam noted that he was tense and vague about his plans to remain off alcohol. For the first time in the past eighteen months Sam openly confronted Alan. "Are you trying to lose your job? Get really sick? You've admitted you're powerless over alcohol, but you haven't admitted that your life is unmanageable. You aren't in control! The addiction is running your life."

Alan responded that no one had ever faced him with it in this way. The following two weeks he seemed to improve and said he had taken his last drink on June 18. Alan described his last drinking episode in some detail and indicated it was like "hitting bottom." Sam was encouraged by this as he felt that such an experience was often a prelude to recovery, but he still intended to monitor Alan closely for awhile.

In the weeks that followed Alan did not return to drinking. He also began to talk about the marriage in a way that Sam had not heard before. He reported that he and Suzanne were doing things together, simple things at first, not requiring them to relate very much, but giving them proximity. They were beginning to discover that they could enjoy one another. Alan was still wary about trusting Suzanne but was also beginning to talk about gestures of affection towards her. He was no longer going to the halfway house after work.

At the end of July Suzanne called Sam Evers. She was no longer seeing Bob Edwards and indicated she felt much better about herself. For the first time in fourteen years she and Alan were talking to each other. Their whole family was going on vacation together. She was not sure if Alan was ready, but she would like a third try at joint marriage counseling. Suzanne agreed that Sam should call Alan for the appointment on their return.

As he reached for the phone, Sam Evers felt that if Alan had returned to alcohol, this could rule out any attempt to do marriage counseling. A serious lapse into alcohol could indicate that Alan was moving more deeply into the addiction than out of it. In this light Alan would need massive long-term therapy which might only be successful if he were completely freed from the destructive patterns of relating he and Suzanne had built up over the years. If this were the case, Sam was prepared for what he considered one of the most painful steps in counseling alcoholics, encouraging a long-term separation or the dissolution of a marriage.

Sam realized that though Suzanne was still dependent on Alan financially and emotionally, even as she had asked him to care for her lover, she would never return to her former servile role. Sam wondered if she might be better off and have a greater sense of integrity and self-esteem if she attempted to manage on whatever she could earn alone for herself and the children.

Yet Sam was deeply concerned by his consideration of separation. For each, the marriage was still important. With counseling, each had experienced a new commitment to themselves and their own individual needs. But was this taking them further apart or closer together? Perhaps most important, Sam realized that the suggestion of divorce would be counter to the strong religious commitment of Suzanne and Alan to support one another in sickness and in health.

Deep in thought, Sam slowly dialed Alan's number.

Commentary

The Fortunate Illness

While the overriding question in this case is the viability of Suzanne and Alan's marriage, there are a number of other issues as well, all of which have a bearing on that decision. What are the major needs of the children and how can they best be met? How should the changes in Suzanne be understood, and should they be supported? Can Alan's alcoholism be controlled, and to what extent is his understanding the reasons he drinks necessary to his controlling his drinking?

SCRIPTURAL AND THEOLOGICAL RESOURCES

There are two ways of approaching scripture for insight relevant to our case. One is to search for specific references to the issues in the case. The other is to examine what scripture has to say about the Christian vocation in general. Marriage is a topic on which the specific teachings and the description of Christian vocation are not always in agreement, and on which the description of Christian life and love is frequently more instructive than the specific teachings.

The positive and useful insights on marriage in scripture are embedded within and often distorted by patriarchal notions of women as men's property, whose claim to virtue rests in fruitfulness, sexual fidelity, an even temper, and housewifely skills. There is virtually no recognition of the personhood of women or of any need for development of character and responsibility in women. Treatment of marriage as covenant, or equations of Christ/church and Yahweh/Israel relationships with bridegroom/bride relationships have presupposed not only the closeness and commitment in these relationships but also the inequalities of power, worth, and initiative understood to be present in the divine/human encounters. Furthermore, scriptural law regarding marriage is inconsistent, so that attempts to apply commands of scripture to this case could lead to wildly contradictory results. Depending upon which part of scripture one selects, we could conclude that Suzanne, Alan, Bob, and the woman at Alan's office should be killed for their adultery (Lev. 20:10), or that Alan (but not Suzanne) could divorce his spouse for any reason merely by presenting her with a notice of divorce (Deut. 18:10). Or we could decide that either can divorce the other because of adultery (Matt. 5:31; 19:8–9), or that neither can ever divorce for any reason (Mark 10:5–12; Luke 16:18). Or we could choose the example of Hosea, whom God instructed to take back his adulterous wife Gomer and love her so well that she would never stray again (Hos. 3:1). Scripture has little advice for wives with problem husbands apart from 1 Peter's suggestion that wives be submissive in order to win over husbands who have not yet accepted the Word (1 Peter 3:1–6).

Although the specific treatment of marriage in scripture is not very helpful, the general message of Jesus has great relevance for this case. Jesus' message was the imminent arrival of God's reign and the need to prepare to participate in it. He clearly subordinated family, including marriage and sex roles, to participation in the work of advancing God's reign, as for example in his comments about his mother and brothers (Luke 8:19–21; Matt. 12:46–50; Mark 3:31–35), on discipleship (Luke 14:25–26; Matt. 10:37–38), and to Mary and Martha (Luke 10:38–42). From this perspective the question in this case is whether the marriage of Suzanne and Alan has the potential to become a channel through which they participate in and contribute to the wider inbreaking of God's reign, or whether continuing the marriage would sap their energy and time to the exclusion of serving others.

The Christian theological tradition has treated marriage in a manner similar to that of scripture. Most of the early tradition revolved around Augustine's teaching on the three blessings of marriage: offspring, fidelity, and sacrament. The chief purpose and blessing of marriage was the creation and rearing of children, with sexual fidelity and the permanence of the marital bond as secondary blessings. Successive theology often noted with St. Paul that licit marital sex helps prevent the greater sinfulness of non-marital sex. The quality of the relationship between the spouses was not in the classical tradition ever a central focus. A major reason for this absence was that Thomas Aquinas, and most other Christian theologians, agreed with the judgment of St. Augustine that when Genesis said that woman was made as a helpmate for man, it meant a helpmate for the work of procreation, "for in any other work a man would be better helped by a man."

In contemporary Christian theology procreation is certainly not the only important purpose for marriage, and for many theologians procreation takes a secondary place to the quality of the marital relationship itself. When theologians of more recent centuries discuss the relationship of the partners they often define it in terms of mutual commitment to the perfection of the other. For some, this commitment to virtue tended to be understood in traditional terms of supporting habits of prayer and avoiding sexual sin. Because of a very real and persistent suspicion in our society about sexual pleasure, even in marriage, some theologians urged on married couples periods of separation and celibacy devoted to prayer and meditation. But increasingly among theologians the marital commitment is understood in terms of friendship, emotional disclosure, and personal intimacy. In fact, so thoroughly has this become the cultural definition of marriage that some theologians now urge that we develop some friendships and meaningful activities *outside* of marriage. For if we limit our intimacy and search for meaning to marriage, our spouse bears the impossible task of making the whole of our life worthwhile. The need for forgiveness, both for sexual infidelity as well as for the small failures to love which plague any relationship, continues as a constant theme in contemporary theological treatment of marriage.

Most Christian denominations today allow divorce and remarriage, though encouraging permanent unions and stressing the need for a process of examination of conscience, forgiveness of self and spouse, and healing after failed marriages. The Roman Catholic church, while not recognizing divorce or allowing remarriage, grants annulments in cases where church tribunals establish that the necessary elements for a true marital union were not present at the time of the ceremony, regardless of the length or fruitfulness of the legal bond. Since Alan and Suzanne, though raised as Catholics, are not involved with the Roman Catholic worshiping community, it is unlikely that they would choose to request annulment even if they would choose to separate.

CHOOSING CRITERIA FOR DECISIONS

While only Suzanne and Alan can decide whether or not this marriage can be rebuilt, it is important to note some criteria often invoked to save marriages in such situations which can do violence to Christian understandings of what it means to live out the gospel.

Neither spouse should decide to continue the marriage primarily out of feelings of self-sacrifice. Self-sacrifice becomes destructive as an end in itself, but can be life-giving when used as a means to restore or promote growth and relationship. Jesus did not come to earth to die, but to usher in the reign of God. His suffering was acceptable and even virtuous in the pursuit of this goal, not for its own sake. When we promote self-sacrifice as an end in itself, we choose to deplete ourselves and others, and are often unaware that we pursue other personal needs which are too uncomfortable to acknowledge.

It is also dangerous to preserve marriage solely for the sake of the children, as is so often done. Parents are the primary models for children in how to live and grow and relate. A marriage which is dead, in which there is no loving energy, but only tolerance and civility, leaves children without hope for forming adult relationships which nourish. Furthermore, the pressure of living in a failed relationship often results in situations of violence and instability, which further undermine the needs of children. Judging from this case, such upheaval could be expected, as the children are already exhibiting symptoms of distress, such as truancy and bed wetting.

Neither should the decision be based on financial criteria alone. Husband, wife, and therapist all consider the financial situation of this marriage as an important factor to be considered in deciding what should be done with the marriage. It is impossible to know from the case how well Suzanne could expect to be able to support the children on her own, though it is clear it would at the least require a reduction in standard of living. This is typical of disrupted marriages. For a number of reasons, in the United States divorced women who head households make up the largest proportion of wage earners within the category of impoverished. Many women who return to work after divorce never obtained or completed education or training for skilled trades. For the majority of divorced women support payments for children run into arrears or total noncompliance after the first year of divorce. And in many areas of the U.S. economy, there is job discrimination against women, which either channels women into lower paying dead-end work, or sometimes pays them less for doing the same work as men. Considering Alan's problems at work and his alcoholism, if Suzanne decides on divorce, she would be wise not to plan on steady economic support from Alan. Though Suzanne's supporting the children would not be easy, avoiding a needed separation in order to protect a more comfortable standard of living has serious problems. The example provided to many children who watch their divorced mothers struggle to obtain education and training and achieve financial independence is invaluable for the children even if those efforts fall short of economic success as that is commonly understood.

Continuing marriages at great cost out of loyalty to law may also be perilous. Both Suzanne's and Alan's interest in preserving the marriage tends to be expressed in terms of living out strongly held beliefs in the permanence of marriage. One hopes that what they are trying to express is a conviction that *this* marriage can still live because it retains some basic residual level of love and desire. For if the loyalty which brings each of them back to the marriage is not to their spouse, but to some abstract principle that marriage is an indissoluble bond regardless of the feelings of the spouses, then there is little reason for either to trust and open up to the other.

SEXUALITY IN MARRIAGE

This case is presented from the point of view of the therapist. Sam Evers does not present any information about the sexual interaction in this marriage, though that must certainly be one of the areas about which he has questioned Alan and Suzanne. Sexual intercourse is not by any means the sole test of marital relationship, but it is at the core rather than the periphery of marital union. Sex is not merely pleasurable activity made licit by marriage. Nor is it merely an *expression* of a love which is built and maintained through other levels of marital relationship. Rather sexual intercourse can create and confirm, and therefore build, the love that it expresses. It is perhaps the human activity which most concretely models the mutual love within the Trinity, for in orgasm one surrenders to complete unselfconsciousness and openness to the other. Sexual intercourse, when it is allowed to be a symbol—an act which creates the love which it signifies—rather than merely a sign of that love, brings about an overflow of love. It spreads love, not only through the biological creation of new human life, but by opening lovers to others, to more loving relationships in the community.

What had Suzanne and Alan's sexual relationship been like in this marriage? Was there a commitment to each other already built and expressed which can, through effort, be re-established? Was sexual interaction ever a channel for Alan's self-disclosure, or did his inability to express his feelings extend to their sexual union as well? Did Suzanne turn to Bob out of a need to express feelings Alan had never been open to sharing, out of hurt at Alan's withdrawal from a mutual sexual expression, or perhaps out of her frustration that his expression of feelings could not grow beyond the sexual union? Can either partner summon up any desire for the other or expect that desire could return? The answers will make a difference for how each partner assesses the viability of the marriage. If trust and love can be re-established, but not desire, then they can have a friendship, but not a marriage. There are various degrees of sexual desire in marriage; for some it is not nearly so important as for others. But the sharing of sexual desire is what distinguishes marriage from other close loving relationships.

UNITY WITHOUT SACRIFICE OF DIVERSITY

The title of the case raises the likelihood that without Alan's alcoholism it is improbable that either Suzanne or Alan would have been forced to the self-analysis and growth as individuals which they, especially Suzanne, have recently undergone. Though it is not clear whether they will be able to salvage their marriage, it is clear that Suzanne has a much more positive self-image than ever before, and that Alan may be moving toward greater responsibility for and knowledge of himself.

The process of growth to which Suzanne was opened as a result of therapy is common for middle-aged women in our society. Many women emerge from adolescence into marriage and devote fifteen to twenty-five years to childrearing. They then discover that they don't know who they are apart from being someone's daughter, someone's wife, and someone's mother. At thirty-five to forty-five they suddenly ask: "Who do I want to be? What do I want to do when I grow up?" These are questions that have been postponed for women who have been socialized to understand marriage and motherhood as constituting identity and fulfillment. Suzanne's new assertiveness—her packing Alan a suitcase and sending him from the house until he sobered up—is characteristic of women beginning to forge an identity for themselves. In American marriages it is common for men to monopolize power for the first years, with women moving toward mutual assertiveness in the middle years to often become slightly dominant after retirement. Change is a normal part of life, but abrupt questioning and change put severe strains on many marriages — marriages much stronger than this one.

Alan's response to the person Suzanne is becoming will be important. Her process of development is both normal and positive, but it comes at a time when her husband is already vulnerable. He has had trouble on the job from his alcoholism. His role in his family seems to have been the traditional breadwinner, which means he is less involved with the children than Suzanne. We do not know whether he can be comfortable with the prospect of a more independent, assertive Suzanne who may finish her education, begin a career, and rival his role as provider. Can he accept and love this Suzanne? Was her dependence an important part of his attraction to her?

A positive criterion of Christian marriage is that it should *promote* the growth and development we see in Suzanne. The two who come together in marriage make something new, a mutual relationship, but they do not cease to be separate selves as well. It is the differences, the individualities of the two, which create the tension, the attraction, the dynamism of the marital relationship. Spouses should support the growth in individuality of the other, for what enhances the other enhances the relationship.

ALCOHOLISM

It seems to be true that Alan is an alcoholic, a person who cannot control his use of alcohol. But it is not necessarily true that he, or anyone connected with him, must live in fear of periodic binges. While experts in alcohol treatment centers insist that once an alcoholic, always an alcoholic, many alcoholics have been alcohol free for decades. Cases like Alan's, in which excessive but seemingly non-dysfunctional drinking went on for years before a crisis hit, are often more difficult to arrest, as the patient thinks that because he managed to drink and be functional before, he can do this again. Sam thinks that Alan has been testing out such an approach. Nevertheless, there is hope for Alan's reform. This requires the will to stop, support from others, and often some understanding of why one drinks. The latter may be a major issue for Alan, as there is some evidence that he has a problem with self-disclosure. This is a common problem among men, the result of a socialization process which conveys the idea that to self-disclose is to both become vulnerable, and to forfeit some part of one's identity. Very low rates of self-disclosure in men have been linked to many physical and psychological maladies, as well at to marital problems. One result of not disclosing one's feelings is an increasing lack of consciousness about what one is feeling. Alan may face a long process of learning to recognize and then to express his feelings before he understands why he drinks.

CHILDREN OF ALCOHOLICS

The best interests of the children must also be taken into account. Sam and Suzanne wonder if she could support the children if she left Alan. But given Suzanne's present worries about the behavior of the children, the children already seem to have fared poorly. Marital discord is terrifying for children, as the parental relationship is a major part of the security on which a child's world is built. The children of alcoholics live with additional insecurity as they can never know from day to day what behavior to expect of the alcoholic parent, or how preoccupied the nonalcoholic parent may be with the alcoholic.

We know from research with adult children of alcoholics that the destructive coping patterns developed by children of alcoholic homes often become an ongoing part of the child's personality, and are much more varied than we formerly believed. It has been known for decades that many disturbed and/or delinquent teens and adults turn out to have been raised in alcoholic homes. But this was interpreted to mean that children who have been harmed by the instability and/or abuse of the alcoholic home become defiant problem children and then young delinquents. What alcoholism counselors have learned in the past fifteen years is that though the problem child in alcoholic homes gets the attention, in fact, it is often more difficult to treat the destructive patterns learned by children who choose other responses to alcoholic parents. In many ways the problem child, if treated early enough, is the most healthy and most amenable to intervention, because the rebel has most clearly refused to accept the alcoholic home as normal or right. There are other responses to the alcoholic home: the child who makes a life of coping, of expecting disaster and upheaval, and who therefore lives without hope; or the child who accepts the blame for the situation and goes through life trying to placate everyone at the expense of establishing a centered self; or the responsible child who tries to create order out of the chaos and takes on the home and the world as a burden to be carried. These children have at some level been damaged by their acceptance of, and attempt to adjust to, alcoholism. And yet the children of alcoholic homes can be freed from destructive coping patterns. The earlier such treatment begins, the easier it will be. Both Suzanne and Alan need to learn about the effects of alcoholism on their children and become active in combating them. If this marriage is put back together and alcohol continues to be a problem for Alan, then one hopes that Suzanne will at the very least take the responsibility for excluding Alan from the home—from the children—when he is drinking, and get counseling help for the children.

REACHING A DECISION

It would be a step toward wholeness for Suzanne to understand what drove her to her affair. It would be good for Alan to ask why he slept with a secretary at work—was it to restore damaged pride or to get back at Suzanne? Both of them seem to have used others—though they themselves may have been used as well—to act out problems in their marriage. Their relationship has thus been destructive not only for the two of them, but also for children, Alan's work, and other members of their community. A Christian approach to this situation would suggest that Suzanne and Alan need to be able to forgive not only each other but themselves. Any movement toward reconciliation depends first upon their ability to forgive themselves for their failure to take charge of their lives responsibly: for the failure of Alan to cope with his alcoholism and the feelings which trigger it, for Suzanne's dependence on Alan even in her adulterous infatuation. If each can manage to forgive herself or himself, they may be ready to move toward forgiveness of the other and true reconciliation. But it will be important that they admit both their own failings, and their anger and disappointment at each other. Wounds must be exposed before they can begin to heal.

Does this marriage have the potential to become a relationship which fosters the growth of both Alan and Suzanne, provides a stable and loving environment for the children, and supports the family in general in contributing to the welfare of the wider community? If it does have such potential, then Christian theology suggests that it should be preserved. For its contribution to the creation of the reign of God would be twofold. First, the value of the vows which were made when Alan and Suzanne married would be reaffirmed, which encourages trust in vows and promises in general. Second, the marriage would become a symbol of the possibility of forgiveness and reconciliation for others, not only in marriages, but in relationships between other persons and between persons and God. Saving their marriage could make them a sign of hope for others.

If this marriage does break up, both these people will carry long unmet relational needs, as well as destructive patterns of relating. Suzanne wants support for the person she has been becoming. Alan does not want to be alone in facing his alcoholism. But need alone is no basis for mutual relationships. Both should beware of precipitate involvements: marriage counselors have discovered that marriages begun less than two years after a marital breakup have an 80 percent mortality rate; marriages two to five years after a divorce have a 50 percent mortality rate, which is the national average. The supposition here is that the intervening time is used to come to grips with the causes of the breakup and to heal the remaining sore spots.

Keeping marriages alive requires a basic attraction between the partners, communication between the partners, and the development of a shared life together which binds them to each other. The partners in this marriage seem to have lacked communication skills, which are only now beginning to be developed. The bond which presently holds them together consists of belief in the permanence of marriage and in their children's need for them, but the relation lacks trust. It is not clear how much of the basic attraction remains.

We cannot hope to indicate from this case what the outcome should be. The decision of both spouses will depend on a variety of factors. Only they can decide if this marriage can become a truly mutual bond of love which strengthens and energizes them in reaching out to their children, their families, their co-workers, their neighbors and friends as co-creators with God of a truly human reign of God.

ADDITIONAL RESOURCES

Black, Claudia. *It Can't Happen to Me: Children of Alcoholics.* Denver: M.A.C. Printing and Publications, 1979.

Dominian, Jack. *Marriage, Faith and Love: A Basic Guide to Christian Marriage.* New York: Crossroad, 1982.

Gallagher, Charles, et al. *Embodied in Love.* New York: Crossroad, 1984.

Jourard, Sidney. "Some Lethal Aspects of the Male Role." In Joseph Pleck and Jack Sawyer, eds., *Men and Masculinity.* Englewood Cliffs, N.J.: Prentice-Hall, 1974.

McLaughlin, Eleanor Como. "Equality of Souls, Inequality of Sexes: Women in Medieval Theology." In Rosemary Radford Ruether, ed., *Religion and Sexism.* New York: Simon and Schuster, 1974.

Preparing the Engaged for Marriage. Videotape of a workshop given by Barbara Markey, SND, in May 1986, in Cincinnati, Ohio. Available from Barbara Markey, SND, Director, Family Life Office, Archdiocese of Omaha, 3214 N. 60, Omaha, NE 68104.

Sales, Esther. "Women's Adult Development." In Irene Frieze, et al., *Women and Sex Roles.* New York: Norton, 1978.

PART II

LIBERATION

Case

Prophets from Brazil

Alan Johnson's chain of thought was momentarily interrupted as the Boeing 747 began its approach to John F. Kennedy Airport, New York. Alan was returning from a three-week business trip to Brazil, and he had been mulling over the meetings with business and church leaders in São Paulo, one of the largest cities in the southern hemisphere. A company conference awaited his report on Monday, and, perhaps equally troubling, the Social Concerns Committee of the Catholic parish he belonged to in Stamford, Connecticut, expected his recommendations.

Questions raised during his trip raced through his mind. Should Brazil be the parish's mission focus for the next year? If so, how should their influence and resources be brought to bear? Should they focus upon the social, political, economic, and religious structures that work to oppress the poor? To do so would mean working with the poor and in opposition to those who hold power in Brazil. Or would it be more responsible to work with those in the hierarchy of the government and church, funnelling money into their hands and agencies so that they could then dispense it in the form of food, medical supplies, educational supplies, and resources to help further evangelism? In short, Alan would have to recommend whether his church should work within or against the established structures in Brazil.

But that was not Alan's only dilemma. There was also the tension between his two roles. Could he recommend that his company expand its business investments in Brazil and at the same time argue that the church should oppose the structures that seemed to be at the root of the oppression of the poor and the violation of human rights in Brazil? Those suggestions would seem to be at cross-purposes. Alan's recommendations had seemed clearer before he had begun serious preparation for the visit. Now after that preparation and the visit itself, he was flying back into New York

This case study was prepared by Robert A. Evans. Copyright © The Case Study Institute. The original case appears in *Human Rights: A Dialogue between the First and Third Worlds* (Maryknoll, N.Y.: Orbis Books, 1983). Case revised in 1987, Alice F. Evans.

confused by the wealth of conflicting information and insights he had encountered.

SOCIAL CONCERNS

On Tuesday evening Alan was scheduled to share his findings during his trip to Brazil with the other members of the Social Concerns Committee of his 1,500-member parish. The parish was composed largely of the families of business executives and professionals, many of whom commuted each day to New York. The committee in recent years had been involved in promoting charitable causes on a local level, such as a children's home, family counseling services, meals-on-wheels, and some mission interpretation for the national church. The year before, a new chairperson, John Andrews, had urged the committee to take an active position on national and international issues of justice, drawing on the expertise and knowledge of several members of the congregation. John declared that the committee's mandate was set by Jesus himself at the beginning of his public ministry. John had read from the prophet Isaiah:

> The Spirit of the Lord is upon me, because he has anointed me to preach good news to the poor. He has sent me to proclaim release to the captives and recovering of sight to the blind, to set at liberty those who are oppressed, to proclaim the acceptable year of the Lord [Luke 4:18–19].

Andrews personally recruited Alan for the committee, knowing that he was committed to issues of civil rights and that he traveled widely for International Electric as a vice-president of the international division. Although initially reluctant to serve because of a heavy work schedule, Alan found the committee work exciting. It was in his judgment, however, too scattered; there were reports to the congregation on everything from drug abuse to world hunger. Alan urged the committee to make an impact upon the congregation through the identification of a specific mission priority for the new year. Given the concerns of several committee members for human rights and for poor in the Third World and the growing significance of South America for both U.S. government and business interests, this area was selected by the committee.

BACKGROUND PREPARATION

In preparation for his trip Alan read briefing documents prepared by the International Electric research department, a 1986 report on Brazil by Amnesty International, the human rights organization, and *Brazil 2000*, a report prepared for Brazil's president. Alan had also consulted with a friend, Tom Perkins, who taught in a nearby university and had access to

U.S. State Department reports. Alan was struck by the startling contrasts in the largest country in South America. One document indicated that in terms of gross national product, Brazil ranked eighth in the world, placing it in the company of countries such as Japan, West Germany, and the United States. Brazil had become the world's second largest exporter of food (following the United States). However, in terms of infant mortality, poverty, and malnutrition, Brazil ranked near the bottom, in the company of nations like Haiti, Nepal, and Bangladesh. According to Tom's analysis, a primary factor was that control of the great natural and industrial wealth of the country was in the hands of a small minority. In addition, several years of drought in northeast Brazil had brought extreme hardship to the area. Hundreds of thousands of landless peasants had migrated south toward the urban centers of Rio de Janeiro and São Paulo in order to survive. At one point a number of years earlier there had been reports that as much as one-third of the total population was in migration. Although many had now returned to the north, countless thousands of homeless remained in and around the urban centers.

By earlier government estimates 45 percent of the nation's 400 million acres of arable land was in the hands of 1 percent of the nation's landowners. Tom Perkins traced these figures historically to colonial policies introduced by Portugal in the sixteenth century. Eager for the new colony to be explored, settled, and defended, the Portuguese monarchy granted vast estates to vassals of the crown. These vassals were given total power in return for a percentage of the taxes and revenues collected. Portugal later moved to appoint a governor general for the whole of Brazil, but the pattern of single family ownership of hundreds of thousands of acres remained. Specific land reform laws were introduced in the early 1960s and in 1985, but the government did not actively pursue enforcement of the laws.

Ninety percent of those who owned these large tracts farmed a small percentage of their land. Alan learned that significant portions of the land which was cultivated were used to grow export crops of sugar, coffee, and soybeans. Beef and leather were also major exports. Alan noted that extensive burning and development of large tracts in the Amazon Basin were proceeding on a massive scale, much of it intended to provide grazing land for cattle and access to mineral and oil deposits. He also read about "irreversible ecological damage" to the rain forests in northern Brazil.

The mid-1980s was a period of great hope that many of these situations would change. From 1964 to 1985 Brazil had been ruled by a series of military dictators. During those years federal and state legislatures had been disbanded, the constitution had been suspended, and strict censorship had been imposed. There had been severe repression, including secret arrests, torture, and murder by the military and police. Following elections, a civilian president, Tancredo Neves, had been installed in May 1985. Congress had approved a constitutional amendment to restore direct elections.

Neves's platform opposed state economic intervention and authoritarian control; he personally vowed to give priority to dealing with the annual inflation rate, then at 230 percent. After five weeks in office, Neves was hospitalized for abdominal surgery. Many questions raised by the national and international press about his subsequent death were left unanswered. José Sarney Costa, who had been elected vice-president, assumed the presidency. Until the previous June, he had led a party which supported five consecutive military governments.

This change from military to civilian rule had inspired considerable hope, and many in the United States assumed that civilian rule would bring about significant changes in life in Brazil. Many people at International Electric and at Alan's church had made that assumption. But, as Alan read the various reports and talked with Tom Perkins, he learned that there were many signs that fundamental changes had not occurred. Two land reform bills were approved in 1985, but wealthy landowners violently opposed implementation, and little had been done by the government to implement the mandated reforms. Amnesty International's 1986 report (on 1985) expressed concern for "an increase in the politically motivated killings of rural trade union leaders, peasants and others during land disputes." The organization "welcomed official inquiries into some of the worst abuses."

Before he had left on his trip Alan learned that in November 1985 the Roman Catholic Church in Brazil released a list of four hundred people charged with torturing political prisoners during the twenty-one years of military rule. The list included several high-ranking officers who were on active duty when the report was released. There was no official response to the report.

On the economic front, Brazil had gone through a period of rapid industrial development, financed by large international loans. The government had amassed an enormous foreign debt. By 1985 its interest payments consumed 27 percent of all exports of goods and services. The United States continued to be Brazil's greatest trading partner.

When Alan arrived in Brazil he knew that Brazil's economy had grown remarkably, but he also learned that functional illiteracy (24 percent of the population) continued to grow at a significant rate. Figures from the nation's industries indicate that as many as 58 percent of the workers are functionally illiterate. Rural teachers, whose salaries are often only $10 per month, have little or no training. Alan read that teachers of the poor had said that "the children of the poor often drop out of school to work or are too restless and hungry to concentrate."

Finally, in the report prepared for Brazil's president, Alan read that the richest 1 percent of the population earned 13 percent of the nation's total income, roughly the same as the poorest 50 percent. Research indicated that 65 percent of Brazil's inhabitants suffer from malnutrition. The report concluded that the "country is reaching the limits of peaceful coexistence between the rich and the poor."

Alan reached Brazil trying to sort out this conflicting and complicated mass of data and the contrasting signs of hope and despair. He hoped that by meeting with business and church leaders he would be able to reach conclusions about how International Electric and his church's Social Concerns Committee could proceed in relation to the social, economic, and political forces at work in Brazil.

THE MISSIONARY

Alan spent the first week of his trip immersed in conferences and formal dinners with Brazilian business executives. The first Sunday afternoon he had free, Alan called on Doug Williams, a friend of a minister who had worked with Alan's pastor in Stamford. Doug had served as a missionary in Brazil for twenty years. Deeply concerned about the reports he had read of human rights violations and the desperate poverty of the people, Alan asked Doug what position his mission had taken.

Doug Williams was emphatic in his response: "Missionaries are the guests of the country and the Brazilian church. It is presumptuous of outsiders to speak out as natives. The task of the church is set by Jesus himself in the Great Commission. We are to go into all the world and preach the gospel. This is a mission of conversion. When people are liberated from sin, they are liberated to change their own situation. Jesus also calls us to minister to the needs of the poor and those who suffer. This is the basis of our mission health clinic, which serves thousands in the *favelas* [slum areas], and of the mission school. If we spend our time fighting the government or the rich, we will drain our energies and resources and will neglect the power of the gospel to change lives.

"I may not always agree with the government's course of action," Williams continued. "However, as foreign nationals we have to understand the position of a government trying to survive in a nation with an enormous gap between the rich and poor, and with political controversy always being stirred up from the outside. The communists are seen by those in power as a threat to the survival of Brazilian life. It is like going into the *favela* and being challenged to a fight. You and I have been taught in our protected society to fight fair. But if the boy who challenges you has sand to throw in your eyes and a broken bottle to cut your throat, to fight fair would be to die. The government sometimes takes extreme measures, which may seem oppressive to outsiders, to survive these foes.

"There are those Christians who have directly challenged the government. However, you must realize that some strategies of confrontation hurt the mission of the church and even the cause of human rights. A number of years ago the U.S. administration took a strong stand on human rights issues. There was broad U.S. media exposure of human rights violations and direct criticism of the Brazilian government's policies.

"And what was the result," Doug asked, "of all this intervention? A greater pressure put on those advocating change and the recognition of human rights. Also a change in policy: for a time no missionaries or church personnel were granted resident visas.

"As Christians, we must continually remind ourselves of our mission. Paul was clear when he warned: 'Let every person be subject to the governing authorities' [Rom. 13:1]. Remember that Paul was speaking of the Roman government which was both cruel and unjust to early Christians. The church is not called to be a political agent. The church is called to conversion."

CALL FOR LIBERATION

Following the conclusion of Alan's business consultations, his company had suggested he spend an additional weekend in Brazil "for personal relaxation." Alan decided to spend much of this time in conversations with members of the Inter-Faith Task Force for Liberation, a group suggested by Tom Perkins and members of the Social Concerns Committee.

It was difficult for Alan to believe that his business associates were describing the same country as those he met at the headquarters of the Inter-Faith Task Force. "Identification of the church with the poor, not the powerful," the Reverend Paulo de Souza declared, "is the only hope for the Catholic or Protestant churches in Brazil." A dedicated group of churchpersons, including priests and lay people, Protestants and Roman Catholics, men and women, had formed the task force to demonstrate the need to "labor together across ecumenical and geographical lines in the name of the universal church of Jesus Christ." They were often criticized by members of their own church bodies, and under the military government in particular they had been harassed, arrested, and imprisoned when they sought to "denounce and expose the violation of human rights and dignity of all God's children."

Father Antonio Cardosa, a Dominican priest and teacher, reminded Alan that over 60 percent of Brazilians were hungry, living far below the poverty line as defined in the United States. "There is enormous wealth in Brazil, concentrated in a tiny portion of the population that exerts power to maintain the status quo. In these circumstances, what does it mean to follow Jesus' command to preach good news to the poor? The critical issue is: How can a people be free? How can the church as church be free? Conscientization of the church would mean moving from focusing on purely spiritual matters to engagement with the community in Christ's name."

Paulo de Souza was clear about the major issues that face the church in Brazil and what was required of those seeking to be faithful. He summarized those issues and requirements while speaking with Alan. He told Alan: "First, the church must become a true companion in favor of justice — an advocate of justice, not in principle only but in concrete situations. Problems of poverty and violence can no longer be ignored by the church.

Second, the church must identify with the populace. In the past the church has always been linked with the powerful. The church can no longer simply react; it must take its place in the struggle and initiate action. Third, identification with the poor — the special concern of God in the Old and New Testaments — involves ceasing to spiritualize the problems of the poor. Poverty in Brazil has a social structure that is a direct result of the capitalist system. This system — nurtured by the U.S.A. and protected by the rich, which includes the present church — breeds injustice. Fourth, there is a built-in relationship between creative pastoralization and politicization. The church is involved in the problems and must work at the issues. Politics is a form of faith for an institution seeking to be a church of the poor. Three elements required are: (a) a practical alliance with the poor; (b) a methodology for the scientific interpretation of social reality; and (c) biblical and theological reflection resulting in the stress on action with the poor, excluding any compromises with power. Fifth, local congregations are inadequate. There is need for a new form of church where believers are not domesticated, but take part in the decisions that affect their lives. Our hope is in the base communities [*comunidades de base*] that are attempting to change the structure of an unjust society. The question is not so much individual rights as it is the social rights of a whole community. Although they may seem threatening to some priests, these lay groups provide new structures of hope for the church."

Father Antonio was in agreement that the new hope of the church was in those same base communities now numbering millions of persons, with fifteen thousand new groups in one year alone. "They have no sacrament and no priest, but are studying the Bible and politics in order to discover a way to liberate themselves and the world. The need is for an honest, aggressive, and compassionate world church that will be willing to suffer with us. Galatians says we are 'to bear one another's burdens.' Let us then do this for one another."

During these conversations Alan was struck with the parallels to one of the church-related human rights reports he had read which stated that to confess belief in the communion of saints meant to share the suffering of brothers and sisters in Christ in every section of the earth. Anything less would be to avoid Christ's call to set at liberty those who are oppressed. As he returned to his hotel, Alan was seriously considering that those who demanded a new position from the U.S. government and a new lifestyle from Christians in the U.S. church may be on the right track.

THE MEDIATORS

Some church bodies, Alan found, represented neither the drive toward structural change of the Inter-Faith Task Force nor the personal, spiritual focus represented by conservative evangelical Christians like Doug Williams. "The mediators," as the Reverend Benjamin Villaca described them, "are the practical moderates present among Roman Catholics, Presbyterians, and some other Protestants. They call for gradual transformation of our Brazilian society. This nation, which occupies over half the land mass of the South American continent, has been characterized by evolution, not revolution. The Brazilians are a relatively gentle and tolerant people who have had such a stable development that even our coups have been relatively bloodless. Realistically, social change will be slow and the church must be present and faithful. The answer lies in the responsible use of the God-given talents of individual Christians in the public service of their people.

"Education and evangelism are at the heart of the matter," Villaca continued. "Religious and secular education of the people provides the foundation for a renewed church and a developed society. Christians must devote their talents to providing better schools, more adequate housing, and medical facilities at every level of society. Evangelism programs will allow Brazilians to see that the church has the key to a better life. The Christian message will take different forms in the *favelas* and on Copacabana Beach in Rio. The Christian is called to be responsible to God, neighbor, and self. Catholics constitute over 90 percent of the overall population in this 'most Catholic nation of our times.' If only 5 percent of them, and the Protestants, who comprise a similar minority, are active, then the opportunities for evangelism are enormous.

"Ecumenical radicals are as much Marxist as Christian. They cannot really affect government or the privileged class despite their claim that 'only a revolution in the structure of society and the church will bring liberation.' Christians are entitled to the fruits of their labor if the gains are responsibly shared with others. The World Council of Churches has been simply ignored ever since it began to support terrorists and guerrillas who only bring violence and loss of life by preaching liberation, not reconciliation.

"The conservatives and Pentacostals are individualistic escapists, unwilling to face their societal responsibilities. Their refusal to dance, smoke, drink, gamble, or in general participate in society simply evades the reality of an evolving society. A few hours of ecstasy each week through baptism of the Holy Spirit is little different from our spiritualist cults. Moral rigidity that judges and condemns all practices except one's own builds enthusiasm for a righteous minority but will not attract those who need the Christian gospel of forgiveness.

"We need," Villaca concluded, "the support of the North American churches as we have usually experienced it, only to a fuller measure. We need more money and trained personnel for schools, hospitals, housing projects, and Christian education projects. Send us aid without strings attached. Help establish better relations with our president. He has promised progress in several areas of life, from land reform to a more active anti-poverty program. This is a religiously oriented nation. The church could help us by encouraging private and governmental gifts. Let your church and companies know we need their continued support."

DOUBLE DILEMMA

After circling for thirty minutes, the captain announced the final approach to New York. Alan's thoughts spun from his confusion on the church recommendation to the business advice he must provide. With over 450,000 color television sets sold in Brazil in one year alone, and with the promise of the U.S. government to guarantee the investment, it seemed good business sense to recommend expansion. There was substantial evidence that the profits for International Electric would be high. However, the 230 percent inflation rate in Brazil, and the standard practice of private lending companies to finance television sets and refrigerators at an 8 percent monthly interest rate, made Alan hesitate. He was disturbed by the loan policies with which newly arrived immigrants in Rio and São Paulo were unfamiliar. They made little more than the $50 a month national minimum wage — if they had a job at all. The buy low, sell high attitude of retailers, coupled with aggressive debt collections, spelled tragedy for low-income consumers, though a boon to the appliance business. The members of the Inter-Faith Task Force had pressed Alan to understand and communicate to North Americans that multinational corporations such as International Electric expected twice as much return on investments in countries like Brazil as on the same investments in the United States; those corporations helped to maintain the often oppressive regimes and political and social structures that fostered the profits at the expense of the poor. Alan gave his mind to that analysis, but then reminded himself that stockholders at home wanted a return on their money, not a speech about corporate social responsibility.

The church report was equally a problem. Should he recommend Brazil as a mission priority? If so, which request by Brazilians should he honor? What is the most faithful and effective: political and economic intervention; lobbying at home combined with a new awareness of the world church; a campaign for major mission funds for education and evangelism; or not recommend Brazil as a mission project because the issues are unclear and involvement from outside is not wanted?

As the clouds parted over Long Island, the face of Carlos de Carvalho — Alan's host, old friend, and an active Christian layman in Brazil — came to Alan's mind. After a lively discussion of the options on the last evening, Carlos had said, "It's a tough decision for you to make and I am not sure what you ought to do. I am convinced the world church must learn to make decisions in light of needs everywhere in the world. To make no decision is cowardice. A sustained strategy is needed. When will the church in America have the courage to be a prophet and not just a provocateur?"

"Fasten your seatbelt, please, Mr. Johnson," the flight attendant said. "The landing in this wind may be a little rough."

Commentary

Prophets from Brazil

Alan Johnson's problem seems simple enough. He has reports to make to the two different worlds he lives in: the world of his suburban parish and the world of International Electric, a large transnational corporation (TNC). Alan's visit to Brazil, however, has added several new worlds, making his problem far more complex. He must now consider the rich and poor worlds of Brazil as well as the world of U.S. foreign policy.

Whose world should he stand in to view the reality of Brazil and the mission of the church? He has the briefing documents of International Electric, no doubt with their eye for profitable opportunities; U.S. State Department reports, which regularly view the rich/poor division in terms of the East/West conflict; a report from Amnesty International and another written for Brazil's president; the outlook of Brazilian business associates, probably urging his company to expand the production of big-ticket consumer goods; the charity-based perspective of his own congregation; Doug Williams's individualistic Christianity; the view of those in the Inter-Faith Task Force who work within the reality of Brazil's poverty; and Benjamin Villaca's reformist approach. With these conflicting worldviews before him, the storm over Kennedy Airport is also in Alan's soul.

The immediate task is the reports. Since Alan is in a quandary, perhaps the frequently used technique of delay in such situations is appropriate. Alan could make preliminary reports and then undertake a more thorough study involving members of his church and business associates. Both research and experiential learning would be part of this study.

Alan would have to decide what his study would entail. Certainly it would have to include something on the history of Brazilian social structures, and how the Brazilian experience relates to other Third World situations. Alan needs to understand the dynamism of the Brazilian economy and the 40 to 60 percent of the people in poverty who do not participate in it. He needs to know how his company contributes to both the economic growth and the persisting poverty. Finally, further reflection on his encounter with Brazilian Christians, perhaps even returning to dialogue further, would help him to identify his options. With this Alan could make more comprehensive reports with recommendations for action. By bringing others along in his study he would increase the possibility for successful learning and implementation. This delay and further study would no doubt ultimately produce a better report, and yet Alan is still faced with the need to reach some conclusions for the reports he must soon give.

BRAZIL: UNIQUE YET REPRESENTATIVE

Alan undoubtedly knows that among countries in Latin America Brazil is unique because of its Portuguese colonial rule and its rate of economic development since 1930. It is the latter which really sets it apart, however, since Portuguese colonial administration and the religious imposition which accompanied it were not substantially different from that of the Spanish. Since 1930 Brazil has industrialized at a rate that proponents of development call "phenomenal" or "miraculous." It is now the richest country in Latin America. Still the same development process has occurred to a lesser degree but with many of the same elements throughout Latin America, so that even with its more rapid economic growth, Brazil can be considered representative of the region. In particular, the division of Brazilian society into a well-off minority and an impoverished majority is characteristic of countries in Latin America and generally in the Third World.

In addition, the same general historical forces pushing Latin American economic and social development also pushed Brazil, only much harder after 1930. From the sixteenth century until the latter part of the nineteenth century the economic life of Brazil was dominated by gold mining and the production for export of sugar, coffee, cocoa, rubber, and hides. Brazil, as was the case in almost all colonial countries, supplied the raw materials for the industrial production of the more developed countries and in turn imported finished products.

While a few Brazilians in the colonial period became very wealthy on this relationship, they made little effort to invest this wealth productively. Much of it was consumed in maintaining a high standard of living. The revolution of 1821, which brought formal independence, did not alter this pattern.

The social system which supported this pattern was based in agriculture, unequal, and dominated by a feudal aristocracy. The Roman Catholic Church mirrored the pattern. It was hierarchical, state-supported, and aloof from the vast majority of Brazilians whose popular religion saw them through life's passages and taught them not to raise questions about inequities. State and church were two well-integrated parts of one system which benefited the ruling oligarchy and left the rest to subsist as they could on a limited range of basic necessities.

As the nineteenth century unfolded, some parts of Latin America began to attract foreign capital. In many countries there emerged a new elite based in expanding commerce; they were called "liberals," in contrast to the landed aristocracy who were known as "conservatives." The political history of the late nineteenth and early twentieth centuries in Latin America was dominated by conflict between liberals and conservatives as now one, now the other, gained control. The two elites had one thing in common, however — disdain for the Indians, mixed-bloods, peasants, and Afro-Americans who did their bidding.

During the early part of the twentieth century almost everywhere in the region liberals gained the upper hand and then joined forces with conservatives to form a fairly tight oligarchy. In Brazil liberal ascendancy is usually dated from 1930 when the export market for agricultural commodities collapsed in the Great Depression. Thereafter Brazil embarked on a period of industrialization marked by the substitution of domestically produced consumer goods for foreign imports.

Industrialization picked up steam in the late 1940s and 1950s fueled by deliberate government policies to restrict imports, to stimulate demand, and to encourage domestic production of consumer durables such as automobiles and electrical equipment.

Important in this strategy were TNCs such as International Electric and executives such as Alan who were called on to provide the needed capital-intensive technologies to advance the domestic production of consumer durables. Attracted by government policies and the prospect of substantial profits, TNCs answered the call. They thrived. What resulted was the cozy relationship, which Alan has inherited, between the TNCs and the small class of Brazilians who benefited from rapid growth and held political power.

Whether the eventual dominance of the TNCs had more to do with their ability to penetrate markets or the conscious choice of a few Brazilians to let them take over is a matter for economic debate. Whichever, today's reality is fairly clear. TNCs own about 50 percent of Brazil's total assets. Forty percent of its largest firms are TNC subsidiaries. TNCs dominate the most profitable sectors, such as automobiles, pharmaceuticals, and electrical equipment, leaving the production of less profitable, nondurable consumer goods to private Brazilian firms. Their domination has given them power over prices, which they have translated into what is known as monopoly profits.

In charging higher prices than would be normal in a more competitive situation and in turn realizing higher profits, TNCs help to redistribute income to the rich inside Brazil who own subsidiaries and to owners in First World countries through repatriated profits. The skewed distribution of income and wealth characteristic of the colonial period has become a seemingly permanent inheritance, even though a few poor people have entered the ranks of the new elite.

During the 1960s Brazil's industrialization slowed down. The Brazilian military, always an important source of stability, stepped in and governed with severe repression, justifying civil rights abuses in the name of national security and the fight against communism. That pattern of military takeover and its justification were widespread in Latin America. As Alan has learned from reading a number of recent documents, in 1985 civilian rule, or at least the veneer thereof, returned to Brazil. Human rights violations were greatly reduced and a measure of democracy was instituted. Effective power, however, still rested with a coalition of military men, bureaucrats, industrial leaders, and wealthy landowners.

In the early and middle 1970s the generals and their economic advisers did manage to set Brazil on another growth spurt. But this spurt ended in the late 1970s with rising oil prices and world recession. In the 1980s the problem became the massive debt which Brazil had run up especially in the 1970s. The debt problem is general to the Third World, but Brazil's more than one hundred billion dollar debt is the highest in the developing world. It is also beyond Brazil's current resources to manage. The tragedy of the debt is that the poor, who received few of the benefits from incurring it, are being asked to foot their share of repayment through austerity measures which feature lower wages, higher prices, increased unemployment, and more emphasis on cash crops and exports.

The U.S. government has had an important role in all this. The United States has supported the Brazilian government through a succession of military and civilian regimes. It has furthered the penetration of the Brazilian economy by U.S.-based TNCs. It has trained Brazilian and other Latin American army leaders and provided them with military equipment. Finally, it has ensured "stability" to the entire region through direct intervention, as in the overthrow of Jacobo Arbenz in Guatemala in 1954 and Salvador Allende in Chile in 1973, and through "low-intensity warfare." The latter is a strategy to destabilize potentially hostile regimes, for example, the Sandinistas in Nicaragua. Combined with military support of friendly regimes, for example, El Salvador, Guatemala, and to a degree even Brazil, "stability" is assured. The U.S. government does all this in the name of the East/West conflict and national security, maintaining that friendly governments are democratic and capitalist and that popular movements keyed to the interests of the poor are totalitarian and communist. One thing Alan must do is weigh these claims carefully and ask if this strategy really ensures long-range stability.

THE REALITY OF POVERTY

Statistics offer some indication of Brazil's two worlds. As Alan learned from the report prepared for Brazil's president, the richest 1 percent of Brazilians harvests about 13 percent of the national income while the poorest 50 percent gleans slightly less. Of the gain in national income between 1960 and 1976, three-quarters was appropriated by 10 percent of the people.

But abstract statistics do not reveal the misery and suffering which Alan Johnson could not have avoided on his business trips. Occasionally such things as mud slides in Rio de Janeiro kill enough shanty dwellers to attract media attention. For the most part, however, the poor are invisible and silent, eking out a subsistence on marginal land or muddling through in urban slums. The truth is that one-third of Brazil's families exist in wretched and miserable poverty with little hope for improvement.

One element in this tragic picture is directly relevant to Alan. In small part the misery of Brazil's urban poor is attributable to the demand which TNCs such as International Electric stimulate through advertising. The poor no less than their better-off cousins develop a "need" for television sets. Food is traded off for a television set in the family budget, and hunger increases. Although the effect is seldom linked to the cause, for Alan's company to increase its sales is to decrease nutritional standards further.

Alan encounters and will continue to encounter conflicting interpretations of this poverty. For supporters of Brazil's "economic miracle" it is temporary. It is the inevitable state of affairs which always accompanies rapid economic growth. These people argue that the need to depress consumption and to increase savings in order to generate capital creates great inequality for a limited time period, as it did in the United States and Western Europe during their industrial revolutions. This short-term side-effect will eventually be overcome as the wealth and income generated by growth trickle down to the poor. When that happens the distribution of income and wealth will improve of its own accord. Thus the antidote for poverty is more rapid growth. This is best achieved by social stability, TNC and World Bank investment, rewards sufficient to persuade entrepreneurs to take risks, and government policies which stimulate demand for consumer durables and protect Brazilian industries.

Alan may wonder why this trickle-down process has been so slow to take effect. Yes, it is true that a few have become fantastically wealthy, and a few more have shifted from the land and found work. Still the reality for the overwhelming majority of poor is the same grinding existence.

In contrast to the official explanations of economic theory, Alan hears from those who hold that the bottom 40 to 60 percent of Brazilian society will remain poor so long as power is wielded by a narrow oligarchy and TNCs buttressed by U.S. military might. There are indeed gains from economic growth, but poverty will persist if these gains are siphoned off by a few, taken out of the country in TNC profits and in deposits to Swiss bank accounts, spent on luxury consumption, and invested in inappropriate technology.

To make matters worse, worsening terms of trade for primary agricultural and mining exports relative to manufactured imports continue to funnel the gains of international trade to the industrialized countries. This brute fact and the need to repay staggering debts keep most poor countries on a treadmill of dependency. They must export more and more to import the same or less, and the anomaly of prime land being used to produce speciality agricultural commodities for export while poor people go landless and without staples will continue.

Perhaps Alan will come to think of Brazil's economy in terms of a closed circle. During the colonial period the circle was tiny. Using slave labor, wealthy landowners exported raw materials and agricultural commodities and imported luxury goods. The circle of the well off increased somewhat with the addition of the new urban commercial class and their military allies, but the post-1930 policies kept the circle closed by concentrating the gains of growth in the hands of a few.

Executives, such as Alan, were invited into the circle because they provided access to financial capital and the technical expertise to produce and market the consumer durables those inside the circle wanted and could afford. These executives also fortified the circle. The gains they brought were appropriated by the few. Their capital-intensive technologies created relatively few jobs so the circle did not appreciably expand. The military preserved the status quo. In simple fact the TNCs served themselves and a few in Brazil, all the time reinforcing the circular pattern.

Moreover, Alan will have to confront what should be for him a very disturbing conclusion. There is no particular reason to expect TNCs to change practices honed to perfection in developed economies just because those practices do not fit the needs of the poor. To change would mean huge new costs developing less capital-intensive technologies and basic products, both of which would be inappropriate to their primary markets. Risk would increase because TNCs are not adept at labor-intensive technologies and the mass production of basics.

In fact it is easier for TNCs to manage Third World economies so that these economies consume what TNCs already produce well. TNCs control modern technology. They have the capacity to set prices to gain monopoly profits. They can create demand through superior marketing skills and advertising. They are large enough to realize the reduced costs of large-scale operations. Finally, they have superior access to financing, the capability to bail out subsidiaries, and the resources to acquire local firms.

TNCs simply are not geared to the needs of poor people. They never have been and never will be as long as capital-intensive markets are their main arenas and profits their major preoccupation. Poor people in Third World countries like Brazil need labor-intensive technologies. They do not have sufficient purchasing power to meet the profit and growth needs of the TNCs. To secure a change in policy and to gain purchasing power they will have to be admitted to the closed circle or force their way into it. For them to be admitted means a redistribution of income and wealth which is of little interest to TNCs, not to mention local elites. Redistribution would in the short run only mean a reduction in consumption and a loss of TNC business as more basics were consumed. Forcing their way in means revolution with its instabilities and threats to growth and profits. It is thus in the immediate interest of TNCs both to promote the status quo and to sell consumer durables to the wealthy.

THE POOR AS THE POINT OF DEPARTURE

Assuming for the sake of discussion that Alan had the power to embark on development plans which did not depend on trickle-down economics but took the poor as their point of departure, what are a few things he could do?

In rural areas, a three-pronged strategy called "integrated rural development" has gained strong support. The first prong of this strategy is concentration on smaller-scale, more labor-intensive and appropriate production which generates more employment and productivity than larger-scale, more capital-intensive production for export. Agrarian reform is crucial. It includes land redistribution and the provision of financial, legal, and technical services to ensure that newly acquired land is used productively and does not revert to former owners.

The second prong involves the integrated improvement of the various dimensions of community life. Nutrition, health, sanitation, education, and family planning are simultaneously addressed along with the promotion of cooperative endeavors and the encouragement of a new sense of self-worth. Some of the more creative plans focus on women as the primary agents of social change.

The third prong is the building of a framework for development by concentrating on the institutions and skills necessary for development. Individuals must learn the techniques of productive agriculture, sanitation, nutrition, and family planning. They must master the organization of regional structures, local cooperatives, and volunteer associations.

In urban areas, concentrating on labor-intensive production with massive subsidies to develop intermediate technologies would be one way to create more jobs. Combined with some form of income and wealth redistribution to broaden the base of consumers, enough demand could be stimulated to soak up the output of labor-intensive production.

Alan might have to conclude for obvious reasons that prospects for development plans which take the poor as their point of departure are not bright. Still, experiments with integrated rural development and the recent movement away from repressive military dictatorships are at least a few steps in the right direction. The electoral process which brings new administrations to Washington at least every eight years also leaves hopes for a changed U.S. role.

The possibility of a new era in Brazil, Latin America, and the Third World generally could even mean opportunities for Alan and International Electric. Perhaps Alan's task within his firm is not the expansion of the market for more television sets but research into ways that a TNC could provide appropriate technologies and financial services to the poor yet still make a profit. He probably will not have an easy time persuading his associates at International Electric, however. That is one reason why their education is so crucial.

THE MISSION OF THE CHURCH

Using his free time well, Alan Johnson managed to touch base with a remarkable cross section of Brazilian Christians. In Doug Williams he encounters Protestant evangelical Christianity with its individualistic bent. The Reverend Paulo de Souza and Father Antonio Cardosa represent the liberation movements in Latin America. Finally, in the Reverend Benjamin Villaca, Alan sees an evolutionary, middle-of-the-road approach stressing political moderation and education. By taking time to experience these perspectives firsthand, Alan immeasurably enhances his understanding. Indeed he represents a model of dialogue which he can encourage members of his congregation and business colleagues to follow.

Protestant Evangelical Christianity

This form of Christianity has enjoyed remarkable growth in Latin America spurred by missionaries from the United States such as Doug. The reasons for its growth are not hard to find. The traditional aloofness of its clergy and its alliance with the landed aristocracy had for centuries put the Roman Catholic Church out of touch with much of Latin American society. Moral values supportive of market capitalism and the tendency to stay out of economics and politics give the evangelicals a natural affinity with the new commercial class. The evangelical approach with its message of individual salvation, its warm fellowship, and its otherworldly concerns appeals to poor people in an unstable and repressive political atmosphere.

For Doug Williams the mission of the church is set in Jesus' Great Commission to his disciples (Matt. 10:35ff.): To preach the gospel of the kingdom of God. The gospel Doug preaches is one which appears to divide human reality into personal and social realms, the former the province of the church with its message of individual salvation, the latter the province of civil authorities with their obligation to maintain order. While he is critical of Brazilian inequality and preaches to the poor the gospel of liberation from sin, he is even more critical of Christians who take direct action to end social abuses and liberate the poor politically. In the final analysis, Christians are to be subject to the governing authorities (Rom. 13:1ff.), and the church's task is to bind the wounds of society's victims and help them to find salvation.

For Doug the way to change society is to change people. Convert individuals to Jesus Christ and the "born again" life, and they will in turn change society from within. To superimpose social change on sinful people is fruitless, for sin will inevitably reassert itself.

Although he does not say it explicitly and is even critical at points, Doug seems generally supportive of the social status quo. The closed circle does not bother him, probably because he considers it outside of his purview and irrelevant to his task. "Life in Christ," he might say, "can be lived inside or outside the circle, it makes no difference."

Much of what Doug preaches is very traditional. Alan needs to ask him further, however, about his tendency to separate individual and social realms and his neglect of social justice questions. Alan might want to say that Jesus Christ is lord of both realms and works to bring liberation from political oppression as well as from sin. He might question Doug on the mission of the church and whether it is so exclusively tied to individual conversion. And will saved souls in fact be agents of social change or supporters of both the status quo and the closed circle? Finally, Alan may wonder if the gospel Doug preaches does not act as a drug salving only the wounds of injustice and ignoring their causes.

Liberation Theology

Liberation theology is a movement that began in Latin America. It is represented in the case by the Reverend Paulo Souza and Father Antonio Cardosa of the Inter-Faith Task Force. This movement arose in Roman Catholic circles, but its rapid growth and popular appeal have carried it to Protestants. As a result, ecumenical groups, such as the Inter-Faith Task Force, have developed. Today liberation theology stands in tension with both traditional Latin American Catholicism, with its hierarchical structure and popular piety, and with evangelical Protestantism, which arose out of the North American experience and its concentration on individual salvation.

In Brazil liberation theologians Leonardo and Clodovis Boff have been especially prominent. Several Brazilian cardinals, for example Aloísio Lorscheider and Paulo Evaristo Arns, have also lent the movement support. The case itself offers a good summary of liberation themes, and a further discussion of liberation theology can be found in this volume in the commentary on "Vietnam's Children."

Liberation theology is an interpretation of Christian faith which emerges from the experience of the poor. It seeks to empower poor people to develop a new consciousness about reality and their faith for the purpose of changing the conditions which oppress them. By liberation three things are meant, according to Peruvian Gustavo Gutiérrez: (1) liberation from social, economic, and political injustice; (2) liberation from false consciousness — an example of false consciousness might be the religious and economic ideologies which support the closed circle of Brazilian inequality and oppression; and (3) liberation from sin. God works on all three levels of liberation.

Central to these understandings of liberation is a critique of existing social institutions and the ideologies which sustain them; this critique is carried out from the perspective of the poor. The thought of Karl Marx is at times used selectively for this social criticism because it can be a helpful tool for understanding the economic and political injustice which the poor experience. Following Marx, liberationists frequently take an historical approach, tracing the path of oppression from the colonial period to the so-called national security state of the present day.

Liberation theology is a "bottom-up" perspective and may as a result seem foreign to Alan, the members of his church, and his business associates. Not only is existing reality viewed from the angle of the poor, but the poor are also to be the agents of their own liberation. Liberated from social repression, false consciousness, and incompletely from sin, the poor will take charge of their own futures. This process begins in small groups called *comunidades de base* (base communities) stressing prayer, worship, Bible study, and community. First instituted in Brazil and now reportedly numbering seventy thousand communities involving 2 percent of the population there, base communities are the platform for broader liberation.

While violence is not ruled out, most liberationists envision liberation as proceeding nonviolently. The overthrow of ruling oligarchies and the shape of liberated societies are both left purposely vague. Liberationists refuse to be "top-down" social engineers. The shape of the new society, they insist, must emerge in the process of liberation from the old and be tailored to the many different situations of the Third World. Social ownership is frequently mentioned although a full-blown socialism is usually rejected in favor of mixed public/private ownership.

The biblical basis for the liberation project is God's preferential option for the poor. God, according to liberation theologians, has taken the side of the poor. God has made this option clear in freeing the Hebrew slaves from bondage in Egypt, in the teachings of the prophets, and preeminently in Jesus Christ. Jesus reading from the Book of Isaiah in Luke 4:18–19 (cited in the text of this case) has become perhaps the most quoted text.

The mission of the church is to be God's servant for liberation. The church cannot liberate the poor, but it can identify and suffer with them, look at reality from the same angle, work for justice, and provide enabling resources. Change will come when the poor take the necessary actions. Individual conversion to Jesus Christ, as in the gospel which Doug Williams preaches, is not sufficient for social change because it ignores the first two forms of liberation and the social impediments to the third in its concentration on the individual.

Liberationists are, of course, critical of Brazil's closed circle and the role TNCs play in it. There is some tendency to see TNCs as villains, but it is the overall injustice of the closed circle which is their target. TNCs do not figure in the vision of the liberated future because in the past TNCs have had so little to offer a process of change from the bottom up.

To executives such as Alan, liberationists might appear simplistic and utopian. They seem to underestimate the difficulty of accumulating capital and organizing the factors of production. Their criticism of TNCs overlooks the valuable contributions TNCs make in assisting rapid economic growth.

On a theological level, Alan will want to ask Paulo and Antonio if they are not subverting the church's traditional message of liberation from sin and replacing it with a political ideology. Alan will have to think through the charge that liberation theologians are guilty of reductionism – that is, that they reduce sin to social institutions, the gospel to the struggle for justice, and Jesus' message to partisan politics. Finally, Alan must also ask questions about the use of Marx's thought. Is it compatible with the gospel? Does it not at least carry the implication of leading toward violent revolution? How much does it control the theology?

It may be difficult for Alan and most North Americans to understand this perspective. What he can understand, however, is what he can see: the degrading poverty of Latin America which is the parent of liberation theology. Whatever he advocates to his two worlds, he cannot overlook this poverty without doing violence to his conscience.

Moderate and Reformist Christianity

This form of Christianity seems to be the vantage point of Benjamin Villaca. The case suggests that he comes out of what in the United States would be called a "mainline" denomination. Benjamin is clear on the mission of the church. Perhaps referring to Doug Williams, he rejects the individualistic escapism of conservatives and Pentecostals. But in the same breath, perhaps referring to Paulo de Souza and Antonio Cardosa, he dismisses the "ecumenical radicals." To his way of thinking they are tied to Marxism, too prone to violence, and finally irrelevant.

He then carves out for himself an evolutionary perspective. Implied in his understanding is a theological balance of individual and social dimensions and realism about the human situation. The persistence of human sin is assumed, and agents of both social change and the status quo must be carefully monitored.

The path of change is evolutionary and is best traversed along the route of education and evangelism. Indeed, those are the two main tasks of the church, although it would not be outside the bounds of his perspective for the church to engage in political action of a moderate, reformist type. He is encouraged by the liberalizations introduced by the government and would seem to support the return to a semblance of democracy.

Given the tenor of his remarks, he is probably in general agreement with the rapid growth policies of successive Brazilian governments, although he would no doubt be critical of the great inequalities and abuses of human rights which have accompanied those policies. Included in his support might also be general affirmation of TNCs and certainly the expectation that they would be open to reform and possibly even agents of a more human direction. He says as much when he asks for financial support.

As with the others, Alan needs to ask Villaca questions. Can the closed circle of Brazilian life be opened by reform? Would it not be better, Alan might think, either to let the current policies run their course with the hope that some benefits would trickle down to the poor, or to seek radical social change and some sort of socialistic alternative? The former might at least bring economic growth and the latter greater equality. Benjamin's reformist perspective runs the danger of achieving neither and being overwhelmed in the process by more extreme options. Finally, Alan may wonder whether Benjamin's perspective, like that of Doug Williams, does not implicitly support the status quo by claiming it is capable of reform.

ALAN JOHNSON'S PROBLEM

So whose worldview should Alan represent? What should he report to his colleagues at International Electric and what to his church's Social Concerns Committee? The same questions are, of course, directed to every North American Christian, if for no other reason than the massive influence of the U.S. government and economy in Latin America.

One thing for sure, Alan cannot return to the charity-based perspective which has dominated his wealthy church in the past. That perspective deals with symptoms, not causes, and is not very relevant to the massive suffering in the Third World. Likewise, business as usual at International Electric is not an option unless Alan wants to turn a deaf ear to the cries he has heard in Brazil. Alan hardly seems callous to the suffering he has witnessed, so it seems that he must either find a way for International Electric to become less of the problem and more of the solution, or resign.

Whatever Alan decides, one thing he can do is share his new insights. In his explorations he has shown great openness in seeking to augment his understanding with genuine dialogue.

In assessing Alan's dilemma and the many perspectives he has encountered, the Christian concern for the poor should play an important normative role. It is a concern with many dimensions: greater equality, political freedom, the correction of human rights abuses, the provision of basic necessities over the long haul, and participation in community. In showing concern for the poor it is not enough to be well intentioned. The task of building durable and equitable political and economic institutions must be added to right intentions in order for justice to be a reality in Brazil.

ADDITIONAL RESOURCES

Berryman, Phillip. *Liberation Theology.* New York: Pantheon; Oak Park, Il.: Meyer-Stone, 1987.

Gutiérrez, Gustavo. *A Theology of Liberation.* Maryknoll, N.Y.: Orbis, 1973; rev. ed., 1988.

Hewlitt, Sylvia Ann. *The Cruel Dilemmas of Development: Twentieth-Century Brazil.* New York: Basic Books, 1980.

Johnston, Bruce F., and William C. Clark. *Redesigning Rural Development: A Strategic Perspective.* Baltimore: Johns Hopkins University Press, 1982.

Newfarmer, Richard, ed. *Profits, Progress and Poverty.* Notre Dame: University of Notre Dame Press, 1985.

United States Department of State. *Sustaining a Consistent Policy in Central America.* Special report no. 124, 1985.

Case

Eye of the Needle

"How do you get people not only to sign a covenant for low-income housing, but to seal it with their commitment and their funds?" Sue Adams was speaking to a colleague during the monthly meeting of HOPE, a loose coalition of church leaders working for adequate housing for the poor of Springfield.

"Hope" was not what Sue was feeling as she left the session a short time later. Six months earlier, following a hotel sit-in crisis, a gathering of the newly formed organization HOPE (Housing Opportunities for People Ecumenically) numbered thirty with a good representation of bishops, executive secretaries, and presidents of church groups. However, during those six months the participation of influential church leaders had declined. As a Puerto Rican friend remarked to Sue when discussing HOPE the week before, "It looks like the power has put it to the poor again. The 'city fathers' and the 'bishops' are off the hook on housing while the Blacks and the Hispanics get co-opted." At the meeting Sue had just left, she was one of two Whites. The other seven present were black clergymen.

Sue Adams knew that the agenda of the next meeting of HOPE was for each member to make specific strategy proposals. As she drove home, she decided she would telephone some of the key figures in the drama. Many persons seemed able to share freely with her, perhaps, she thought, because she had no clout of her own.

As an officer on the administrative board of the Methodist Church of Chesterton, Sue had become involved in the struggle for low-income housing through a telephone call from the associate pastor of her suburban church of seven hundred and fifty members. Acknowledging Sue's current involvement in the city as a volunteer English teacher for Hispanics, he had

This case was prepared by Robert A. Evans and Alice Frazer Evans. Copyright © The Case Study Institute. The names of all cities and case characters are disguised in order to protect the privacy of the individuals involved in this situation. A longer form of this case appears in *Human Rights: A Dialogue between the First and Third Worlds* (Maryknoll, N.Y.: Orbis Books, 1983).

urged her to join a demonstration at the Springfield Sheraton to protest the eviction of eighteen Hispanic families from the temporary shelter provided by the city. She had little idea then how her acceptance was to affect her life. She reflected now on the last six months, which were so much more involved with the problems of the inner city than when their family of four had lived in suburban St. Louis. Sue's husband was often away on business, their two teenage sons were fairly independent, and her own career as a writer allowed time for volunteer involvement.

BACKGROUND TO THE CRISIS

The background to the housing crisis of Springfield, with a population of two hundred and thirty thousand, was effectively summarized by a series of articles in the *Springfield Daily News*. Fifty percent of the city's population was black, 35 percent Hispanic. Springfield had one of the highest infant mortality rates of any city its size in the United States; unemployment was double and triple the national average among the black and Hispanic communities respectively; only one-third of the city students who entered high school graduated, and many of them with only a fifth-grade reading level. All these conditions existed in stark contrast to what the executive director of the Council of Churches called the white noose of affluent suburbs that ringed the city. Among these was Chesterton, where the Adams family lived.

The Springfield Housing Authority reported that five thousand families were on the waiting list for public housing — nearly twice the number waiting eighteen months earlier. Another fifty-five hundred families were waiting for federal rent subsidies provided through the city's Public Housing Corporation. Another fifty families had been forced out of their apartments by fire, housing code violations, or redevelopment projects.

Gentrification

The 1980 census showed that over thirty-three hundred housing units were lost in Springfield during the past ten years. Despite the fact that this was the only major city in the state to have a decline in housing units, there was no shortage of housing for those who could afford more than $500 a month for rent. There was general agreement that the housing crisis was primarily limited to the poor.

A major factor appeared to be the relatively new phenomenon of "gentrification": developers and speculators were buying numerous units of low-income housing, turning them into large, luxury housing units for the middle class, and selling them at ten times the original investment. Sue recalled reading an analysis of the process by the manager of a low-income housing project: "The huge profits go to the investors. The city council praises the increase in the tax base, and other landlords raise their rents, convert to condominiums, or abandon the buildings as not economically viable. The poor are the ones who lose."

Sue's husband, Frank, had openly disagreed with parts of the analysis. Though affirming the need for adequate housing for the poor, he said that "ultimately the poor will win if the city can regain a stable middle class. No solid tax base means no social services. This kind of 'gentrification' restores fine old buildings and can turn the tide of 'white flight' to the suburbs."

City Hall Sit-In

Several Roman Catholic priests of Springfield, including the auxiliary bishop, held a news conference in September. They called upon the populace, in the name of the Christian gospel, to examine its attitude to the poor and to support low- and moderate-income housing. Not long after the priests had taken this public stand, a group of eighteen homeless Hispanic families, in cooperation with the Puerto Rican Center, decided to protest the lack of emergency housing for the homeless. They occupied a public meeting room of the city council in City Hall. The occupation ended after city and state officials agreed to house the families temporarily at the Springfield Sheraton Hotel.

After a week, the city had not located permanent housing for the eighteen families. At this point, the corporate owners of the hotel, who were in the process of negotiating its sale, took legal action to have the families evicted. Individuals at the Puerto Rican Center then made appeals to the priests of the diocese, to the ecumenical coalition of churches serving the city, and to suburban church members to resist the eviction and stand in solidarity with the homeless and suffering.

Sue responded to this appeal issued through her associate pastor and drove the fifteen miles into downtown Springfield to stand in the street outside the Sheraton with about twenty other supporters of the Hispanic families. The same day a superior court judge issued a temporary restraining order barring the eviction of the forty-seven homeless persons and urged the parties to reach a settlement. Sue participated in some of the daily demonstrations which followed. Ranging from twenty to over a hundred participants, they drew regular TV and newspaper coverage.

The Call of the Spirit

During these demonstrations Sue became acquainted with Norman Thompson, who headed Urban Ministries, Inc. (UM). This coalition of a Roman Catholic parish and six Protestant congregations sponsored inner-city programming in areas of hunger, housing, health, education, and counseling. When Sue asked Norman about his involvement in the present hotel confrontation, he had responded that the original request from the director of the Puerto Rican Center was "a genuine call of the Spirit, a call to action. However," Norman added, "I've got some real conflicts about this situation. The media have characterized some of the families as 'freeloading newcomers' who want to use the confrontation to jump past the five thousand already waiting on the subsidized housing rolls—some waiting over two years.

"Now, the black city manager who placed the families in the Sheraton is a member of one of our sponsoring congregations. He is already infuriated by accusations that the city is trying to avoid the issues being raised, that it cannot—or will not—find permanent homes for the families and is unable to develop a comprehensive housing plan. We ultimately need him on the side of the poor—and not as an antagonist, if that is at all possible. Then look at another side of this: the two corporations that own the Sheraton are major contributors to our UM budget. The main reason all this is so threatening is not the financial base, but that the staffs of UM churches have been asked to give up not only power but control of the situation to those families. Putting our lives in the hands of others calls us to live out 'homelessness' ourselves for a moment. If this situation comes to arrest and jail, as was true in the sixties, I'm not sure if we have the commitment or the courage to hang in there. Will I release control over my life even though I'm sure of the cause—but not sure of all the motives?"

Second Sit-In

By Thursday morning, some two weeks after the eighteen families had entered the Sheraton, four families had still not been placed in permanent housing as promised by the city. Sue knew that many of the apartments had been found by UM staff, not by the city housing department. As that process had gone on, the restraining order on the evictions had expired. In anticipation of the arrival of the police to process the eviction notice, a group of one hundred persons, most of whom were church-related, gathered at the hotel entrance. A joint statement was issued by four church leaders calling on all persons in Greater Springfield to take responsibility for the housing crisis and in the name of human dignity to stop discrimination against the poor and elderly in the city.

By 12:30 P.M. it seemed apparent to Sue that the police were not going to confront the crowd. It was rumored that the police were going to wait until that night when the crowd and cameras had retired. Suddenly, the closely guarded doors of the hotel burst open and it was announced that there would be a march to City Hall four blocks away; the families during the last thirty minutes had slipped out the back of the hotel and quietly reassembled to reoccupy the council chambers of City Hall. All those present were invited to join in a confrontation with the mayor and city manager. They were asked to commit themselves not to leave City Hall until all previous promises were met. Sue joined the parade not quite sure where this action might lead.

About fifty persons occupied the city council chambers from 1:00 P.M. until about midnight. With the exception of reports of Hispanic persons "hassled" by the police for entering City Hall, the events had what one participant called an atmosphere of "empowerment and celebration" for the families involved.

Hector Hernandez, a militant Hispanic leader speaking on behalf of the families, held a news conference and condemned the city, business, and media for "their neglect of all poor residents and for inadequate housing, education, and employment opportunities." Puerto Rico was described as "a colony of the U.S." used for American profit and as an "American defense base in the Caribbean." Hernandez, his voice shaking with emotion, shouted: "U.S. capitalism makes profit, not people, the value. All the poor — Whites, Blacks, Hispanics — are treated like animals; it only happens Hispanics come last and are the least respected." He also charged the media with "unfair coverage of events at the Sheraton."

From her vantage point in the crowd, Sue thought the five clergymen who were asked to sit beside Hernandez looked uncomfortable at several points in the statement and during the heated exchange between Hernandez and the press that followed.

Negotiations with city officials resulted in promises of acceptable apartments for all families. This led to a celebrative, prayerful adjournment of the crowd of supporters about midnight. In the elation that followed, Norman had shared with Sue his reaction to the outcome: "Moving the principalities and powers is what we were about. The church of Jesus Christ has been visibly present on the side of the poor and oppressed. The ecumenical church declared to the powers-that-be, 'If you do it to one of the least of these my brethren, you do it unto me.' Our presence helped humanize the process. That is what the church is for."

Mission to the Corporate Boardroom

Sue knew, however, that others, such as Father John O'Shea, had serious reservations about what some described as the "victory" in the City Hall confrontation. For eight years he had played a role as a leader of UM as well as being a city pastor who held key positions in housing coalitions and regional foundations. Sue suspected that John knew his way around the city bureaucracy as well as any of the local clergy. "I would have wanted to know more about what was going on in the corporate world. The corporations that owned the hotel may have been willing to compromise and defuse the situation in a way that would have benefited the ultimate goal of housing for poor people. Some want just a fight. I want to win.

"The involvement of the official church in the dialogue shows the importance of integrating economics and theology. The greatest mission of our time may be to the corporate boardroom. I don't automatically see business as the enemy. Business has the resources to solve the problems. People in power need to become aware of the problems in terms they understand. We must compromise as well as confront.

"The Springfield priests had begun to experience the housing problem from the perspective of the poor through contact with 'Mi Casa,' the successful 'sweat equity' housing project in which Hispanics contribute time and labor toward acquiring adequate housing. Priests were just beginning to understand the basis of Latin American liberation theology—to be for the poor as Jesus was. I am convinced that the central factor in the priests' new awareness was a decision for each man to donate $1,000 from his personal income to establish a symbolic role for the church in the housing problem.

"There is danger in compromise," John admitted, "for it may allow one to avoid militancy when it is needed. You must remember the church is against change. Clergy are stabilizers, not confronters. Experiential theology is a big jump for priests. The confrontation became a consciousness-raising event which led to an ecumenical act in solidarity with the poor. Ultimately the consequences may be important, but I have concerns about what the confrontation itself accomplished for the poor."

PUBLIC RESPONSE

Sue was perplexed when she found the bulk of the public response to the sit-ins negative, particularly to the Puerto Ricans. She made this judgment based on newspaper letters to the editor, radio talk shows, and conversations at dinner parties, grocery stores, and even church coffee hours in Chesterton. The strongest negative voice was that of the vice-president of the city council, Leonard Stout, who attacked the Puerto Rican Center for organizing the event, and the families and clergy for participating. Stout declared, "It is most important that we stress John Calvin's ideas about the work ethic." Stout suggested that "if housing and welfare benefits are too generous, we will have all the homeless in Mexico City moving to Springfield." He went on to introduce a resolution in city council that cited the four clergymen who had issued a joint statement of responsibility at the second sit-in. Stout proposed that religious institutions help solve the housing crisis in the city by freeing millions of dollars they received in bequests from wealthy benefactors. He referred specifically to funds in the Catholic and Episcopal dioceses and accused a local seminary of destroying existing housing units to construct a new building. Stout concluded the statement by declaring, "Being in the housing business is not the city's function."

The city manager joined Stout by suggesting the families' own inability to manage their welfare grants was partly responsible for their difficulty in obtaining affordable housing.

Suburban Anger

Sue found a number of middle-class suburbanites angered by a remark of one of the Hispanic mothers housed at the Sheraton: "Who'll take care of us?" The response of one of Sue's friends was, "Who has the right to demand that the city take care of them?" On another occasion Sue encountered Sam Barnes, an irate Chesterton storekeeper who said that he had once rented two of his Springfield apartments to Puerto Ricans. "I'll never do that again," he declared. "Those people didn't pay the rent and then got legal-aid lawyers—supported by my hard-earned taxes—to take me to court when I tried to evict them. Those people don't even care enough about our country to learn English."

Sue's husband, Frank, offered an assessment that paralleled a number of the responses from her friends: "There has been a slow deterioration of the cities ever since the massive welfare programs began, as far back as the thirties. The handout system has evolved as ridiculously costly and cumbersome, open to absurd abuse by both white-collar clerks and welfare recipients, and, I believe, is ultimately destructive of the people it was intended to help. We must reverse this trend. Give corporations and the private sector a chance to respond to the needs of the people in a more responsible way."

Sue had retorted in frustration, "Can't you see, Frank, programs like legal aid, food stamps, and housing subsidies, which you seem to think are superfluous, are understood as the only means of survival by many of the poor in Springfield. How can we ask them to sit around and wait until big corporations or affluent citizens decide to toss them a few crumbs?"

Sue agreed with the assistant pastor who called on the congregation in Christian love to initiate a low-income housing program in Chesterton. Frank and other members voiced strong opposition. Several stated that low-income family housing would "lead to slum conditions and would isolate Hispanics from their own people. The church should not meddle in social policy—especially if it is ill-informed." Sue regretted that Orlando Gonzalez was not present to give a persuasive response.

Economic Structures

The Reverend Orlando Gonzalez, pastor of a small Hispanic church in Springfield, was one of the persons Sue had come to know during the demonstrations. As they discussed the negative media image Gonzalez felt had been portrayed of the Puerto Ricans in the hotel, he asked, "Why do people refuse to understand that Puerto Ricans are American citizens and Puerto Rico is a commonwealth of the U.S.? Puerto Ricans and other Hispanics contribute in a significant way to Springfield. We pay taxes far beyond our fair share." Gonzalez's comment reminded Sue of a study by the state university that showed that state residents who earned $5,000 a year paid 18.4 percent of their income in taxes, while those who earned $50,000 a year paid the state only 7.6 percent in taxes.

"If we did it, why can't they?" was the question Sue found raised again and again by the affluent middle class. Professor Lopez, a Puerto Rican at the state university, agreed that "people assume poverty is a matter of lack of incentive, determination, and aggressiveness." He, however, argued that "poverty is systemic. There are elements of our economic system that maintain poverty. While 6 percent of the people control 57 percent of the wealth, 44 percent control only 2 percent. It's no surprise where Blacks and Hispanics fall on this scale."

Lopez indicated that an integral part of the whole economic picture was the system of "queuing." Essentially the theory held that the last immigrant group "queues" behind the social power and economic control of the former groups in line. The historical control of income is modified slightly, but poverty is maintained for the low-skilled, low-educational-level immigrant group. They are needed by the affluent to do the jobs that the more affluent resist. The new poor also carry a disproportionate tax burden because they do not have the funds or knowledge for tax write-offs, loopholes, and exemptions. The tax exemptions for home owners and landlords are prime examples of how even the middle class benefit from their place in the system.

Sue thought about the historical queuing pattern of Springfield with successive immigrant groups: Irish, Jews, Italians, Southern Blacks, and Hispanics. When economic times are hard, the last group to queue suffers unemployment and deprivation of even minimal social benefits. In Lopez's words, "If local labor gets too expensive, businesses ship out manufactured goods to be assembled in Hong Kong or Taiwan. The queuing system effectively maintains poverty, because it keeps alive the myth, especially for new groups, that if new arrivals try hard enough, they too can break through and make it big in the system. So we highlight the token millionaires, professionals, or government representatives from the queuing groups."

THE CHALLENGE

In Sue's judgment it was Leonard Stout's public challenge to the churches following the sit-ins that initiated the formation of a loose coalition, or as members preferred to say, "a movement" of religious leaders for human dignity through housing. In his role as the vice-president of the city council, Stout issued a public statement to the institutions linked with four of the protest leaders. In effect, the challenge was to "put up or shut up." All four, without prior consultation, Sue understood, responded to Stout's challenge as if it were a genuine call for cooperation between the city and the churches to solve the problem.

An ad hoc informal group of about twenty persons who had been involved in the demonstrations gathered in Episcopal House to chart a response to Stout a few days after his statement and about a week after the second council chamber occupation. The group agreed to attempt to meet on a monthly basis.

HOPE

In Sue's mind there were three turning points that shaped the formation of HOPE. First was the decision of this group of twenty to seek more significant cooperation with the black religious community. Only two black leaders had been involved in the occupation. The move to join with the Black Clergy Association (BCA) expanded the composition of the group and moved their meeting location into the inner city. According to the chairman of BCA, black and white church leaders prior to this had had little history of sustained communication or cooperation.

Secondly, the organization now called HOPE arranged to be on the agenda of the next city council meeting to respond to Stout's challenge. Almost a hundred people from city and suburbs attended this meeting and stood in solidarity when the Catholic bishop read a statement. He rejected the direct use of church bequests for housing because "these had legal restrictions." However, he pointed out that the leaders of HOPE sought concrete forms of cooperation with the city council and its committees. Following the council meeting one council member interviewed by the press stated that the conversations had "opened up new lines of communication and established a more cooperative stance." However, no specific programs emerged.

Thirdly, the members of HOPE developed a theological statement with a focus on the God-endowed human dignity that makes adequate housing a human right. The statement pointed out that housing was only an entry point to the systemic issues of poverty. The document called for an advisory board composed of affected persons and groups, ranging from the poor to business, labor, and government representatives. The document also summoned commitment from religious institutions in the form of (1) expertise based on a number of low- and moderate-income housing projects previously sponsored by churches, (2) personnel, and (3) funds.

Little money was forthcoming, however. Except for the Roman Catholic gift from the Campaign for Human Development projected before the formation of HOPE, there had been no major, concrete contributions toward low-income housing during the months following the statement.

The Search for Allies

Following the March meeting of HOPE, in which members were challenged to construct concrete strategies, Sue began to call key church leaders whose opinions she valued.

"Rich churches in America will not do anything on their own about housing." Sue was listening to the Reverend James Phillips, pastor of St. Luke Methodist Church in Springfield's North End. Phillips had spent fifteen years as a black pastor in the inner city. "Those highly endowed city churches put a little change in UM, but they aren't going to do the big project until they are forced to. When you moved the HOPE meetings to the North End and out of Episcopal House, and the bishops and executive secretaries started sending their representatives, we should have known we were in trouble. That took the pressure off the power.

"If we really want to affect housing, before the developers buy up the North End," Phillips continued, "then the rich churches need to do a *real* model, low-income housing project with easily accessible health, social work, and welfare services. Previous projects simply concentrated poor people and their problems."

Phillips continued to reflect on the current situation: "You can be 'ghetto' or 'middle class,' but not *both*. Most city employees and officials live outside Springfield, in the suburbs. There are no real alliances inside the city. Blacks and Hispanics aren't closely related. It's no surprise there were few Blacks involved in the hotel occupation. They didn't see it as their fight. Puerto Ricans don't want to be identified with Blacks, and Blacks look down on Puerto Ricans. As survival services are cut, tensions increase among the poor. On the other hand, many of my church people have become middle-class home and tenement owners interested in protecting their investments. Strategy is almost impossible if you are counting on the middle-class black or white churches to help."

Feeling discouraged about how she or the middle-class white church she represented could respond to the housing issue, Sue then called the Hispanic pastor, Orlando Gonzalez. Gonzalez linked the Sheraton and City Hall occupation strategy to the black protests of the sixties by quoting the former president of the state office of the National Association for the Advancement of Colored People. Gonzalez said: " 'It won't solve any problems, but it does attract attention.' " He then went on to state: "We Puerto Ricans embarrass the city administrators, but unfortunately for them we do necessary work. Next to acceptance as full contributing human beings with a right to dignity and respect, the priority for Hispanics is housing.

"The most obvious result of the Sheraton sit-in," Gonzalez continued, "was that the Puerto Rican Center lost all of its federal funds. City Councilman Stout not only managed to cut off all federal community development block grant money of those agencies that were critical of him, but he also tried to get United Way to cut off funding. If you fight the powers, they will silence you. The problem is we lack unity and understanding between Blacks and Hispanics; Blacks look down on Puerto Ricans as new immigrants who compete with them for funds and jobs.

"The only good thing that came out of the Sheraton event was HOPE. The church has some unity here, and because of this we may have a chance to affect the city. The only enemy the church has is itself. If it fails to act for the poor, this will be out of self-interest for its own institutional survival. The trouble is, the leaders don't really trust each other enough; perhaps God will give us trust as a gift of the Holy Spirit."

ON THE BRINK OF SOCIAL CHAOS

As she began to prepare her family's evening meal, Sue decided to make her last phone call one to Dr. Curtis Wilmore, an African Methodist Episcopal pastor who was now in education work and was one of the Blacks present on the Sheraton picket line and present at the last meeting of HOPE. "Those struggling for survival can't see others' views, can't applaud the gains of others," Wilmore proposed. "Blacks felt the hotel occupation was a Puerto Rican issue and therefore did not identify with those who could be natural allies. The powers in the city cultivate this lack of cooperation. If people can be kept divided by fighting over a limited number of grants, jobs, or houses, it keeps them off the back of those in control. I am not sure whether community leaders self-consciously discourage coalitions or whether that just occurs.

"Though HOPE has brought an offensive posture to the encounter that is important, look at our last meeting. Where are our white and Hispanic brothers? Is it bad communication and too many personal agendas, or is it more than that? In housing we don't need conversation, we need houses for low-income people of all races. The priority is to lobby businesses and government and to get them involved in specific projects.

"In my opinion," Wilmore continued, "the government scene is a disaster. Recent political decisions have been devastating for the poor. With the current minimum wage, people who work full-time — even two shifts — are unable to pay rent and utility bills, much less health and day care. UM has been swamped with calls over this past year. The growing pressure may crush the instinct to survive and can lead us to the brink of social chaos."

Wilmore added, "The church must agitate, not just consciousness-raise. The white church has never been revolutionary. Maybe that is why our white brothers, especially the bishops, are so busy lately. The white church has a chance with HOPE if it becomes a community in solidarity with poor people. No significant impact of the gospel as a social phenomenon has had an individualistic base. Civil rights and anti-Vietnam war movements were not based on personal salvation, but on God's will as perceived by the community. Blacks learned that to save souls one-on-one means your body still belongs to the oppressor. You may be saved but are not whole. You can't have freedom on the installment plan."

ARMS STAMPEDE

In trying to assess the impact of government policies on the poor of Springfield, Sue's mind kept returning to the administration's decision to apply the bulk of the billions saved by recent social service program cuts to the defense industry. This issue had been raised during a UM-sponsored conference on peacemaking last March. Sue now recalled some of the data as she sought to envision how a strategy for peacemaking might affect the Springfield housing situation.

It was clear in the presentations that the money saved through the social service cuts had been used to supply arms to support procapitalist governments such as those in Brazil and El Salvador and to build SSN nuclear attack submarines to add to the U.S. firepower, now capable of destroying the USSR many times over. Of the billions spent in the entire world on armaments, the U.S. spent more than one-third of the total.

The figures always overwhelmed Sue, but what she had learned was that there was a direct relationship between armaments and the issues of urban ministry. Was the cost of that one trident nuclear submarine worth eliminating all the food stamps, school lunches, and rent subsidies in Springfield for several years?

When Sue came home with euphoric reports on the conference and the call to peacemaking, Frank challenged her with the reality that their state had the highest per capita dependence on the defense industry in the United States. The clear implication of peacemaking for their state was a direct challenge to job security for thousands of workers.

STRATEGY FOR HOPE

The conference on peacemaking and the conversations with community leaders had raised what Sue felt were critical questions, yet ones she was reluctant to face. Was the issue really the system and not housing? If persistent discrimination against the poor maintained the self-interests of the affluent, then was there any real possibility of change coming from the middle class? Sue could not imagine her affluent neighbors abdicating either their comfort or their power. Was it not fruitless even to attempt to change the historically established economic patterns Dr. Lopez had illustrated?

In the same way, if the churches were also captives and promoters of the system, there seemed to be no acknowledgment of it and certainly no attempts to change. The status quo worked too well for established churches. As Norm Thompson had said at the last HOPE meeting, "It's back to business as usual. We still have no long-range plan. The bonding we have established won't affect the powers. We're not tithing, not sacrificing—not even challenging our own institutions."

Sue felt the drain of energy and the resistance of her family and friends. Everyone agreed there was a housing crisis. Even the mayor could say that without fear of rebuke. The issue was strategy for change and at what cost. Wilmore reminded her that "everyone, including the clergy, is still thinking more about what is fiscally feasible, not what is best for people at any cost.

Poor people are considered ultimately transformable or expendable."

A simple, comfortable, gradual solution of the problems for the poor and middle class is what Sue confessed in her heart she wanted. No one else should suffer needlessly. HOPE was *becoming* a community, but was not one yet. Could it really be a Christian community in solidarity with the poor and oppressed?

As Sue thought about the next meeting of HOPE, now only a week away, she was a little overwhelmed. The problems were so massive, complicated, and systemic. How could one take concrete, practical action in the name of the gospel to feed and house the suffering? Who should she believe, or support? Or should she just retire for the summer?

Norm Thompson kept raising the most uncomfortable issue for Sue by his own lifestyle as urban-centered, autoless, raising interracial children, struggling with the city and the church. The "eye of the needle" was Norm's question. Norm had challenged Sue with these words: "Do rich men and women, which most Americans are in the global context, really want to pass through the eye of the needle to enter the kingdom of heaven? Jesus said, 'Sell everything and give to the poor.' "

Sue was tempted to answer, "Not everything Lord—not yet anyway. First we've got to think about the kids' education, retirement plans, and mortgage payments." Maybe she had been co-opted during the last six months, or maybe her personal turmoil was a sign of conversion? She began to think of the personal price involved in what Wilmore and Thompson called solidarity with the poor.

Just then Sue Adams's sixteen-year-old son, yelling from the outdoor grill, broke into her thoughts: "Mom, the steaks are burning!"

Commentary

The Eye of the Needle

Sue Adams raises two basic questions from her exploration of Springfield's crisis in housing the poor. They are: (1) What obligations do middle-class Christians have to the poor? and (2) How should we formulate strategies for dealing with the lack of housing for the poor? The first question is one demanding theological reflection; the second demands the integration of social analysis and theological reflection.

RELIGIOUS OBLIGATIONS TO THE POOR

The basic Christian obligation according to Jesus is to love God with all our heart, all our soul, and all our mind, and to love our neighbor as ourselves (Matt. 22:34–39). To love God is to commit ourselves to the fulfillment of God's intentions for creation, in which love of neighbor is central. Furthermore, Jesus taught that love of neighbor is evaluated in terms of meeting the needs of our neighbor, which thus gives priority to the neediest. To come to the aid of the needy takes precedence even over formal worship, as Jesus taught in the parable of the Good Samaritan, who stopped to aid the robbery victim after the priest and levite passed him by because they were unwilling to risk ritual uncleanness which would temporarily bar them from Temple worship.

Many scriptural scholars find it important to note that Jesus' warning that it is easier for a camel to pass through the eye of the needle than for the rich to enter the kingdom of God may not have referred to the eye of a sewing needle, but to the pedestrian gate of a city, which was also called "the eye of the needle." The implication is clear. It would be difficult for a camel to enter the pedestrian gate. It might require kneeling, and it could not be done if the camel were carrying a full load. But it was certainly possible. The issue is not the size of the camel, but the *condition* of the camel: how much unnecessary burden the camel carried. The implication, then, is that a radical conversion to the "right condition" is necessary if the rich are to enter the kingdom of God. Part of that right condition involves aiding the neediest; theological reflection thus must focus on choices and strategies for aiding the needy, for that is part of the core of our Christian values and commitment.

In pursuing strategies for loving our neighbors, especially the needy, we need constantly to reflect back on the gospel's understanding of poverty. Poverty in both the Old and New Testaments is sinful, an affront to God whose intentions are that all persons live in dignity and community. The sinfulness of poverty is demonstrated by its destructiveness. Poverty damages the human spirit, destroying self-respect and responsibility, breaking bonds between families and neighbors as each is pressured to pursue personal survival at the expense of others. Poverty breeds despair, despair that in our society manifests itself in alcoholism, drug use, violence, crime, suicide, and broken families.

COMPLEXITY OF HOUSING FOR THE POOR

Sue is dismayed to discover the complex nature of the issue of housing for the poor. She is uncomfortable with the personal antagonisms that have sprung up around the conflict. Such antagonisms often occur, for it is tempting to understand sinful social situations in terms of personal sin. Those committed to housing for the poor often view the "hard-heartedness" of government officials as the root of the problem, and officials tend to blame the plight of the homeless on their inability to budget their wages or welfare payments. Understanding social sin in personal terms is tempting because the solutions are easier: those committed to the homeless hope to either convert unconcerned officials to care for the poor or to unseat them from positions of power, and officials who blame the poor for their plight can renounce responsibility for the homeless. These are much simpler solutions than reconstructing entire social systems, but they are not adequate.

Most cities are hard pressed to deal with the issue of housing for the poor. The shift of the middle class to the suburbs and the move of many industrial plants from northern cities to the South or to Third World nations have severely shrunk the tax base of many cities. Federal money for low-income housing has dried up in recent years. Increases in unemployment, gentrification trends, and cuts in welfare and food stamps have increased the need for low-income housing at precisely the time that cities are hard pressed to continue basic services such as police, fire, street repair, and schools. Housing for the poor cannot be dealt with in isolation from these other issues.

One important part of analysis of the housing problem is articulated by Sue's middle-class friends. They ask why the city should be responsible for housing the poor, why middle-class people should be responsible for paying to house their own families as well as those of the poor. It is easy for some to dismiss these questions, as well as the anger of Sam Barnes (whose Puerto Rican renters didn't pay rent but resisted eviction), as un-Christian, for such middle-class people seem to call for ignoring the needs of the poor, for blaming the poor for their poverty. But frequently in rushing to condemn such positions we settle for solutions little more beneficial to the poor.

Our intention must be to meet the needs of the poor, but the needs of the poor go beyond food, shelter, and clothing. The poor are human persons who are called to be contributing members of society, responsible for themselves and willing to help others. Work is the primary need of the poor. Through work human persons earn their livelihood, contribute to the common good, and help shape themselves into the persons they want to be. Some form of work, of contribution, is essential for human dignity.

While it is necessary to feed and house the poor on an emergency basis, outreach ought not be structured in such a way as to make the poor permanent dependents. This is the danger in a welfare society. Welfare is in structural terms a buying off of the poor. It makes people dependent, robs them of pride, and marginalizes them from responsible citizenship. Their very dependence on welfare for the minimum for survival prevents them from effectively protesting their marginalization. Permanent welfare prevents both those who receive it and those who provide it from respecting the humanity of recipients. It is necessary to have welfare programs, but the policy goal should be to make their use temporary, for periods of disaster and job transition. This, of course, is only possible if we can reconstruct our society so as to offer decent employment to all.

WORKING FOR FULL EMPLOYMENT

Providing employment for all should be a primary social policy goal, but it is the subject of a great deal of debate. Should we have make-work programs such as the government founded during the Great Depression when youths were employed to work in conservation programs in forests and farms, when urban unemployed were put to work building stairs, walks, and retaining walls in parks and neighborhoods, when unemployed artists were hired to adorn public buildings? Or should we use tax incentives to encourage hiring by private corporations and businesses, and expand job training and placement services? These are important questions, and we have no space to explore them here. But often it is not the case that we must choose only one of our options; sometimes it is not advisable to do so.

Larger and larger parts of our population are becoming surplus labor. This not only means a larger unemployed base and second and third generations of family joblessness, but it also means that wages for those working in unskilled and semiskilled jobs are kept low. With so many out of work, employers do not need to raise wages to obtain or keep workers. Many jobs, even in skilled work such as accounting or nursing, are becoming less than full time, which means not only lower salaries, but often loss of benefits such as health insurance and pension. Workers in such jobs have little chance of becoming homeowners, or creating savings which could see them through emergencies. The lower middle class is shrinking, with some joining the upper middle class and the majority sinking into the working class/ poverty sector. The biggest increases in jobs for some years have come in the low-paid service sector of the economy, with the bulk in the fast food business where workers earn minimum wage for twenty-five to thirty hours per week. The process at work is gloomy: fewer jobs and more of them incapable of supporting a family even at minimum levels.

STRATEGIES

There is no one area to concentrate on, no single plan for solving our housing problems. We need to continue seeking ways to house the millions of poor who roam the streets of our cities. We need cooperation among federal, state, and local levels in planning, legislation, and funding. We are beginning to see interesting cooperative plans among governments, universities, research centers, and private business in some cities. Cities should at the very least provide emergency shelters. They should also attempt to regulate gentrification, for example by heavily taxing speculation or by requiring developers to include low-income units in their projects. If cities and the federal government would enforce such existing agreements made by developers in order to secure tax-free financing, many more units would be available to the poor now.

There are many private housing groups in existence now which can help to meet this crisis. Some are community land co-ops, which buy housing in poor neighborhoods to keep it from gentrification. They then rehab it and lease it to the poor at nonprofit rates with payments accruing toward ownership. The property is permanently protected from gentrification because the co-op continues to own the land, and has first option on the housing should the owner decide to sell. Habitat for Humanity represents another type of housing group working for the poor. It is a nondenominational Christian group with affiliates all over North America and abroad. Habitat uses donations of material and labor to build or rehab housing for the poor at cost, with long-term, no-interest loans. There are hundreds of variations on such groups around the country. As the experience of such groups has grown, they more and more see their work not as a gift for the poor, but as a partnership with them. Many of the poor who have received such homes not only worked on their own units, but are involved in volunteer work to provide housing for others.

Churches have an important role to play in such groups. A first step is often involving ministers and priests on the boards of the groups. As they become exposed to the housing problem and to the work of these groups they often become enthusiastic about involving their congregations in such work. They can arrange for presentations to the congregation, have their church boards consider pledging a portion of the church's outreach funds to the work, solicit donations of labor and materials from individuals in the congregation, and thereby gradually expose even the middle-class members of suburban churches to the problems and perspectives of the urban poor.

Norman Thompson, who heads Urban Ministries, Inc., makes a valid point when he insists that antagonizing the city officials was not a good idea, that supporters of housing for the poor must involve the city. Federal and city agencies can be a great help to such groups. City officials have great expertise which can be of use to housing groups in planning where to build or rehabilitate—those officials know the whereabouts of abandoned/condemned buildings which could be acquired cheaply and rehabilitated, and they know how to meet zoning requirements or obtain variances from the many rules governing construction. The city can expedite paperwork around building permits and variances, and give low-income housing priority in scheduling inspection visits or lowering fees for inspection or construction permits.

Confrontation is sometimes necessary. It is often the case that city officials are supportive of developers involved in gentrification because of the tax benefits to the city. City officials are often as removed from the plight of the poor as Sue's middle-class friends. But there are different ways to confront those whose policies we oppose. Father O'Shea has a point when he says, "Some just want a fight. I want to win." Winning here means obtaining housing for the poor—not just for these few families, but all the poor. Persuasion should always be exhausted before turning to confrontation. If confrontation is necessary, it should be done in such a way that those confronted are challenged to co-operate, not to greater efforts in opposition. Too frequent recourse to confrontation can undermine its effectiveness, and result in the group's being dismissed as crank protesters; but reluctance to confront can be equally paralyzing.

It is important to remember the fact that the social systems which are in place did not just happen by themselves. They have some purposefulness: they serve the interests of some. It would be naive not to anticipate opposition to changing the way systems operate. Sue's husband Frank articulates the classic liberal argument for allowing the market to structure the economy without government intervention. If developers are allowed to gentrify the city, the tax base will expand and the city will have more money for social services, including housing for the poor, he says. According to this same logic, if businesses were not regulated and taxed, they would expand and hire more workers. The assumption of this analysis is that the benefits of allowing unfettered capitalism will filter down to all. When government interferes through regulation and costly taxes to support welfare and low-income housing, the poor not only lose the incentive to work, but there are fewer jobs open for them, because taxes absorbed funds which could have been used for expansion.

Christians have debated and will continue to debate whether this theory's priority for capital rather than for needy persons is compatible with the gospel. But there can be little debate that in this decade the theory has not accurately described our situation. Taxes have been lowered, especially for corporations and the wealthy, and regulation of many kinds lessened, but resulting increases in capital have not gone to expanding production in the United States. Instead they have gone to fund both costly corporate takeovers of existing firms and the expansion of production abroad. Benefits have not trickled down to the poor to any appreciable extent. Gentrification in particular urban areas has attracted some small numbers of middle-class persons into the cities. But the tax gains have not nearly offset the losses of housing for the poor. Gentrification projects inevitably displace many more persons than they attract, since the middle class is accustomed to occupying more personal space than the poor.

Father O'Shea may be right that the greatest mission of our time is to the corporate boardroom. The boardroom is not the place most congenial to the gospel, but it is a major source of power in our society, peopled by human persons who, like those in Sue's suburban church and neighborhood, must be somehow connected with the lives and aspirations of the poor. Applying the gospel to economic life leads to the conclusion that the test of any economic or political theory is its effect on the dignity and well-being of the poorest and weakest.

WHAT PATHS FOR SUE?

What does a preferential option for the poor demand in terms of lifestyle? Is Sue obliged to sell all she has and give it to the poor? If she is not ready to do that, has she then rejected Christianity? She asks whether she has been converted or co-opted. But perhaps the choice is not so simple as that. Conversion is not an event, but a process. Sue has begun the process; she is beginning to view her context from the perspective of the poor. The challenge is to continue the process of conversion and to overcome, one piece at a time, the co-optation or complicity in sin which characterizes all of us.

Because poverty is sinful, it should not be pursued. Sue should not give away all she has in order to be poor and thus virtuous. Jesus' challenge is not to be poor, but to love the poor, which entails action on their behalf, a commitment to the elimination of poverty. The first step is to recognize the needs of the poor as Sue has begun to do. She has begun to act politically on behalf of the poor, but she recognizes that demonstrations have a limited effectiveness in two ways. In political terms, as Orlando Gonzalez remarked, demonstrations garner attention for problems, but do not solve them. And in terms of personal conversion, demonstrations seldom connect even their participants, much less their spectators, in deeper commitment to the poor. It is too easy to make space in unredeemed lives for a few hours of picketing. Sue wants to know where she should go from here.

Her choices are many. She can volunteer to work with existing agencies procuring low-income housing, or in emergency shelters for the homeless, or in solicitation of necessary services (medical, dental, tutoring) for those in shelters. She could help the homeless obtain job training or placement, or throw open her own home as a shelter. In all these options Sue would be moved to question her level of consumption and the separation it creates between her and the homeless. This process will lead to a reduction in her consumption.

Perhaps her problem is that the options are so many. There are two major criteria for Sue to use in deciding to what particular work she should commit herself: (1) Where does she see the greatest need for her services? (2) In which option would Sue continue to be pulled into the life of the poor, continue to grow in love for these sisters and brothers? If she continues to make choices using these criteria, lifestyle questions will be dealt with each in its own turn. As her life penetrates deeper into the lives of the poor, her needs and desires will change, her lifestyle become more simple.

The real challenge Sue seems to anticipate is not that of giving up things, but of risking relationships. She already experiences her initial level of commitment as estranging her from her husband, friends, and associates. The implicit threat is that the rift will grow ever larger until the relationships fall into the resulting crater. If she is to continue her commitment, she needs to attempt to involve her family and friends in her work, to continue to expose them to the perspective of the poor in the hopes that they, too, will begin a conversion. At the same time she must cultivate support for herself from other persons involved in this same work. The work must provide Sue with signs of growth, solidarity, and joy if she is to be able to risk what Jesus warned us we must risk to follow him: "For I have come to set a man against his father, and a daughter against her mother, and a daughter-in-law against her mother-in-law; and a man's foes will be those of his own household. He who loves father or mother more than me is not worthy of me; and he who does not take up his cross and follow me is not worthy of me. He who finds his life will lose it, and he who loses his life for my sake will find it" (Matt. 10:35–39).

ADDITIONAL RESOURCES

Holland, Joe, and Peter Henriot. *Social Analysis: Linking Faith and Justice.* Maryknoll, N.Y.: Orbis/Center of Concern, 1983.

John Paul II. *Laborem Exercens.* Washington, D.C.: U.S. Catholic Conference, 1981.

Piven, Frances Fox, and Richard A. Cloward. *Poor People's Movements: How They Succeed, Why They Fail.* New York: Vintage, 1977.

Schiller, John A., ed. *The American Poor.* Minneapolis: Augsburg, 1982.

Wineman, Steven. *The Politics of Human Services: Alternatives to the Welfare State.* Boston: South End Press, 1987.

PART III

VIOLENCE/
NONVIOLENCE

Case

Vietnam's Children

"What should I say to Chris?" Martin Paxton questioned himself. "Should I remain silent, press my ideas on my son, or merely point out the options? What Christian perspective makes sense in a world of fifty thousand plus nuclear weapons?"

Then Martin's memory, or perhaps it was his conscience, began to work. The images of his own Vietnam experience came flooding back like an ever-flowing stream. He is "gun boss" on a U.S. Navy destroyer with six five-inch guns. Routine mission: to shell "Vietcong positions" from two miles off the coast of central Vietnam. "Battle stations," booms the ship's public address system. The radio crackles the coordinates of the target. One round on its way. The spotter over the target in a light plane responds with a "left four hundred yards, down two hundred yards." Another round, another spot. Then in an electric voice the spotter yells, "You've got 'em on the run. Shoot! Shoot!" A quick correction to fire control, then the command, "Thirty rounds, fire for effect!" The noise is deafening. The shock shakes loose the accumulated dirt of twenty years from the pipes overhead. The spotter's voice returns even more excited, "You got 'em, you got 'em!" The combat center erupts with cheers. The captain races back from the bridge to congratulate everyone. Back slapping, hugs, and handshakes follow. God, it feels good! Until the wee hours of the morning, that is. Then the small voices began to work: "Why did the gunners want to paint coolie hats on the sides of the gun mounts? Why did you hesitate? Why did you finally say, 'No, I don't think coolie hats are appropriate'? What are you doing here in Vietnam? Why did you enjoy killing the Vietnamese so much? Who are you anyway, a killer, a Christian, or both? Why didn't anyone prepare you for Vietnam or killing? Why didn't you think these things through before you got here?"

The questions never were answered. Discharge, graduate school, an oc-

This case was prepared by Robert L. Stivers. Copyright © The Case Study Institute. All names have been disguised to protect the privacy of the individuals involved.

cupation, several jobs: life has a way of intervening to block introspection just as the decisions of one's children have a way of releasing it. Chris, his son, was almost eighteen and required by law to sign up for the draft.

Martin's question to his son as he was on the way out to a basketball game was innocent: "What are you going to do about the draft?" The reply was quick and without reflection: "Sign up, I guess, and declare conscientious objection, whatever that is." The door slammed and the sound of Chris dribbling the ball down the walk faded away as the old questions reasserted themselves.

Martin was not without resources for the questions and the new context of Chris's decision. A recent adult education class in his church had studied Christian views on violence and nonviolence. The class had helped him sort out a few things. The early church, he learned, had been pacifist, and a continuing tradition had carried the option of nonviolence to the present in what Ronald Smith, the class instructor and professor of religion at the local college, had called "the way of the cross."

A Mennonite from the local area, Jacob Kaufmann, visited the class on the first Sunday and explained his own pacifism. He identified with the position represented by *Sojourners Magazine* and spoke of how important the community of the church is to the way of the cross. "The church," he said, "takes its cue from the nonviolent but socially active model of Jesus in the New Testament." He went on to explain that the early Christian community followed Jesus and his nonviolent ways not because Jesus demanded it, but because faith motivated it. "When Christ is truly in you," he said, "nonviolence is your automatic response. Love engenders love. That is the message of Jesus. I can never be a soldier."

Martin's friend Jim Everett had pressed Jacob in the question period which followed. "How can I follow the way of the cross in a fallen world?" he asked. "What would you do if your wife and children were attacked?" Obviously Jacob had heard these questions before because without hesitation he replied, "We are called to follow Jesus, not make the world turn out right. Ultimately, we are called to suffer before we inflict suffering. And in any case, we do not need to kill the attacker. There are other alternatives."

Jacob's assurance had a certain appeal to Martin. The way was simple, straightforward and seemed to fit Jesus' radical call to discipleship. Jacob himself was active in the community on justice issues in the tradition of Gandhi and King.

Still, Martin was not convinced. "Justice is as important in the way of the cross as nonviolence," he thought. "On occasion a large measure of justice might be gained for a small measure of violence. Why prefer nonviolence to justice in these situations? And who does the dirty work of keeping order in a violent world?"

The next Sunday Ronald Smith presented a position he called "Christian realism," out of which comes the doctrine of the justifiable war. Historically,

Ronald explained, this position emerged after the emperor Constantine converted to Christianity in the early fourth century and the church achieved a favored position. Christians took political office and became responsible for the general welfare. The ethical and political task for Christians of this view, Ronald continued, is not perfection or the literal following of the way of Jesus, but the use of power to push and pull sinful reality toward the ideal.

"Not best, but better," he insisted, "because best is impossible in a fallen world. The way of the cross may be lived personally, but it is not immediately relevant to politics. We in our freedom can ignore the power of God in our midst and alienate our neighbors. God doesn't set things right or organize them for us. We have been given dominion and are responsible for the use of power. To serve one's neighbor, to steward resources, and to achieve higher levels of justice in a sinful world mean a Christian must compromise and occasionally use means which are not consistent with the way of the cross. This is how anarchy is avoided and tyranny prevented. This does not mean the way is irrelevant and God does not work in the world. God acts like a magnet pulling us out of sin and moving us to higher ethical levels, and we have a limited capacity to respond. God's power and this capacity are the basis of hope and make 'the better' a constant possibility. Simply put, those of this view are realists because of sin and Christians because there are resources for making this a better world."

Ronald went on to draw the justifiable war tradition out of this realistic perspective. "Nonviolence is the norm," he insisted, "but on occasion violence is permissible if it clearly meets certain criteria." He then set forth the criteria and indicated that they make both violence and selective conscientious objection moral possibilities. He also observed that if every nation took the criteria seriously, all war would cease. He paused and added, "but that is a big 'if'."

Martin remembered leaving the class attracted to this position as well. But he was also troubled. How can realism be consistent with the picture of Jesus in the New Testament? Does not the idea of a justifiable war open the flood gates to misuse? Even Hitler claimed his cause was just, not to mention what Martin himself had been told in Vietnam. And how about nuclear war which would always violate one or two of the criteria? The very thought of a just nuclear war is preposterous. Religiously, do the realists take the power of sin too seriously and the power of the Holy Spirit not seriously enough?

The next Sunday a Salvadoran refugee offered still another position, called liberation theology. Her name was Maria, or at least that was how she was introduced without further explanation. Martin found her difficult to understand because of her Spanish accent, but her perspective was clear enough. Maria spoke of centuries of oppression in Central America. In emotional terms she related the violence done to her family in San Salvador by right-wing death squads. She described her own participation in a "base community," and how a grass-roots movement of the poor is spreading through Latin America. She insisted the movement was Christian and spent most of her time linking it to liberation themes in the Bible.

"Yes," she admitted, "we use Marxist analysis to understand our situation. We also seek an alternative to the dependency created by international capitalism and the oppression of political and religious oligarchies." Maria concluded with a passionate plea for justice for the poor and an end to violence fomented by the rich against the poor.

When asked if she advocated violence in response, Maria looked down, paused, and slowly replied, "Sometimes there seems to be no other choice. I feel called to relieve the suffering I see and reluctantly to fight for liberation."

Martin was deeply moved by Maria, whose position seemed to be a variation of the justifiable war tradition, but with important differences, of course. Still Martin was bothered by her references to socialism and Marxism. The former did not seem very efficient as a way of economic organization, and the latter not much help when it came to creating something new. What both attracted and bothered him most, however, was her passion. He worried that passion easily yields to fanaticism and fanaticism to new forms of tyranny.

The final week of the class Ronald Smith explained the crusading tradition in Christianity, but without much enthusiasm. He had not been able to locate anyone to represent the position. This does not mean the crusade is dead, he suggested, only that few are willing to state it in its classic form. The best example is the willingness on the part of many Christians to use violence in putting down "godless communism."

In the Christian tradition, he went on, crusaders base their violent actions on the holy war texts in Deuteronomy, Joshua, and Judges. They see as God's clear command the call to stamp out evil and the designation of themselves as God's agents. Serving in the army of the righteous is a Christian responsibility.

Ronald dismissed the position by claiming it improperly literalized the biblical texts and then misapplied them. Faith in God is the real significance of the texts, and they are hardly directly relevant to modern warfare with all its destruction. He added that the portrayal of God as commanding violence was incompatible with the biblical witness taken as a whole and that crusaders often fail to see their own sin. He concluded by observing that crusades are usually the bloodiest kinds of wars. He cited the religious wars of the seventeenth century and the Iran-Iraq conflict as examples.

Martin agreed but reflected on the depth of the good/evil dualism in each of us. "Wouldn't we all like to stamp out evil if we could?" he mused. "And how like us it is to represent our own cause by our best ideals and our opponents' by their worst deeds!"

Martin sifted through the options one more time. "I might be able to quiet my own conscience, but what do I say to Chris? Should I advocate the way of the cross and conscientious objection? Should I suggest a more realistic option which allows for justifiable wars in oppressive situations and selective conscientious objection in others? Or should I tell him to sign up, do his duty, and serve his country as millions have before? After all, that's what I did."

Martin had now been in thought for over an hour. He was drawn out of those thoughts by the sound of Chris dribbling a ball back up the walk. Chris entered the house and asked, "Dad, you wanted to talk about registering for the draft?"

Commentary

Vietnam's Children

A generation has matured since the Vietnam War. It knows little about My Lai, the Tet offensive, Khe Sanh, or the final capitulation. The troubled waters stirred up by injustice, massive demonstrations, rhetorical flourish, and challenges to traditional authority have stilled. But beneath the surface, currents of conscience and unresolved identity created by the Vietnam War still run deep. Like the powerful currents which circle in the great ocean basins, these undercurrents of conscience circulate without resolution. Martin Paxton, on the occasion of a chance question to his son, Chris, finds himself in one such current of conscience with a chance to break out and simultaneously to help Chris make a decision about conscientious objection.

To see that Vietnam and Chris's decision about conscientious objection are related is important. They are related on the personal level through the exchange of thoughts and feelings between father and son. They are also related through the four Christian perspectives on violence presented in Martin's adult class. Finally, they are related through the education Chris has received in the Paxton family. Martin's conscientious ambivalence, which includes his lament about not being prepared for killing, has no doubt been communicated to Chris. Vietnam's children, whether they realize it or not, are now making decisions about draft registration with their parents' and their society's moral perceptions of the Vietnam War as important ingredients.

CONSCIENTIOUS OBJECTION

Chris's disconcerting and quick reply to Martin's question about signing up does not make clear whether Chris objects to all wars or merely to unjustifiable wars. This may just be a lack of information in the case. More likely, Chris does not himself know the difference between conscientious objection and selective conscientious objection, and how the law treats each.

From 1948 through 1972 the U.S. government used a combination of draft and voluntary recruitment to fill the ranks of its armed forces. In 1971 the draft was put on standby status and voluntary recruitment became the sole source of new soldiers. Draft registration continued until 1975 when it was suspended. In 1980 registration was reinstated.

That is the status of the law today. All males ages eighteen to twenty-six are required to register by filling out a form available at the post office. Failure to register can result in a fine, imprisonment, or both. After registration, the name of a registrant such as Chris is entered into a computer for possible future use.

To make use of these names to induct draftees into the armed forces would require an act of Congress with the signature of the President. In an emergency a law to classify and induct could be passed on very short notice accompanied by all the emotions of nationalism which cloud clear thinking.

Were such legislation enacted, local draft boards would quickly form, classify all those who are registered, and begin calling individuals for induction, first from the twenty-year-old age group according to a rank order of birthdays determined by lottery.

Once Chris was classified 1A and his name came up, he would receive an induction notice and have ten days to report. It is within this ten-day period that he would have to set in motion the machinery for deferment or exemption on grounds of conscientious objection.

Once Chris made application for conscientious objection, the draft board would postpone induction and set a date for a hearing where he could present his case. His application would be judged on the basis of three criteria: (1) that he is opposed to participation in war in any form; (2) that his opposition is by reason of religious training and belief; and (3) that he demonstrates sincerity.

If the application were successful, Chris would be reclassified in one of two conscientious objector categories. If not successful, the local board would have to declare in writing the reasons for its rejection, which Chris could appeal.

The vast majority of conscientious objectors are registering for the draft, but a number of alternatives exist, including refusal to register and the indication of conscientious objector status in the process of registration. The task for Chris is to think through the ethical implications, decide if he is a conscientious objector and what type, and make his decision about registration. If he elects to be a conscientious objector, he should seek the advice of a draft counselor and begin preparing his supporting material.

THE VIETNAM WAR

The Vietnam War is not over. The hand-to-hand combat has long since ceased, but the meaning of the experience has not been settled. The Vietnam upheaval has never been adequately worked through, and as time passes, it looks more and more as if it never will be. Americans either cannot or will not come to terms with it.

Martin appears bothered by two things. The first is the destruction of a social myth about the United States, the second the destruction of a personal myth about himself. For Martin and many other Vietnam veterans the destruction of their social and personal myths and the lack of adequate replacements have resulted in lost identity and the inability to comprehend what they went through.

The 1950s saw the apex of American power. Victorious in World War II and economically unrivaled, Americans had reason to be content with themselves in spite of serious unresolved social problems. They also had a vision with roots. American social mythology depicted a new city which is set on a hill free from the cynical entanglements and imperial ambitions of old and decaying Europe. Stories of the American frontier told of rough but moral and hard working pioneers pushing back the frontier and bringing civilization in their wake. Those who resisted were pictured either as uncivilized and in need of American technology and virtue, or evil and in need of a crusade.

The frontier closed in the nineteenth century, but its mythology remained open-ended in spite of changing conditions and rude shocks such as the Great Depression. The mythology was skillfully manipulated by politicians like John F. Kennedy with his New Frontier. It was exploited by those who saw the spread of communism in Asia as the latest evil in need of a crusade, and the Vietnamese as candidates for American technology and virtue.

In the end this pervasive social mythology was not able to carry the day for an entire nation. The harsh realities of racial violence and the injustice and inconclusiveness of the Vietnam War combined to explode the myth for a vocal minority. For men and women such as Martin Paxton the bell is now cracked and no new bells have yet been cast.

Martin could not have avoided participation in this mythology. He would have been brought up on westerns, war movies, and patriotic instruction. The path of least resistance would have led him to the conclusion that for the first time in history, here was a moral nation. Because he was brought up in a middle-class America that almost without question saw itself as morally right, he probably saw himself and his nation as inheritors and purveyors of that morality. Abundance would have shielded him from the violence of poverty and class conflict. Entering the Navy was probably as natural as a trip to Disneyland.

That beneath the mythology of the American dream and his own peace in it lay a different reality would only have been dimly perceived. It apparently was not the injustice of Vietnam or the oppression of racism which revealed this reality to him, at least not initially. Rather it seems to have been his participation in and apparent enjoyment of killing and the acids of uncomfortable dreams stimulated by a vigorous conscience. The combat center erupted with the "happy" news of death, killed Martin's false consciousness, and left him with a good dose of guilt.

In a like manner Vietnam blew the top off the dormant volcano of the American dream. Martin's crisis is the nation's crisis. The problem for both Martin and other Americans is how to build new mythic mountains to give order and justice to their landscapes. Martin may be building one in his Christian journey.

In Christian terms the problem is repentance and new life. Repentance must be the foundation of his building. The first stone is to realize that he is one of those individuals who is capable of killing and enjoying it. Such an admission is hard for most individuals. It forces the sacrifice of the proud self and produces vulnerability. For modern nations it is much harder because pride is so strong and so central to national identity. For corporate America with its glowing self-image and righteousness to admit that the Vietnam War was unjust may be too much to expect.

The guilt Martin feels and the continuing discussion about Vietnam are signs of God's judgment and first steps toward repentance. But the recognition of judgment is not the end of the story. God forgives and this forgiveness opens the door to new life. As soon as Martin goes through the door of repentance, the process of coming to terms with his role in Vietnam will begin. There are indications this process has already started.

The prospects for America in its continuing mental struggle over the Vietnam War are not as good. Nations have far fewer resources for coming to terms with their own injustices. The current infatuations with nuclear weapons and increased armaments do not improve the prospects. The church will have an important role to play in whatever rethinking takes place, for it has resources for announcing judgment, for coming to terms with guilt, and for moving beyond it.

Any rethinking that goes on must address Martin's question and lament: "Why didn't anyone prepare me for Vietnam or killing?" That question points up a shortcoming in the education of children in the United States. Experiences differ, of course, but a child of Martin's generation would normally have been exposed only superficially to peace education. History texts of his generation emphasized kings and great victories. The pacifist side of the Christian tradition was a well-kept secret, even in Sunday school. The media glorified violence and past wars much as they do today.

It is no wonder Martin found himself on the firing line before he had thought things through. His option, stated at the end of the case, was "sign up, do your duty, and serve your country." Is it not a problem that the state sees its internal cohesion as so important that it tries to make certain that this is the only option which can receive a hearing? Has the church failed to present the full range of options out of its own traditions? Or is the failure to question, to explore, and to reflect Martin's?

The answer is yes to all three, and from an ethical perspective the point is that those who are forced to make life and death decisions ought to be exposed to moral perspectives on violence. The state's need for compliance with its will and certainly the church's role in supporting the state do not warrant the exclusion of such perspectives. Young men and women have the right to have access to the different options.

CHRISTIAN OPTIONS

Available to Christian thinking on conscientious objection and the Vietnam War is a normative tradition of great variety and richness. No less than four distinct options are presented within the case itself. The Mennonite Jacob Kaufmann offers the pacifist option. Professor Roger Smith discusses both the crusade and Christian realism, which includes the justifiable war tradition. And finally, Maria presents liberation theology in its more militant form. Liberation theology may or may not be a fourth option. Its theology is certainly distinct, but on the use of violence its proponents are not in agreement. Some are pacifists, while others see violence as justifiable as a last resort in oppressive situations.

Pacifism

Pacifism appears first in the case. Christian pacifism is linked with what is called "the way of the cross." Jacob Kaufmann presents a modern version of this very traditional perspective, a version often associated with theologian John Howard Yoder.

The way of the cross starts with and stresses what it takes to be the New Testament view of Jesus Christ. According to this perspective, Jesus unambiguously models and calls Chris and Martin to one radical option which is normative for life in society. No other options are valid, no other path but discipleship that is authentically Christian.

This radical option takes its cue from Luke 1:46ff. and 4:5–8. In these texts Jesus is announced as an agent of radical social change who scatters the proud, puts down the mighty, exalts those of low degree, and sends the rich away empty. These texts portray Jesus in a new light. Jesus introduces a nonviolent but politically active way of life for Chris and Martin to live in the midst of the world. This way is best seen in the cross where Jesus stands up to Pilate but does not resort to mob violence or coercive political power to achieve his ends.

The way of the cross is not a new law. It cannot be forced on Chris or Martin, for its essence is freedom. It must be chosen by the disciple with recognition of its true costs, the ultimate being readiness to suffer. While all are called, few will follow because of the high costs. The few who follow will gravitate to small, sharing communities, for the church is the essence of the way.

The way of the cross almost always runs counter to the prevailing culture because the world cannot bear its ethical rigor. No compromises with secular values are brokered. A distinct lifestyle emerges. As disciples, Chris and Martin are called to live simply, bear hostility, serve others, and to be dominated by God's self-giving love.

The way is emphatically nonviolent. Violence is antithetical to God's love even when some other good seems to justify it. Jesus makes clear that an authentic witness to the world is possible without resort to violence.

Nonviolence is not passive nonresistance. Jesus did not condone sin. He resisted it at every turn. Nor did he give in to the power of Rome. Likewise Christians are to resist up to the point at which they would have to use violence to continue resisting. At that point resistance takes the form of suffering. Gandhi, King, and the tactics of nonviolent resistance offer a model for those who choose this option.

Finally, the way involves a radical break with calculations of consequences, power balances, and prudence. As followers of the way Chris and Martin would not be responsible for getting results, making things come out right, or moving society to some higher level of moral endeavor. If good results come, fine. If not, then they persevere. They are called first, last, and always to the way.

For Chris the way of the cross points unambiguously to conscientious objection. To Martin it calls for repentance and in the future active resistance to all forms of violence.

Christian Realism

Roger Smith presents the second option, Christian realism, which is presumably his own. In our time the best-known exponent of this position was the American theologian Reinhold Niebuhr.

Christian realism has its roots both in Luther's two realms doctrine and Calvin's call to transform society. The nomenclature reveals the essence of the perspective: the holding together of idealism and realism.

Idealism is a disposition to be loyal to norms or to some understanding of goodness or right. Christian idealists usually look to the Bible and the tradition for their normative understanding and stress adherence to the rules and principles which they find in these sources.

Realism is the disposition to take full account of sin and other elements which frustrate the realization of the ideal. It starts with the way things are and stresses the brokenness of history, limitation, and the pride of individuals and groups. Instead of pushing single-mindedly toward the ideal, the realist asks: "Where do we go from here?"

In Christian realism Chris and Martin must keep the ideal or normative pole of the tradition together with the realistic pole of the way things are. Realism without vision degenerates into cynicism, idealism without a sense of sin abstracts into illusion.

Chris and Martin are called in this view to live in freedom on the knife edge between idealism and realism and to act politically to move the present situation toward the ideal without the illusion that they can or must achieve the ideal. The political task for them is not the rigorous following of the ideal, however important the ideal may be, but the use of political and sometimes even military power to establish the most tolerable form of peace and justice under the circumstances.

The idealism in this perspective comes from an understanding of God's work in Jesus Christ. Jesus Christ reveals the wisdom and power of God to be self-giving love untainted by self- or group-interest. This ideal is not achievable by Chris or Martin because of their own sin. Nevertheless, approximations of the ideal are possible for them because God's power of love is constantly at work in human affairs and their lives.

God's love judges and convicts Chris and Martin. It breaks their pride and prevents illusion. It brings humility and repentance. As a result, Chris and Martin can undertake political tasks motivated by God's love but with a healthy sense of their own sin as well as the sin of others.

The cross and resurrection free Chris and Martin to work in the midst of horror and contradiction and to serve without need of reward. God's love is also a power at work in the world. It creates the possibility of justice and peace and sustains Chris and Martin against the power of sin.

The realism in this perspective comes from an analysis of human sin. Sin is the inevitable alienation which results from self- or group-centered attempts to gain security against the anxieties of the human condition, for example, using guns or waging war in response to political frustrations. This tendency to seek security in and through the self or he collective is strong in individuals, stronger still in groups. While the individual has a limited capacity for repentance, for shifting from self to God, and for relationships with other persons, this potential is greatly reduced in groups. It is impossible, for example, for groups to love each other.

Such realism does not lead to pessimism and withdrawal. Rather it leads to a new awareness about groups. Different norms apply. If groups cannot love, then the appropriate norm is justice under law. Groups can achieve some semblance of mutual regard and justice by balancing power against power.

This view of groups as having a different set of norms than individuals is called the two realms doctrine. In it the earthly realm is governed by justice, law, rules, and the sword; the divine realm by love, the gospel, and sensitivity. Chris and Martin, provided they find their center in the divine realm, are freed by the cross and resurrection of Jesus Christ to live and work in the earthly realm and to get their hands dirty as soldiers.

Indeed, the task for Chris and Martin is to serve in the earthly realm doing within reason what is needed to make it a better place to live. They are called to exercise power and insofar as they are able to move the inevitable power balances which are prematurely called justice to higher levels of freedom and equality.

The call to exercise power in as ethical a manner as possible leads to the principles of the justifiable war. In the best of times Chris and Martin should work for justice and peace using nonviolent means. In the worst of times, when neither justice nor peace is possible, violence is sometimes the lesser of evils.

In such situations Christian realism considers violence, if not good in itself, at least acceptable as long as certain conditions are met. There are seven conditions or criteria for a justifiable war:

1. Last resort: All other means to achieve a just and peaceful solution must have been exhausted.

2. Just cause: The reason for fighting must be the preservation or restoration of a morally preferable cause against a clearly unjust adversary.

3. Right intention: The intention of violence must be the establishment or restoration of peace with justice.

4. Declared by legitimate authority: Only legitimate authority may declare war. Private, self-appointed defenders of justice are disallowed.

5. Reasonable hope of success: While success does not have to be guaranteed, the useless sacrifice of soldiers no matter how just the cause is ruled out.

6. Noncombatant immunity: Civilians without direct connection with the opponent's war effort must not be intentionally attacked.

7. Proportionality: The force used should be proportional to the objective sought. The good sought should exceed the horrible evil of the violence.

This perspective puts pressure on Chris and offers several alternatives on Vietnam for Martin. Christian realists do not reject military service out of hand, but are prepared to resist fighting in an unjust cause. Unfortunately, the current draft law does not allow for selective conscientious objection, which is the logical outgrowth of the perspective. Realists must therefore either serve or take the legal consequences in the event resistance is conscientiously selected.

Martin, should he accept this perspective, must decide on the justifiability of his own involvement in Vietnam and what to advise Chris. If he sees his involvement as unjustified, which seems to be the case already, he should seek forgiveness and new life in Jesus Christ. He should also relate to Chris the lessons he has learned over the years as his conscience has reacted to his experience in Vietnam. For the future he should be prepared to support just and resist unjust causes. His advice to his son probably should be to register for the draft and to be prepared for selective objection with all of its ambiguities and perils.

Liberation Theology

Maria offers the third option, liberation theology. What is distinctive about this theology is its perspective—its constant touchstone is the concrete reality of the oppressed poor of the Third World. In order to understand the causes of that oppressive reality it employs a variety of tools, among them the biblical witness and the social sciences, including some elements of the social theory of Karl Marx. Liberation theologians must work to understand the political and economic causes of poverty and oppression so that they can better help the poor in eradicating those causes. Liberation theologians also employ the social sciences to give factual insights to the biblical witness, the essence of which they argue is commitment to the poor.

Using the social sciences, liberation theologians have scrutinized historical developments in Latin America from Spanish authoritarianism to liberal democracy, to the current control exercised by the military in most countries. What emerges from their reading of history is a long train of abuses. Economic elites have combined political, economic, and military power with other-worldly, pietistic expressions of Christianity to exploit the Indians, mixed-bloods, peasants, and Afro-Americans of the region.

Today the combination of transnational corporations and local elites, buttressed by the military might of the United States and marching under the ideological banner of economic development and conservative Christianity, is continuing the oppression begun under the Spanish. The oppressed majority, awakened by their new consciousness of this situation, have two options: continued bondage under the status quo or liberation.

Liberation theology enters at this point as a challenge to conservative theologies and as the Christian basis for seeking liberation. The incarnation places Chris and Martin squarely in the midst of life, not in some idealized spiritualized realm apart. An incarnational approach affirms Jesus Christ as the measure and power of God's work. It also affirms history as the place where God's work of making and keeping life human will reach fulfillment. The key for interpreting God's presence and hence for setting social priorities is social justice for the poor.

Liberation theologians see the essence of the gospel in the struggle for liberation on three levels. The first level is the elimination of social, economic, and political injustice. At a deeper second level liberation is historical. It expresses the struggle of the poor to come to a new consciousness about history, rejecting what has been mediated by ruling classes and realizing the liberating power of Jesus Christ. This second level is concerned with freedom, specifically the freedom of the poor to determine their own destiny. The third level is theological. It is liberation from sin through faith in Jesus Christ. It is also the most fundamental level, for sin is the root of all oppression.

These three interdependent levels are played out in the Bible in concrete historical situations. Liberation theologians see the beginning of God's act of liberation in the Exodus, which becomes the paradigm for all levels of liberation. The Israelites were freed from Egyptian political and economic bondage and came to a new sense of identity as a people. This activity of God continued in the work of the prophets who challenged the unjust social conditions and reigning ideologies of their times.

In Jesus Christ something new is added. God takes Israel's place as the suffering servant and reveals a willingness to suffer that humanity might be fully liberated. Jesus sets human understanding on a new course of justice and liberation. Jesus himself rejected perverted forms of kingship and the role of the messianic leader of an armed revolt, but not the use of human power itself. Jesus incarnates God's just and liberating rule creating a new consciousness of liberation which is to be carried out by Chris and Martin in their own situations.

The relevance of Jesus' ethic is direct. The realm of God is not merely foreshadowed, but actually present and operative in historical struggles for liberation. Thus liberation theology would challenge Chris and Martin first to try to understand the perspective of the oppressed and then, working from that perspective, to determine how best to participate in the fuller realization of the kingdom as it breaks in to transform society.

Liberation theology does not offer a distinctively new perspective on violence to Chris and Martin, since all of the traditional options are found in it. Instead it asks them how they can participate in God's so-called preferential option for the poor. For Chris this means close scrutiny of U.S. military involvement in the Third World and preparation to resist or support such involvement depending on a new criteria: how it hurts or helps the least advantaged. For Martin it presents a new view of Vietnam through the sights of the poor instead of those of his ship's guns and his own culture. Finally it calls both to a new, topsy-turvy biblical awareness and to action in cooperation with the world's poor.

Crusade

The final option presented in Martin's class is the crusade, which historically has been an option but does not appear to be so in this case. One reason the crusade has been popular is its simplicity. It divides reality into good and evil. The crusader is always on the side of the good, the enemy always the incarnation of evil. God wills the eradication of evil, hence the crusader is justified, even commanded, to kill. Another source of its popularity is its compatibility with tribalism, that seemingly natural human inclination to favor one's own group and accept without question its rituals, perspectives, and aggressions.

The crusade has had its moments in Christian history. It was at work in the conquest of the Promised Land by the Hebrews. Pope Urban II used it successfully in the Middle Ages to rescue the Holy Land temporarily from the forces of Islam. Today in some Christian circles it is encountered in the call to oppose "atheistic communism."

In the case study the crusade is seen as foreign to the teachings of Jesus. Its dualism of good and evil is simplistic in the extreme, especially in its naiveté about the sin of the crusader. Its embrace of violence is so alien to the central Christian experience of faith as to make a mockery of it. For these and other reasons Ronald Smith, the teacher, was correct in dismissing it as an option. It is out of the normative bounds of Christianity and offers no guidance to Chris or Martin. Its ethical importance today is that of an historical artifact and an example of what to avoid.

ADDITIONAL RESOURCES

Bainton, Roland H. *Christian Attitudes toward War and Peace.* Nashville: Abingdon, 1960.

Gray, J. Glenn. *The Warriors.* New York: Harper & Row, 1959; rev. ed., 1967.

Gutiérrez, Gustavo. *A Theology of Liberation.* Maryknoll, N.Y.: Orbis, 1973; rev. ed., 1988.

Míguez Bonino, José. *Doing Theology in a Revolutionary Situation.* Philadelphia: Fortress, 1975.

———. *Toward a Christian Political Ethics.* Philadelphia: Fortress, 1983.

Niebuhr, Reinhold. *The Children of Light and the Children of Darkness.* New York: Charles Scribner's Sons, 1944.

Sider, Ronald J., and Richard K. Taylor. *Nuclear Holocaust and Christian Hope.* Downers Grove, Ill.: InterVarsity Press, 1982.

Stone, Ronald H. *Reinhold Niebuhr: Prophet to Politician.* Nashville: Abingdon, 1972.

Yoder, John Howard. *The Politics of Jesus.* Grand Rapids: William B. Eerdmans, 1972.

Case

Crossroads

The Reverend Roger Kenner sat at his desk uneasily mulling over his options. The life and death struggle in the black squatter village of Crossroads seemed so far away from his home in this quiet all-white section of Cape Town. The study door was closed to keep out the noise of the television program his children were watching. He had not had much time with Tom (age seven) and Kim (age nine) these last few months. They had a hard time understanding why his duties as minister of a local congregation and his involvement in the Crossroads community took him away from them. Roger wished he could just spend the rest of the afternoon playing with them. But today was not the day.

It was now Tuesday afternoon. In less than an hour Roger was to meet with leaders of the Crossroads squatter village. They would want his answer. Late Sunday afternoon armed vigilantes, identified by white armbands and under protection of security forces, had attacked an area of Crossroads, setting on fire homes in Community A, one of twelve separate communities or sections designated and governed by the Crossroads residents. By the end of the day six hundred homes had been completely destroyed. On Monday the vigilantes returned and continued a systematic attack through the community. When residents tried to stop the vigilantes and protect their homes and families, the police would shoot. Roger had gone to Community A in Crossroads late Monday afternoon. He was able to get through the police roadblock only by proving he was a member of the clergy. As he viewed the smoldering ruins, a sharp early winter wind ripped at his coat. Thousands of people were homeless. Though some could crowd into other homes, most would sleep that night with no shelter at all. Then this morning, Tuesday, a group of leaders from several communities in Crossroads had come to Roger's church and asked him to buy guns and ammunition

This case was written by Elizabeth Wieman and Alice Frazer Evans. Copyright © The Case Study Institute. The names of all persons except public figures have been disguised to protect the privacy of the persons in this situation.

for them to use against the vigilantes. Some of their homes had already been attacked. It was obvious the band of vigilantes would return during the night or the next day. At the current rate homes were being destroyed, other sections would be demolished in a few days. Roger was aware of the risk. It was illegal to own a firearm without a permit, and very few Blacks were allowed permits. Though Roger did have a permit and could buy guns and ammunition, to purchase arms for another person, particularly for resistance to state security, would clearly be seen as an act of treason. If Roger were caught, he could be sentenced to life in prison. And now they wanted to know, would he do this for them? He had agreed to meet them at the church in late afternoon with an answer.

Images of Roger's past relationship with the people of Crossroads flooded his mind. He had come to know the community when he was a theology student involved in helping poor black families through student outreach programs. He organized clothing drives and gathered canned goods. As a student deeply committed to nonviolent action, he imagined participating with the people of Crossroads in a nonviolent resistance campaign. Roger was convinced there were clear biblical strictures against killing. As a Christian he believed that Christ's call to "turn the other cheek" and "to love your enemy as yourself" were calls to nonviolent resistance. His work with the people in Crossroads had strengthened this conviction. It had also taught him a great deal about his role in the struggle as a white South African.

GOVERNMENT LEGISLATION
AND DEVELOPMENT OF CROSSROADS

The 1913 Native Land Act, which made it illegal for Black South Africans to own land outside of existing reserves, was the parent of Crossroads. The Natives Trust and Lands Act of 1936 more clearly designated the reserve areas. Apartheid policies solidified after 1948 when the Nationalist Party came into power. The entire population was divided into categories of White, Black, Colored (mixed race), and Asian. Under the Group Areas Act of 1950 and the Bantu Self-Government Act of 1959, all of South Africa was designated for the exclusive use of one racial group or another. The cities and prime land were almost entirely reserved for Whites. Until the 1986 establishment of a tricameral legislature, which gave limited representation to Coloreds and Asians, only Whites were considered voting citizens.

Since passage of the Bantu Self-Government Act, two million Blacks, and proportionally smaller numbers of Coloreds and Asians, had been forced to leave their homes and resettle during periods of "forced removals." Many had held title and land deeds which were invalidated by the new laws. A small number of Whites in rural areas were also resettled. Black South Africans, who make up roughly 75 percent of the population, were assigned 13 percent of the land. This was divided into a patchwork of disconnected rural reservations. Blacks were to hold citizenship and vote in these reservations. Some of them, later called Bantustans and then homelands, had fertile areas; the majority were barren with little road or rail transportation. Roger recalled the graphic phrase of colored leader Allan Boesak, who referred to the homelands as "human dumping grounds."

Some 50 percent of the black population continued to live outside of the Bantustans. They provided unskilled labor for the cities and lived in designated areas called townships, which were on the outskirts of major white urban areas. Under the Influx Control Law, black families were required to have a resident card in order to remain in the townships. These cards were given to those who had been born there or who had established work records of ten years of steady employment. Although holders of resident cards could build their own homes in the townships, they could not own the land, for which they paid rent to the government.

Under the migratory labor system, men were expected to leave their wives and children in the Bantustans and live in one of the all-male hostels in the townships. Hostels in the larger cities housed as many as 40,000 men. In the Cape Town area the hostels housed 16,000 to 20,000. Only when workers received a resident card could families come and join them. For men who could not afford the transportation costs, this meant seeing their families only once a year.

If Blacks lost their urban jobs, they were supposed to return to the Bantustans, where unemployment is often over 50 percent. Malnutrition is rife in most Bantustans. The rate of black infant mortality is ten times higher than for Whites. In some areas 25 percent of the children die before their first birthday. The statistics carried painful and vivid images for Roger. When he had been invited into areas of the Ciskei, he had seen the swollen stomachs of thousands of children suffering from life-long hunger.

There had always been families who refused to be separated. Rather, they chose to form small squatter communities and settle illegally around the outskirts of the cities. These small communities were easily and frequently dispersed by the police or government military forces. In time Crossroads had become an exception.

Roger learned that before 1975 there were a number of squatter communities of both Blacks and Coloreds living on the outskirts of Cape Town. In that year government troops, in accordance with the Group Areas Act, moved the Coloreds to two areas eighteen and twenty kilometers from Cape Town. Within time, government housing for colored families was provided in both areas. Blacks were sent twenty-five kilometers away from Cape Town to the area which became known as Crossroads. This was declared by the government as a place where black male migrant workers would be allowed to squat. The government maintained that women and children had no right to be there.

The first time Roger saw Crossroads was in 1980. Then there were 60,000 people in the settlement, in an area of about two square kilometers (one and three quarters square miles). Many of the men in Crossroads had come from the Bantustans of Transkei and Ciskei to work as migrant laborers in Cape Town. Most had menial jobs which required few skills and paid poorly. Families with three and four children were living in one-room structures built of wooden sticks and sheets of plastic. A good wind or rain easily tore the plastic walls. There was no running water or electricity. Seven pit toilets served the entire community. The government refused to provide sanitation services, and garbage littered the ground. Since Crossroads was an "illegal community," the government also refused to build schools or health facilities.

Roger had come to respect and admire these poor black families who refused to be separated because of the laws of apartheid. He had come to understand what it meant to them to have their own community, even if the only visible sign of that community was a collection of fragile structures. In eight years Crossroads grew from 20,000 to 100,000 people. Wives and families continued to come from Transkei and Ciskei. The people had divided themselves into twelve communities. Each community had elected an executive committee. Roger worked closely with many of the community leaders and was aware that some were involved in extortion and bribery. In spite of this, decisions were made and owned by the communities as a whole. Roger considered Crossroads one of the few truly self-governed black areas in South Africa.

CROSSROADS COMMUNITY LIFE

Roger remembered the first community meeting he attended, six years before. Over six hundred people gathered at a meeting called by Sipho, the chairperson of the elected executive committee. He began by explaining that the evening before the police had come into Crossroads and destroyed one hundred homes, leaving about four hundred people homeless. This was hardly new. Homes had been routinely destroyed in Crossroads since its beginning. This time the police commander had warned that if the community rebuilt the homes, the women and children who were there illegally would be put in jail. The question posed by Sipho was how they should respond as a community.

Mildred Lesaba stood to speak first. The night before, she explained, she was awakened by the sound of voices. She saw flashlights moving down the street, became anxious, and woke her husband. A policeman's voice came over a loudspeaker telling everyone to get out of their homes because they were going to be destroyed. Mildred and her husband quickly discussed whether they should get out of the house or stay inside and make the police force them out. That would surely involve a beating. Because of the children, they decided to leave. They watched the police move from house to house, tearing the plastic sheeting off the wooden posts and chopping the poles with axes. After destroying all the homes on the street, the police loaded the building materials onto a truck and left. Mildred, her husband, and their three children spent the rest of the night huddled together on the metal bed under a single blanket.

Florence Goba spoke next. Her husband had secured employment with a construction company in Cape Town five years before. He had come to the city and lived in an all-male hostel. She and their four children remained in Ciskei, living with her parents. She did not see her husband for three years, but he continued to send money. It was too expensive for him to take the twelve hour bus trip back to Ciskei. Then two years ago her husband wrote that he had fallen in love with another woman who was pregnant with his child. He still loved Florence and wanted the family to come to Crossroads. Her husband lived with them part of the time and with the other woman part of the time. Things were working out until this morning when their house was destroyed. Now she had nowhere to go.

Roger, angry at the injustice and deeply admiring of the courage, sat for hours listening to the stories. Finally, a woman named Margaret stood up and spoke for the whole community: "We are going to rebuild our shacks. We are the ones who will go to prison and take the consequences." They knew what would happen. The women and children would be arrested and charged with illegal squatting. They would be put in a dirty and crowded prison for a week and charged a fine of R50 (approximately U.S. $50). Margaret turned to Roger and asked, "Will the churches help pay our fines and give us new building materials?"

Roger had said yes, and then had worked with staff members of the Council of Churches to provide legal defense, court fees, and new building materials. Roger also worked with the Crossroads community to plan a strategy for when the women were arrested and for buying and distributing the building materials. Roger had finally lost count of how many times the process was repeated. Each time homes were destroyed, the people would discuss whether they should passively resist or actively fight to protect the community. They were angry, humiliated, and tired of being pushed around by the government. How long did they have to put up with the abuse? But they knew, as President Botha had warned, that the government had not even begun to flex its military muscle. Violent resistance would probably do nothing but increase the violence of the government. So after considerable debate, the communities always decided to resist with nonviolence, hoping the press would publicize their plight, humiliate the state, and force the leaders to make policy changes.

Roger had not always agreed with the community decisions, but he had learned the importance of people being able to make their own decisions. He had become a strong believer that white Christians needed to be committed to the process of liberation without controlling it. Sometimes that meant support when the people decided to do things that he thought were unwise. He remembered when the government had forcibly taken several hundred people back to Transkei, promising employment if they stayed. Roger thought it might be better for them to stay in Transkei and make a go of it. But the people immediately began the week-long walk back to Crossroads. Roger reluctantly secured busses, even though he doubted the people's decision.

KHAYELITSHA AND INCREASE OF GOVERNMENT PRESSURE

The systematic destruction of homes in Crossroads continued for nine years, until 1984. Finally, the executive committees of the twelve sections were able to negotiate a moratorium on tearing down homes. However, tensions increased sharply in 1985 when the government announced a forced removal of all Crossroads residents to a new development named Khayelitsha, which was several miles away. In contradiction to previous government promises and an independent foundation study which proposed specific plans for upgrading Crossroads, government officials now declared this an "impossible task" because of overcrowding. The people of Crossroads had not been consulted about Khayelitsha and voiced strong suspicions. Many had experienced forced removals before and found that promises were never kept. Others were convinced this was the government's way to gain control of the squatter community.

Johnson Daka, director of the executive committee in the original squatter community and the most powerful and respected leader in Crossroads, had spoken strongly against going to Khayelitsha: "We will not be told where to live. Crossroads is our home and we do not intend to move!" Demonstrations erupted in the streets. Several policemen were beaten and one was nearly stoned to death. The government quickly called in more security forces.

Johnson was arrested and imprisoned on charges of provoking public violence. His bail was posted at R25,000, an unusually high bail which signaled the government's seriousness. Then suddenly all charges were dropped, and Johnson was freed.

Strong opposition to the move to Khayelitsha continued. Government officials began to approach individual members of the executive committees. Roger remembered the day Matthew, a member of Community D's executive committee, walked into his office and said, "I'm telling you this and I'm telling you in case I'm dead by tomorrow. Our executive committee was invited to speak with the government officials. We told them we were not moving to Khayelitsha. Then Mr. Brown offered each member of the committee R3,000 if we would agree to move. You know as well as I do that a full-time bricklayer makes only R3,500 per year, and most of the men have not worked for at least a year because they felt they needed to be at home to protect their families. All of our committee members voted 'no.' However, of the other eleven executive committees in Crossroads, I have learned that four committees have agreed to take their people to

Khayelitsha. Eight communities have declared they will not be moved."

In addition to the opportunity to build a more permanent home on a pre-set concrete slab, people were also told there would be a water tap and a toilet for every two families. Those who agreed to move were also promised temporary residence cards. This gave them the right to live in Khayelitsha for eighteen months, even if they did not have work. They were also granted the right to look for work. Rent for the structures which they would build would be paid to a committee elected by the people and agreeable to the government.

The government pointed out the numerous benefits of the new location. Roger was also aware of factors which troubled the people. Most troubling were the design and location of Khayelitsha, thirty-five kilometers from Cape Town. In contrast to Crossroads, there was no rail line into the city and only limited bus service. More than one family would not be permitted to live in a home. There was only one road in and one road out of a community planned for 30,000 people. The entire area was surrounded by high wire fences, and powerful lights beamed down into the compound. Two military bases were nearby.

On the day when a group was to be moved to Khayelitsha, people were given official papers and loaded onto big trucks and taken away. Many of those who remained in Crossroads attempted to upgrade their situation by taking vacant shacks better than their own. However, these homes were immediately torn down by the defense forces and the areas cordoned off by barbed wire. From May 1985 to May 1986, less than one-third of the people in Crossroads moved to Khayelitsha. Though pressure for total removal continued, Roger knew that there was room in Khayalitsha for less than half of those still living in Crossroads. He was concerned that once communities were separated, individual families would not be able to resist being removed to the Bantustans.

BREAKDOWN IN NEGOTIATIONS AND INCREASED VIOLENCE

Leaders of many of the executive committees continued to meet with government officials. Johnson Daka was not among them. Negotiations with the government finally broke down completely. The Minister of Cooperation and Development, who had a major responsibility for the resettlement of black communities, continued to insist that Crossroads was illegal and people must either move to Khayelitsha or return to Transkei and Ciskei. Roger was told that the leaders responded with one question: "Mr. Minister, when a law is unjust, doesn't it cease to be a legitimate law?" The minister was unmoved.

Shortly after the negotiations broke down, the military presence in Crossroads increased. Security forces patrolled the community regularly, and armed tanks were stationed on the hill overlooking Crossroads. On several occasions large areas of Crossroads were tear-gassed in the name of "riot control." Friends shared with Roger that the police were becoming much more aggressive, at times randomly shooting into homes of black families. When questioned by the press and members of the clergy who continued to come into Crossroads, the police explained their actions by saying they were looking for murderers and terrorists. One family came to Roger's office with an unexploded hand grenade that had been thrown into their home by the police.

For the first time in the history of Crossroads, the leadership was divided. Though Johnson Daka had continued to attend meetings of community leaders and to voice his support for staying in Crossroads, Roger suspected that he had secretly agreed to work for the government before his sudden release from prison. A government worker in Roger's congregation showed him a copy of a letter Johnson had written to the Minister of Cooperation and Development in which he had laid out plans for the redevelopment of Crossroads. Roger noted that the plan designed by Johnson assumed that the four largest communities would be eliminated.

Roger also picked up rumors that a vigilante group had formed to work in cooperation with the government. Several people reported that the police had given some of their neighbors guns and ammunition. Then this past Sunday afternoon, a group identified as vigilantes gathered at the north end of Community A. Huge tanks moved down the street. The vigilantes followed, setting each house on fire. Those who tried to stop the vigilantes were shot.

The same thing occurred on Monday in a section adjacent to Community A. By the end of the second day ten thousand people were homeless, and a vast area of Crossroads was in ruins. When Roger tried to estimate the number dead or wounded, the residents could only reply that "many have been shot and their bodies taken away." The police refused to say which hospitals received the dead or wounded. News reporters who managed to enter the area through roadblocks had their cameras smashed and were turned away by shouting vigilantes. Newspapers on Tuesday morning reported "black-on-black" violence in Crossroads.

It was this same morning that a delegation of over forty leaders from Crossroads executive committees came to meet with Roger. They said to him, "We are weak. These people are killing us. They have courage only because we are defenseless. Some of us have guns, but we have nothing to put in the guns. You have white skin, so it is possible for you to get us the ammunition and guns we need. If we show our strength, we will surprise the vigilantes, and they will have to turn away. Unless we can protect our homes and our families, our fight will be over and our people will be killed."

Roger had always argued for nonviolent resistance. He had believed that the only Christian response was to turn the other cheek. He had a deep respect for the way the Crossroads community had used nonviolent strategy in the past. Roger had also learned from the people of Crossroads that nonviolence was crucial for human dignity. But Roger was struck with the sudden realization that if his wife Mary and their children were threatened, he would do all in his power to protect them. Could he ask more of his Crossroads friends than he would be willing to do himself?

Roger asked the delegation many questions. Were they ready to spend time in prison? How could they be sure that one of them wasn't an informer? They didn't understand what people would do under pressure. Remember what happened to Johnson? Did they stand any kind of a chance against the might of the South African security forces? In response, the leaders assured Roger that they had asked all of these questions and had decided that a violent response was the only way to avoid destruction.

After the delegation left with Roger's promise to let them know his answer by late afternoon, he sat alone in his church office. In his mind he could still picture them as they stood before him. These people, just a few weeks before strong and determined, had come to him depressed, desperate, and without hope or purpose. Maybe violence was the only avenue left to them.

Roger called his wife, Mary, who agreed to leave her office and meet him in town. As a secretary in a local business, Mary was not directly involved in the Crossroads community, but she had always been supportive of Roger's work. This was particularly important for Roger when his anti-apartheid stance and activities had brought him into conflict with some members of his congregation and his own church leaders. In recent months, however, as more and more white, black, and colored religious leaders had been detained by the government, she had become anxious for his safety and concerned for the children. Initially, Mary had supported him and said he must do whatever his conscience and his faith commitment called him to do to support the Crossroads community. But this afternoon she was having second thoughts. What would happen if he were caught? What would it mean for the children to have their father in prison and a criminal? Roger admitted to Mary that he was afraid. Then again, maybe he was asking the wrong questions.

Roger and Mary called a close friend who was familiar with the Crossroads community and this kind of request. They hoped he might help. Bill shared his concern about the number of people who knew about the request to Roger. There were established channels for some in the black community to acquire arms, and the leaders of Crossroads had not used these channels. Yet there might be very good reasons why they had not used them. He told Roger that it would take him at least three or four days to check this out.

Mary had gone back to work, and Roger had come home to meet the children after school. Roger spent over an hour in his study, praying, reviewing the issues, and trying to understand what being in solidarity with these people, whom he deeply cared for, was all about. The leaders were clear that if they waited for several days, their community would be destroyed. They needed an answer this afternoon.

Commentary

Crossroads

Ethical decisions focus on a conflict of values in a specific context. The pressing problem of Crossroads is one of tactics in a struggle for liberation. How does a member of the privileged middle class, an advocate of nonviolent strategy, respond to the specific request for weapons by members of a poor and oppressed class with whom he seeks to be in solidarity? In the eyes of the Third World residents of Crossroads who approach Roger Kenner, their request for arms is an issue of self-defense. This is not so much a problem of ethics as one of survival. Roger Kenner, a First World citizen of a Third World nation, faces an ethical problem. At the roots of the dilemma for Roger are the legitimacy and the effectiveness of a strategy of violence or "counter-violence" in this particular context.

The *context* of Roger's problem is a request for support for a decision already made by a group of disenfranchised and threatened members of a black majority at a particular time in the history of South Africa. The reader is challenged to consider the Christian *norms* that would inform Roger's response. And Roger's personal dilemma involves the authenticity of his *relationship* with his family, his church, and the people of Crossroads. Roger has assumed roles as father and pastor, but he also feels a strong commitment to work with the people of Crossroads and has declared his solidarity with them in the struggle for human dignity and self-determination. Context, norms, and relations all bear upon the decision for Roger and ultimately for all of the members of the global human community who are committed to respond to the moral crisis of South Africa's policy of apartheid.

The case challenges the reader and Roger Kenner to empathize with a view from the "underside of history." This means viewing history from the perspective of the dispossessed and marginalized. Encompassed in this view is the understanding that God sides with the downtrodden in their struggle to reshape history. It is from the perspective of the poor and oppressed, with whom God has already demonstrated solidarity, that the appropriateness of an armed strategy of self-defense will be evaluated. The context will demand for many readers that they attempt to see with new eyes and hear with new ears the cry of these people.

CONTEXT: THE CONDITION OF THE PEOPLE

The dehumanizing reality of staggering poverty, malnutrition, and unemployment among the approximately thirty million people of color in South Africa is documented in the case. This reality stands in stark contrast to the wealth and privilege of those citizens classified as white in South Africa. The inequality is illustrated perhaps most shockingly by the fact that a black child dies of hunger every fifteen minutes in what is acknowledged as the most prosperous African nation in terms of agricultural and natural mineral resources. The infant mortality rate in rural black South Africa is ten times that in white areas. In public, segregated education seven times more money is spent on each white child than on each black child.

The legal system includes several "pillars of apartheid." These include the Population Registration Act and the Group Areas Act, which sustain the system of segregation. Domination by four and a half million Whites who are eligible to vote is legally guaranteed, while twenty-six million black Africans are deprived of any meaningful voting rights. Another four million who are classified as Indian or Colored hold restricted representation in a new tricameral legislative system which was boycotted by the vast majority of those voters. With no Bill of Rights and no functionally independent judiciary, there are severely limited opportunities for people of color to appeal to the courts for effective recourse. While other nations may currently have violent and repressive regimes, South Africa has one of the most oppressive systems enshrined in law in modern society.

This context is made even more tragic by conditions which followed the declaration of the partial state of emergency in 1985. This declaration granted blanket powers to police and military, known collectively as the security forces, in specific areas of South Africa. This included the Western Cape Province where Crossroads is located. Members of the security forces were declared free to detain persons without charge or trial for up to six months and to deny the right of movement, assembly, or speech of any persons deemed a threat to national security. Any statement which "discredits the government" could be considered a treasonable offense. This included statements in the news media and at funerals and services of worship. All actions of the security forces were protected by law, and members of the security forces had "total endemnity," which meant they could not be charged with any crime in the pursuit of duty. Though the state of emergency was lifted for a short time prior to the outbreak of the vigilante movement in Crossroads, the stage was set for increased and autonomous actions on the part of the security forces.

The context for a decision on the use of counter-violence is the condition of suffering not only in Crossroads but also for the majority of the people of color in South Africa. This setting is coupled with the refusal of government administrators to negotiate seriously with the leaders of Crossroads or at all with the African National Congress (ANC), considered the leading representative of most black South Africans. In the words of Frank Chikane, a black leader and General Secretary of the South African Council of Churches (SACC), "The intransigence and violence of the apartheid regime has created a pastoral crisis as more victims of apartheid resort to the use of force as the only option left to stop this racist, inhuman, brutal and violent system."

The majority of white South Africans exist in virtual isolation from the inhuman conditions of most Blacks, with contact often limited to Whites dealing with domestic servants and shopkeepers. Isolation is reinforced by stringent censorship of the media and the arts. Since the 1985 declaration of a state of emergency, the white population seems increasingly dominated by fear. Political forces to the right and left of the Nationalist government of P. W. Botha denounce even the modest reforms that have emerged as, respectively, either sellouts to black South African independence or manipulative gestures that are "too little, too late." Negotiations are seen as politically impossible for an embattled Botha. The constant pressure of fear and anxiety, plus the potential loss of power and privilege, make it difficult for many Whites to hear and believe the assurances of the majority of black leaders that white minority rights would be guaranteed through a new constitution and bill of rights. This fear is probably understandable, even in the face of the ANC's Freedom Charter, which is committed to a liberated South Africa as a "non-racial, democratic society."

There is already warfare in South Africa. The reality for residents of the black townships and even more for those in squatter camps like Crossroads is that a revolutionary struggle is underway. Violence in those people's lives is direct, structural, and pervasive. The question is not how to avoid violence but how to contain it.

The isolation of the white population is being penetrated by acts of sabotage in the cities, by young people joining the "end-conscription campaign" and refusing to serve in the all-white South African Defense Forces, by an occasionally distressing sermon or newscast, and by a growing economic crisis in the country sometimes attributed to international campaigns for disinvestment and sanctions. For a growing number of Whites the illusion of the restoration of peace and order without a radical change in the condition of the majority of South Africans is just that—an illusion.

Frank Chikane makes it clear that the debate on issues of violence and nonviolence can continue only when there is a "space" before the war has begun or where the participants experience no immediate threat to their lives. "People in the black townships of South Africa consider this 'a luxury' of which they have been deprived," declares Chikane. Those dominated by the society can no longer participate in an illusory debate because a state of war has already been declared, and any "space" has been completely eliminated. The Reverend Chikane observes, "Faced with this reality one can either run for one's life or fight back in self defense. . . . There is time only for responding to the violence of the system." Often those in power will use violence to create an artificial space in which they will then discuss and condemn violence.

Finally, the view "from below" makes it clear that the war is between economic classes which are defined primarily along racial grounds. South Africa is engaged in a struggle for liberation by the poor against the non-poor.

NORMS: THEOLOGICAL RATIONALE

Seventy-two percent of South Africans claim to be Christian. Those on all sides of the conflict call on different components of the Christian gospel to support their positions. The Dutch Reformed Church (DRC), the largest Christian denomination of white South Africans, has traditionally justified apartheid through biblical interpretation. The term "apartheid" is an Afrikaans word meaning "separateness." The DRC has taken a strong stand against any violence toward the state and offers theological justification for actions deemed necessary for the preservation of the state. A new confessional statement from South Africa entitled the Kairos Document identifies this position as "state theology." "State theology" gives "divine" authority (Rom. 13:1–7) to the state in the name of "law and order" and renounces all violence toward or critique of the state.

Many other South African Christians, including millions of Blacks in independent African churches, while condemning apartheid, refrain from any direct political involvement in the struggle. They advocate a clear division between issues of church and state. This position is known as "church theology." "Church theology" does not involve any analysis of society and applies traditional themes of reconciliation, justice, and nonviolence while supporting a blanket condemnation of all that is called violence.

Roger Kenner has already rejected both of these positions. Through words and actions, he has stated that his central concern is solidarity, to stand with and view the world from the perspective of those who are struggling for liberation. Therefore, the theological norms that inform his reflection on whether or not to purchase arms and ammunition for the Crossroads residents are influenced by the distinctive view of a theology or Christology "from below." This view from the underside of history and the perspective of oppressed people may challenge traditional theological norms on violence and nonviolence. Church historians remind contemporary Christians that in pre-Constantinian days the church was identified with the poor and outcasts of society. Christians were known as "dangerous subversives." In the centuries following Constantine, the church became identified with the ruling classes and with Western civilization. In a conflict of values the church came to identify with the dominant values of ruling regimes and frequently legitimized the use of violence by these regimes and opposed revolutionary violence to overthrow them.

Another theological tradition, one that distinquishes between oppressive state violence and the use of violence in self-defense against aggressors and tyrants, may be helpful to Roger. This perspective, sometimes known as the "just war" tradition, allows for a theological understanding and at times a theological legitimization of revolutionary violence. This understanding supports not only the theological *right* to resist tyranny, but the theological obligation to do so in "obedience to God." Although nonviolence is still normative for the church, the alternative just war tradition has been rediscovered by numerous Third World liberation theologians, including the framers of the South African Kairos Document.

The Kairos Document takes its name from the Greek word meaning the "present time"; the term conveys a sense of crisis (Luke 12:56). Seen by many as one of the most important theological documents of the twentieth century, the document was developed by an interracial group of over one hundred fifty professional theologians, lay theologians, and church leaders as "a Christian, biblical, and theological comment on the political crisis in South Africa." The document was intended to stimulate discussion and action. Citing some of the themes from the Kairos Document may suggest theological norms for many in South Africa such as Roger Kenner who might not call themselves liberation theologians but who are committed to a liberated South Africa and therefore would be about the work of liberation.

The Kairos Document rejects both "state theology" and "church theology" while proposing a "prophetic theology" that views apartheid as heresy and the current government as tyranny without legal or moral legitimacy. This particular theological position is based on an interpretation of the Christian gospel that establishes a method and several norms for decision and action.

A social analysis of this particular "kairos" is the first step in the process of developing a prophetic theology. The methodology employed is one of "praxis," which involves dialogue between experience and theological reflection and which begins with the experience of the people. The social analysis of South Africa in the Kairos Document reveals "a conflict between oppressor and oppressed" with "irreconcilable causes or interests." One side seeks to sustain at all costs, even that of millions of lives, an unjust system of power and privilege. The other seeks at all costs, even their own lives, radically to change the structure of society with a goal of justice. They see reforms or modifications in the system by the present government as attempts to insure that the system is not radically changed. Following this first step of an in-depth social analysis to identify the causes of suffering, injustice, and violence, the Kairos Document goes on to an application of several norms.

1. *God is the liberator of the oppressed.* The Bible makes this clear in the Exodus story telling of the liberation of the Israelites from bondage in Egypt (Exod. 3:7–9), and in the Gospels with Jesus' identification as the one

prophesied by Isaiah to bring "good news to the poor, . . . release to the captives, . . . and . . . liberty [to] those who are oppressed" (Luke 4:18). Oppression is seen as a basic category of biblical theology and God has taken sides. God is concerned about the rich who benefit from oppressive structures and God calls them to repentance, not simply to compromise or reconciliation. The first norm is to name and resist oppression and support God's liberating activity in the world.

2. *God calls us to seek justice* (Mic. 6:8). Since tyranny is the enemy of the common good of all the people, it is the enemy of God and must be eliminated. There is a moral right and an obligation to resist a tyrannical regime because it violates the image and likeness of God in the people. What the tyrant does to the least of the people is done to God (Matt. 25:49). The current South African government is judged by the majority of the people to be tyrannical and thus the enemy of God. Christians are called to love their enemies (Matt. 5:44); the way to do this is to eliminate oppression for the sake of the oppressors as well as the oppressed. Several methods of eliminating oppression by the apartheid state are suggested as a challenge to action: taking sides as God does with the oppressed; participating in the struggle for liberation and justice; transforming all church activities into signs of solidarity; civil disobedience; and providing moral guidance on the duty to resist oppression and to curb excesses. There is no specific recommendation on violence in the document, but it is clearly not condemned in prophetic theology. The second norm, then, is to identify and resist tyranny and to seek justice through concrete action.

3. *The hope of Christ is confidence in a kingdom of love, justice, and peace.* Faith means hope. Tyranny and oppression cannot last forever. Real justice, authentic peace, and genuine reconciliation are assured by God's grace in the coming of the kingdom which Christ initiated. The struggle will be difficult, costly and conflictual. But, the Kairos Document declares, "At the very heart of the gospel of Jesus Christ and at the very center of all true prophecy is a message of hope." The third norm is to act with confidence that hope for liberation and justice is already a reality in Jesus Christ and the kingdom of God.

UNDERSTANDING VIOLENCE

Understanding violence is crucial to Roger's decision. It is sometimes helpful to distinguish between the "force" of the state and the "self-defense" of the oppressed. However, violence is generally understood as an "all-inclusive act of compulsion or restraint," according to South African scholar Charles Villa-Vicencio, who suggests several propositions which may clarify issues of violence within the particular context of South Africa.

1. *Some form of violence is an inherent part of the political process.* From Mahatma Gandhi to Martin Luther King, Jr., nonviolent resistance to the force of the state did not guarantee restraint on the part of authorities.

Peaceful demonstrations by children in Soweto in 1976 resulted in their killing and imprisonment. By definition the state is the holder of the final means of force. Regardless of tactics, some degree of violence is inevitable.

2. *There is a difference between state violence and tyranny.* A state which genuinely represents its people may resort on occasion to the use of force. However, when a state lacks the consent and respect of the governed, as in South Africa, it becomes an illegitimate regime or a tyranny and maintains its power by the use of violence.

3. *Revolution is an inevitable response to state tyranny.* Liberation is a human desire; history suggests that people will eventually resort to violence if necessary to gain freedom. The church must be as concerned with the morality of indifference as with the morality of violence.

4. *Not all violence is revolutionary violence.* Most frequently overlooked are institutional and structural violence such as dehumanizing apartheid laws, poverty, and the resulting hopelessness. There is the direct violence of police and vigilante groups but also the anarchic or purposeless violence that can occur in the struggle for liberation.

5. *The spiral of violence needs to be broken.* Violence and counter-violence will not change the structure of a society like that of South Africa. The need is to build a different kind of society that is more equitable and sustainable.

RELATIONSHIPS: COMMUNITY AND INDIVIDUAL APPLICATION

Roger Kenner has a conflict of values as he faces an ethical decision in the specific context of South Africa, which is at its own distinctive "crossroads." The context discloses the boundaries of the path even as Roger struggles to see the turning points in the nation's journey through the eyes of the victims of poverty and the apartheid system. The norms for the work of liberation, justice, and human dignity provide a map or series of signposts along the way with which he can consult to reorient the trip. Roger's ethical decision is not determined by either the context or the norms, but should be informed by both.

The relational dimension of Roger's ethical decision may be as important as the context and norms. What will his decision mean for the whole community of Crossroads as well as his friends Mildred, Florence, Johnson, and Matthew? What implications are there for the congregation in which Roger serves, with the leadership espousing nonviolence as a principle, not just a strategy. What might his decision mean for the country which he loves and is struggling to change? What are the implications for his children and his wife, who is increasingly anxious? There are obviously many approaches which Roger could take. His concern to stand in solidarity with the people of Crossroads, however, and the thesis of seeing his decision "from below" suggest two primary avenues of choice: counter-violence and active nonviolent resistance. These approaches are advocated out of different sets of relationships and are informed by distinctive histories and different perspectives according to social class.

OPTION: COUNTER-VIOLENCE

Roger's relationship to the community of Crossroads and the individuals with whom he has shared the struggle could provide the basis for a positive response to the request for arms. The leaders of Crossroads have already discussed alternatives and decided to ask Roger for help. His positive response would confirm his commitment to support their leadership and their struggle for liberation.

A "social analysis" suggests that armed resistance would be an act of self-defense. There is a struggle for survival by the oppressed against a vigilante group which, at least in part, has become an instrument of the tyranny of the state. The vigilantes are protected and may have been armed by the state. The vigilante strategy impedes the struggle for liberation. The state appears to have co-opted the leadership like Johnson Daka, bought the loyalty of the vigilantes, and divided the people through purported "black-on-black" violence. It could be argued that this is clearly a case in which there is both the right and the obligation of Christians to resist tyranny for the sake of liberation.

In the long view supplying arms could also be seen as the containment of greater violence or what some call the "minimalization of violence." This may be a decisive moment to contain not only the direct violence of the vigilantes but, even more important, to resist the structural violence that culminates in employment of one part of an oppressed community against another in order to maintain a system of privilege. It may be one part of the revolutionary struggle encouraged by a revolutionary gospel. The war, especially in reference to institutional violence, is already in full force. Camilo Torres, a Colombian sociologist and priest, reflected on the revolutionary struggle, for which he later gave his own life, saying that Christianity focuses on *effective* love of one's neighbor in terms of food, housing, and education. Torres believed revolution was not only permissible but obligatory if it became the only effective and far-reaching way to make love for all people a reality.

A decision to provide ammunition and arms made under these conditions may be theologically justifiable even for a person who primarily seeks an active nonviolent form of loving resistance to tyranny. On this occasion Roger's relationship to the people and the lack of time to pursue other alternatives may support the implementation of counter-violence as a strategy of self-defense. However, the dilemma is sharper because the dangers are great, not only for Roger but for the people of Crossroads. The threat to innocent noncombatants in a community of 100,000 and the degree of force that may be unleashed by the army and vigilantes could render this option an unacceptable risk in light of "Christian realism."

Paid informers have become a reality of life in the black ghettos. Roger has already been offered reasons to doubt Johnson's loyalty to the wider community, and there is no reason to believe he is alone. The possibility of an informer is high, especially since so many people know about the request. The plan could be intercepted by the arrest of Roger and the group even before an act of self-defense could occur. The risk of detention and imprisonment on a charge of treason is possible for Roger as well as the leaders of Crossroads. Roger might consider publicly denying the request to the total group, while privately supplying arms to one trusted member. Yet even here can Roger, as a member of the privileged and powerful social class of oppressors, in good conscience protect himself in ways that are not possible for those with whom he seeks to be in solidarity? This is not to dismiss the authenticity of Roger's relational obligations to his own family and his responsibility as father and provider, which imprisonment would clearly impede.

There is an apparent conflict in expectations that pits personal against communal values. As most readers will understand the force of family responsibilities, these require less elaboration. It is often the community obligations which are more difficult to see because of the power of one's dominant ideology. This has been referred to as the "cultural cocoon" into which all persons are born and through which reality is viewed. Captivity by one's cultural and class cocoon is often in tune with a theology that in practice regularly supports the values of the dominant class. The reader knows little about Roger's congregation, but as white and middle class, there is strong statistical evidence that the vast majority of members would view Roger's decision about arms from the perspective of the white power structure. Historically, the church, while regularly condemning violence, has frequently supported violence in the name of patriotism in wars of questionable justice.

One could ask many questions. Are a few arms enough? Why haven't the regular channels for arms been working? Could they be installed quickly? Why are there no weapons after over twenty years of a military wing of the ANC? But all of these may avoid the ultimate question of solidarity with the people of Crossroads, which Roger has posed as a central concern. It is not clear that Roger has come to terms with his own conflict in class values. He continues to benefit from the system of apartheid with which his friends are at war. He lives in an all-white suburb and has the power of choice as to whether or not he supplies arms. Probably few citizens of the First World cultures of North America or South Africa have faced the contradiction of protected privilege and claims of solidarity. To refuse the request may be the continued condescension of a white clerical elite deciding for the oppressed people what they really need—that is, a theology of control—rather than participating in the struggle through a theology of accompaniment. Since the question in this context is not just about the morality of violence but also about the morality of a revolutionary struggle for liberation, the stake in the decision is even higher. The hope of God's ultimate victory and loving forgiveness, no matter what is decided, will be as important to Roger as it is to those who face the implications of solidarity with the poor and oppressed.

OPTION: ACTIVE NONVIOLENT RESISTANCE

Roger's alternative of refusing to provide the ammunition and guns would strengthen, at least initially, his relational bonds with family and many within his church community who may fear for his security. For those in the community of faith who support either a pacifist position or one of active nonviolent resistance, a refusal by Roger to cooperate could also be seen as the most effective strategy for genuine solidarity. Identifying with the poor and oppressed may mean solidarity with their interests and causes, not necessarily compliance with this specific request. However, Roger must be prepared for possible consequences of this decision in light of his relationship to the community leaders. His denial might threaten the relationship of trust which obviously exists for the request to have been ventured. The leaders of Crossroads may be looking at "nonviolence" with new eyes. Some black South Africans have declared that "nonviolence" and "reconciliation" are coming to be hated as much as apartheid. The suspicion is pervasive and not unjustified that the repeated calls for nonviolence and reconciliation have helped to maintain the status quo and have thus become instruments of oppression.

An alternative social analysis of the context could suggest that armed resistance is not the only viable and effective means of resisting and ultimately replacing the current "tyranny" of the state. Taking up arms would only lead the people to participate in the spiral of direct violence for which the state is much better equipped. In other words, to engage the enemy of God and of the people on their own grounds, while it might be theologically justifiable, would be a tactical error in the legitimate struggle of the oppressed for liberation. An armed encounter would invite a disastrous loss of life on both sides and would make the "reasonable hope of success" unrealistic and proportionate cost so high that it could not be the "last resort." Genuine hope must lie in confidence in God's care for those who are willing to pursue what may be a more vulnerable act of faith than direct violence.

Should Roger refuse to supply arms, however, there are other ways to demonstrate his solidarity with the people. One of these could be through a creative, sustained program of active nonviolent resistance to apartheid which may have more hope of saving the Crossroads community and transforming South African society than the use of direct violence. This approach could entail, for example, challenging the Crossroads leaders and supportive members of Roger's own church community to an active role in defense of the residents by literally standing between the residents and the vigilantes.

Though the residents of Crossroads have many years' experience in passive resistance to attempts at removal, this approach would challenge them to become even more aggressive. It would also mean that the churches must not only talk about nonviolent resistance but actually engage in it. This decision by Roger would draw on a theological tradition different from that of many liberation theologians prominent in Central America. It calls for a rediscovery of the work and thought of Mahatma Gandhi, who began his life's work in South Africa. Another source is what Martin Luther King, Jr., called "active love" in a civil rights movement profoundly rooted in the Christian tradition. Nonviolence was for King, as for Gandhi, first of all a way of life; to use it as a technique is the first step in one's own transformation. King confessed, "I believe the unarmed truth and unconditional love will have the final word in reality." Many proponents see this form of active nonviolent resistance as reducing the danger of continuing—in a liberated society of the future—the militarization of the state and the glorification of violence.

Nonviolence, as developed in the biblical tradition, is a commitment that is not passive but active, not careful but costly, and not safe but fraught with suffering. It is especially identified with Jesus. A fresh understanding of scriptural passages such as "turning the other cheek" and "going the second mile" (Matt. 5:38–41) need to be appropriated. Rather than passive submission, they can be seen as acts of meeting force with ridicule or humor that demand the striker or commander recognize the humanity and dignity of the person who is being oppressed. Professor Walter Wink, a New Testament scholar, has explored this alternative reading of scripture. His perspective is cited in the SACC (South African Council of Churches) Emergency Convocation on Non-Violence as he recalls the success in the Philippines of nonviolent "people power" that led to the flight of a tyrant and the turn to greater democratic possibilities. The resources are present in South Africa for a similar response, but it requires nonviolent training and preparation for people to be willing to suffer and even die rather than retaliate. This kind of nonviolence challenges people to refuse to cooperate with an evil system by withholding whatever the system requires to exist. This may range from votes and labor to personal security. Gandhi declared that "non-cooperation with evil is as important as cooperation with good."

There may still be time for Roger to try to mobilize Christians, both clergy and laity, to be shields of love between the residents and the vigilantes of Crossroads. This could be an alternative step to armed resistance in breaking the cycle of humiliation. Some elements in the South African church are calling for a new surge of nonviolent action and training. This is a call for levels of costly resistance that may be more dangerous and sacrificial than a prison term. Mary Kenner may have more to fear from Roger's leadership in a spiritually empowered, active nonviolent resistance movement, however, than from a treasonable act of supplying arms. Advocacy of and participation in nonviolent resistance is as illegal in South Africa as armed resistance.

Whatever Roger decides, in prayer and integrity, he will need the empowering and transforming relationships of his family, his church, and the Crossroads community. The present debate in South Africa has tended to force a choice between violent and nonviolent responses to apartheid. However, South Africans as a whole and those who are global observers are not necessarily required in conscience to choose between strategies of the minimalization of violence and nonviolent resistance. Those who desire a new society in South Africa can afford not only to tolerate but to affirm both. In the struggle for liberation both positions may have a place. Archbishop Desmond Tutu has staunchly maintained a stance of active nonviolent resistance, but has refused, not on political grounds but on moral grounds, to condemn those who feel compelled to pursue an approach of counterviolence.

THE CALL FOR ACTION

Signers of the Kairos Document call for discussion, debate, reflection, prayer, and, most of all, action. In South Africa where ultimately the issue of liberation will be settled by South Africans themselves, there are areas in the spheres of counter-violence and nonviolence that are yet to be tested. Conflict, suffering, and death are unlikely to diminish immediately with either approach. Some have predicted, however, windows of hope opening along the way before the situation leads to a bloodbath. Signs of hope rest with nonviolent tactics already underway: black labor unions and the withholding of labor; boycotts of schools or essential goods and services produced in the white community; the end-conscription campaign promoted by white students and young professionals; the strategy of making the townships ungovernable by rejecting black puppet leaders through rent strikes and roadblocks; young people refusing to cooperate with puppet black authorities in the so-called independent homelands; and the actions by some churches in the SACC to take seriously the role of active nonviolent resistance.

The declaration of a national state of emergency in June 1986, however, has made all of the above nonviolent tactics illegal and given the security forces extraordinary power to arrest and detain those suspected of violations. The Reverend Frank Chikane describes the months following this declaration as "the darkest part of the tunnel in the life of the people of South Africa." Government actions have included "the banning of all June 16 commemoration meetings [of the Soweto student uprising and the massacre of school children]; the detention [without charge or trial] of more than 30,000 South Africans, thousands of whom have been tortured and placed in solitary confinement; the detention of thousands of children; the harassment and brutal assaults on many South Africans by the security forces; the emergence of vigilantes and assassination squads; the deliberate creation of conditions for the so-called 'black on black' violence, causing the hundreds of deaths of innocent people; the attack on the church and the detentions of hundreds of church workers and some church leaders; the attack on the labor movements including a sophisticated military attack on the building of the Congress of South Africa Trade Unions (COSATU). . . . The list is endless."

A negotiated transfer of power to the black majority toward a nonracial, democratic South Africa, with protection of minority rights, is still an option, though the present lack of space for negotiation makes this increasingly difficult. The majority of white South Africans will not, many believe, fight to the death to preserve their positions of power and privilege. With appropriate pressure and encouragement black majority rule with continued white presence can become a reality as it has in the transformation of neighboring Rhodesia to Zimbabwe, in substance as well as name. In Zimbabwe international solidarity with the black liberation movement and pressure against white domination were both necessary to bring about change.

The Harare Declaration, drawn up in December 1985 by a world-wide group of church leaders, calls on Christians from around the world to support the struggle for liberation in South Africa. The declaration ranged from a call for continued prayer and fasting for the end to unjust rule in South Africa to specific global responses such as support for the trade union movement and "immediate application of international, comprehensive sanctions to South Africa." An ethical response to the ethical debate over South Africa may help lead to the moment of truth (kairos) for South Africa and the world community. Allan Boesak, a colored South African church leader, and Alan Brews, a white South African Methodist clergyman, reflect the spirit of the multiracial gathering in Harare when they conclude, ". . . for the majority of oppressed Blacks the issue is not violence but liberation." This perspective from the "underside of history" challenges Roger Kenner and those in power in the global community to respond to the dilemma of Crossroads and South Africa with a new understanding.

ADDITIONAL RESOURCES

Boesak, Allan, and Alan Brews. "The Black Struggle for Liberation: A Reluctant Road to Revolution." In Villa-Vicencio, ed., *Theology and Violence* (see below), pp. 51–68.

Chikane, Frank. *The Church's Prophetic Witness against the Apartheid System in South Africa.* Johannesburg: South African Council of Churches, 1988.

———*No Life of My Own: An Autobiography.* Maryknoll, N.Y.: Orbis 1989.

Crisis News, no. 21 (April–May 1988). Published by the Western Cape Council of Churches, 41 Salt River Road, Cape Town, South Africa.

Evans, Alice Frazer, Robert A. Evans, and William Bean Kennedy. *Pedagogies for the Non-Poor.* Maryknoll, N.Y.: Orbis, 1987.

From South Africa: A Challenge to the Church. From Theology in a Global Context Program, 22 Tenakill Street, Closter, NJ, 07627. Contains the Kairos Document and the Harare Declaration.

Villa-Vicencio, Charles. *Trapped in Apartheid.* Maryknoll, N.Y.: Orbis, 1988.

Villa-Vicencio, Charles, ed. *Theology and Violence: The South African Debate.* Grand Rapids: William B. Eerdmans, 1987.

Wink, Walter. *Jesus' Third Way.* Philadelphia: New Society Publishers, 1987.

PART IV

THE ENVIRONMENT

Case

Snake in the Grass

Erica Mann sat in her den still working at 10:30 P.M. after a long Friday at her office in the Federal Building in downtown Phoenix. At thirty-eight, Erica was a respected research biologist and conservationist, even though she had earned her Ph.D. in zoology only three years earlier. She was proud of her success, which she felt was the result of hard work, self-sacrifice, and high ethical standards.

Erica was the Endangered Species Coordinator for the Western Division of the Federal Wildlife Agency (FWA). A unit of the Department of the Interior, the FWA had a Congressional mandate to enforce and carry out the provisions of the Endangered Species Act (ESA) of 1973, which directed federal agencies not to carry out, fund, or authorize projects which jeopardize a threatened or endangered species or destroy habitats critical to their survival. Erica's job was to identify threatened and endangered species in her district, see that they were listed in the Federal Register, and enforce the ESA. Another of her agency's functions was to assess the likely effects of proposed federal construction projects on any endangered species. These assessments normally were included in a project's Environmental Impact Statement. Her job of protecting endangered species had not been made any easier by a 1978 amendment to the ESA which provided for a seven-member review committee to grant exemptions to the strict provisions of the act if economic benefits were substantial.

Erica was also the chair of the Conservation Committee of the International Herpetological Society (IHS), a worldwide organization of over 2,200 herpetologists. Although the society's chief role was the promotion of scientific research on reptiles and amphibians, it also provided information for public education and conservation purposes. Erica's involvement with the society reflected a love of reptiles stemming from her childhood infatuation with dinosaurs.

Until recently her dual roles as FWA Endangered Species Coordinator and IHS Conservation Committee chair had blended smoothly, combining the best aspects of vocation and avocation. Now it looked as though a national environmental group, the Environmental Preservation Club, was preparing to sue the federal government over a case in which the IHS and the FWA were involved on opposite sides.

The problem had arisen the previous July when Erica proposed that the Sonoran desert snake be listed as an endangered species. The snake was already listed as endangered by the Arizona State Wildlife Office and was threatened with extinction because it has a restricted habitat, and there was a possibility that that habitat would be destroyed. This species could be found in only a few isolated places in the desert near the Bailey River, a tributary of the Colorado River in western Arizona. An independent study conducted for the FWA by a biological consulting firm had documented previous local extinctions of the Sonoran desert snake due to flooding of the habitat by dams along the river. The investigators had concluded: ". . . the real hazard posed by any new dam is a large increase in the probability of total extinction of the species."

In September, the U.S. Bureau of Inland Waters presented the FWA with plans to build Blevins Dam on the Bailey River to provide water for irrigation, recreation, and the projected growth of industry and new homes in the area. The bureau requested an assessment of the Sonoran desert snake for the Environmental Impact Statement. Erica's FWA report, delivered to the Department of the Interior in December for approval, had ended with the following statement:

There are no known measures which can be implemented in conjunction with the Blevins Dam to avoid jeopardizing the Sonoran desert snake or adversely modifying its natural habitat. Our advisory recommendations are that the water supply needs of the area be met through the development of an alternate water supply source. We considered the possibility of improving the survival outlook for the snake through creation of artificial habitat in the area adjacent to the proposed reservoir. However, we determined that this alternative is not viable because detailed knowledge of the habitat requirements of the Sonoran desert snake does not presently exist. Such information would require several years of extensive and intensive field and laboratory study to obtain.

In May Erica was shocked to read the Bureau of Inland Water's Environmental Impact Statement for the Blevins Dam:

Artificial habitats that will allow the species to carry out all phases of its life cycle can be created and maintained. Areas adjacent to the new lake could be planted with vegetation species endemic to the areas in which the Sonoran desert snake occurs naturally. A team of biologists could then engage in extensive trapping of the Sonoran desert snake in areas threatened with inundation as the lake fills and relocate the species to the new artificial habitat. Long-term commitments to best management practices within the newly created habitat would be maintained by all parties concerned (i.e., the U.S. Bureau of Inland Waters, The Federal Wildlife Agency, The Blevins County Municipal Water Management Authority, and the Arizona State Wildlife Office) to facilitate successful colonization of the Sonoran desert snake in these areas.

Stunned by the bureau's reversal of her FWA recommendation and the twisting of her analysis, Erica called Susan Winston, a friend who worked for the FWA in Washington, D.C. "The word through the grapevine," Susan said, "is that Senator Elder promised his constituents that the project would proceed even if he had to gut the entire Endangered Species Act to do it. He seems willing to call in every political debt to get this dam built. You know he has been in the Senate for over twenty years and served two House terms and as governor before that. If you ask me, it looks fishy. Orders probably came down from the secretary as a result of pressure from Senator Elder, and your report was misrepresented accordingly."

Not long after talking with Susan, Erica received a telephone call from David Miller, the country's leading snake biologist. "Erica, the top is about to blow off the Sonoran snake issue," David said with authority. "I was just at a meeting with lawyers from the Environmental Preservation Club, and they are saying it could be the test of the Endangered Species Act they have been waiting for. The Blevins Dam project is so clearly in violation of the act and the plans for that artificial habitat are so patently weak that they are sure they can win. Everyone knows that no new field studies were conducted on the snake between your December report and the reversal in the Environmental Impact Statement in May. There is absolutely no biological basis for building artificial habitats, and no reason to think that the snake can survive in them. The IHS leadership wants to throw the full weight of the society behind the Environmental Preservation Club. As IHS Conservation Committee chair, we are expecting you to take a leading role in this."

Walter Jackson was District Director for the FWA and Erica's immediate superior. He had held the position as Endangered Species Coordinator before his promotion to director two years ago. Walt was a close friend and a respected colleague. It was he who had suggested that Erica apply for the vacant coordinator position. Walt approached Erica in the Federal Building cafeteria at lunch. "I am as upset as you are at having to swallow that new report," Walt had said, "but sometimes we have to forgo fighting a battle when we will lose the war, Erica. You and I know that the Environmental Preservation Club is crazy to think they can make a case on this one. No judge or jury in any Western state will ever defend a snake against the water needs of humans. Worse, you are clearly faced with a conflict of interest if this thing goes to court. I would hate to have you lose your job over a lost cause. You are a good coordinator, Erica, and we will need your help to fight other battles we can win. Stick with the agency on this one and then you can help me go after that timber company operation that is threatening the eagle nests up north."

Dick Gilsey, professor of environmental ethics and Erica's teacher in college, called after reading *Fight for Wildlife,* the Environmental Preservation Club's activist newsletter. "Erica, you know that each of God's creatures exists for a particular purpose, even if that purpose is hidden from us. Remember the Rosy Periwinkle, that inconspicuous tropical flower you learned about in my course. Who could have guessed that it could provide drugs for treating childhood leukemia and Hodgkin's disease? The loss of genetic diversity means the loss of opportunities for future generations — for medicine, industry, and agriculture. There is the possibility, no matter how remote, that this snake holds some irreplaceable value for our health and welfare. I admit we do not know what it does out there in the desert. Maybe it will never have any direct value for us at all. But at the very least it fills some functional role in the ecosystem, even if we do not yet understand what it is. In any case, does dominion over the earth mean that we have the right to destroy other species that inhabit this planet with us, or does it mean that we have the responsibility as God's stewards to care for them? Extinction is forever, Erica. Once that snake is gone, its functional contribution to the ecosystem, its genes, and its potential gifts can never be brought back."

Erica sat back at her desk and thumbed through the Environmental Impact Statement for the Blevins Dam Project, stopping at the section entitled "Local Involvement: Citizens, Groups, and Individuals." The many letters from local residents appended to the report were nearly unanimous in their support for the project. She read aloud excerpts from several of the letters:

Animals are sacrificed in laboratories for science. If the Sonoran desert snake has to be sacrificed for the sake of water for human beings, I see no difference.

If the environmentalists had to have their water supply rationed in the heat of the summer, maybe they would agree that we cannot live without water.

This is what the Bible says about the value of a snake in Genesis 3:14: "So the Lord God said to the serpent, 'this is your punishment: You are singled out from among all the domestic and wild animals of the whole earth to be cursed.' "

I hope there are enough good people with good common sense to outweigh those radicals with all their priorities in the wrong place.

We desperately need water in this state to support mining and agriculture. I am reminded of the Book of Genesis, Chapter 1, verses 26–29, where God gave human beings dominion over the earth and "over every creeping thing." Gentlemen, I am concerned about protecting our environment as much as the next person, but this issue of the Sonoran desert snake borders on the ridiculous when it comes to the survival of the mining and agricultural industries of Arizona.

Closing the report, Erica picked up the letter she had received two days ago from Jack Knight, President of IHS. After glancing at the clock, she reread the closing paragraph:

Conservation issues are important for the Society. It is important to protect natural populations from catastrophic habitat modification and inappropriate exploitation. Although I appreciate your uncomfortable position as an employee of the federal government, I must know for certain whether you will stand with the IHS on this issue. I will call this Friday night at 11 P.M. for your decision.

As Erica put the letter on her desk and glanced at the clock again, the telephone rang.

Commentary

Snake in the Grass

The problem is deceptively simple: the snake or the dam. Given the arid Southwest's thirst for water and the low status of snakes since Genesis 3:14, all the makings for a quick decision are present. Why not cave in to Senator Elder and the compromisers? Over against the great benefits to people of water on otherwise useless land, what is the worth of the insignificant Sonoran desert snake?

Actually, the snake has considerable worth as a symbol, as a contributor to human welfare, and as an intrinsic good. As symbol, this snake represents the rapid extinction of species resulting from the destruction of fragile ecosystems worldwide. The snake is a potential contributor to human welfare because its irreplaceable genetic material might afford options for scientific efforts to improve human health and to increase the food supply. As for the intrinsic good of the Sonoran desert snake, the authors of Genesis 1 are quite clear that God created it and all other species good.

Moreover, an additional dam in the desert of western Arizona may be difficult to justify. Dams have their uses: irrigation for an increased food supply, flood control, recreation, electricity for homes and industry, and clean water for drinking. But this dam may not be well suited for these purposes, and the costs of construction and maintenance may be greater than the financial benefits. There is even a certain amount of foolishness in encouraging settlement in the arid Western United States where only limited numbers are sustainable unless huge, expensive, and complex transfers of water between river basins are undertaken.

When the deeper ramifications are considered, the simple snake versus dam arithmetic becomes a more complicated calculus. The task is to see the Sonoran desert snake in terms of this more complicated calculus.

The Christian tradition, especially as it developed in Western Europe, is not without problems in all of this. Since the Industrial Revolution, a utilitarian view of nature has dominated this tradition. The command to take dominion of the earth in Genesis 1 has generally been interpreted as license to use nature willy-nilly for human purposes. The side of the tradition which sees nature as intrinsically good has been muted. Today species extinction, environmental degradation, and new questions about sustainability call into question this dominant utilitarian view and invite Christians to consider alternatives.

This case also raises two ethical issues which have appeared in other cases. The first is the dilemma of sticking to principle or seeking effective compromise. Should Erica rigorously follow the ethical and professional instincts which brought her in on the side of the snake, or should she work responsibly within the federal bureaucracy and understand that politics is the art of the possible and that giving in to special interests now may yield important dividends in the future?

The second question has to do with those special interests themselves, symbolized in the case by Senator Elder and the distortion of Erica's report. The history of water projects in the United States, particularly in the South and West, is one in which special interests and pork barreling have been pronounced. The Sonoran desert snake has no voice, and the few who will come to its defense seldom have anything to gain and are chronically underfunded. Were it not for a strong of love of nature among Americans, the snake would not have a chance.

SPECIES EXTINCTION

The extinction of the Sonoran desert snake would not be an isolated event. It would be just one of an unprecedented number of species extinctions resulting from human destruction of habitats.

Scientists have estimated the total number of species to be between 5 and 10 million. This remarkable diversity is a result of 3.5 billion years of evolution. Perhaps as many as two-thirds of all animal species that ever existed are now gone. Historically as many as six periods of mass extinctions can be documented in fossil remains, most induced by climate changes. These periods have lasted as long as two million years, as was the case with the extinction of dinosaurs.

Unlike earlier periods, in the last 100,000 years human beings have increasingly been the cause of extinctions. Today the contraction of biological diversity is proceeding at a faster rate than ever before, or so the fossil record seems to indicate. This is cause for alarm. Especially worrisome is the loss of tropical rain forests which cover only 7 percent of the world's land area but host about 40 percent of species.

Humans cause extinctions through such activities as hunting, forest clearing, conversion of virgin land to agricultural use, the pollution of air and water, the construction of dams, and the control of predators. Hunting works directly, the other activities indirectly through destruction of habitat.

Some species are already well along in a natural process of extinction which human intrusion only hastens. Others are well suited to their environments but do not possess traits which allow adaptation to human interventions. Still others reproduce slowly and cannot bounce back from a rapid loss of numbers. Finally, there are those with narrow habitat requirements, usually having to do with feeding, which are doomed when their narrow habitat is disrupted. Without further information it is difficult to determine to what extent these factors are at work with the Sonoran desert snake. The threat of human intrusion is obvious, however—flooding the snake's habitat with a dam will have a major impact upon the snake's environment.

PRESERVATION?

The case for and against preservation rests on four considerations: the usefulness of the snake for humans, the usefulness of the dam for humans, the Christian tradition's view of nature, and the goodness of the snake in itself.

Usefulness of the Snake

So what is the usefulness for humans of the Sonoran desert snake? For one thing the snake is part of a functioning ecosystem which could be destroyed with the loss of a particular species. This dire outcome is unlikely given the rarity of the snake, but in its own fragile system the snake plays some roll as predator and prey. Humans have much at stake in the preservation of healthy ecosystems. Whether this particular snake and this particular system are of great significance is not the point. They represent something very precious. Healthy ecosystems are the very foundation of life.

Second is the matter of genetic diversity which is contracting at an alarming rate. Again the Sonoran desert snake represents something larger than itself. As total genetic diversity decreases, so does the genetic pool for further evolution. More significant for humans, new techniques of genetic manipulation make even the most insignificant species potentially important. Rare plants and animals often provide the genetic material which can be spliced into more common varieties to enhance survival, increase productivity, and provide new raw materials for further developments.

In agriculture genetic manipulations have already led to new or much-improved strains of many plants and animals. One foundation of the so-called green revolution is the capacity of geneticists to develop new strains which vastly increase productivity. This capacity in turn rests on the availabilty of hitherto undiscovered genetic potential. This is also true in medicine where rare species regularly provide the genetic material for life-saving drugs. In short, to preserve this potential, the genetic diversity should be maintained. No species should be thoughtlessly destroyed.

Third, plants and animals have more direct uses in agriculture, industry, and medicine. None of these uses is indicated in the case, but until the species is thoroughly studied nothing can be assumed. In medicine even apparently rare and useless species have proven significant. The Rosy Periwinkle mentioned in the case is a classic example.

Fourth, plants and animals are important to a clean environment and to climate. Some species, for example, break down pollutants. Tropical rain forests are sources of oxygen and influence the amount and pattern of rainfall.

All these factors add up on utilitarian grounds alone to a substantial argument in favor of conserving biological diversity and preserving endangered species. The strength of this utilitarian argument will vary from species to species and system to system, but it always should be a factor in decisions about endangered plants and animals.

Usefulness of the Dam

Unfortunately for the Sonoran desert snake the good for humans has another dimension in this case: the utility of an ample water supply provided by the dam. The potential usefulness of an obscure and seemingly useless snake is pitted against the known usefulness of the best dams.

Water is essential to the mining and refining of metals, to the manufacture of chemicals, to the production of oil, pulp, and paper, and to food processing. A dependable water supply can make the desert bloom, increasing the amount of land producing food for a hungry world, boosting yields per acre, and giving peace of mind to farmers with huge capital investments. Municipalities use water for drinking, cooking, bathing, washing, and other activities. Dams can also harness water's energy in order to generate electricity. Hydroelectric power is clean, efficient, and wastes very little water.

All these uses add up to a considerable benefit and to heavy and increasing demand, in this case fueled by Arizona's population growth rate of 30 percent per decade for the last thirty years. It is no wonder that planners want to build a new dam.

From the resulting sum of benefits must be subtracted the costs, however. As the best dam sites are used, and generally they have been in the Southwest, the number of cost effective sites diminishes and the price of projects goes up. At some point costs exceed benefits and the dam is not worth building on economic grounds alone.

Irrigation in the desert is no panacea. High evaporation rates mean lost water and increasingly salty soils. Reservoirs behind dams silt up. As they do and high costs rule out dredging, benefits are reduced and eventually the dam must be abandoned.

The costs in terms of extinct species such as the Sonoran desert snake must also be counted. Unfortunately, because this cost cannot be quantified with precision, it tends to be overlooked and the lost species undervalued.

Finally, the addition of new dams in arid regions has a circular effect. If the water resources are not priced at their true cost, which they have not been in the Southwest, inordinate numbers of new settlers are attracted and come to assume sufficient supplies at low cost as a natural right. Officials who do not supply ever-increasing amounts of cheap water are viewed as irresponsible and quickly lose favor at the polls. So an increasing amount of water is supplied and this in turn attracts even more settlers with the same expectations.

Unless this circle is broken with a pricing policy which makes the consumer instead of the American taxpayer pay the cost, the nation more and more will squander its resources. There is little reason to subsidize expensive irrigation projects when overproduction in more humid regions is a problem. At some point the Southwest will be forced to live within its means, that is, unless Senator Elder and others continue to be successful in transferring costs.

The preceding considerations and the role of Senator Elder in this case force a discussion of politics. In the United States the control of water, especially in the West and South, has been a well-documented combination of Byzantine intrigue and pork barrel politics. These things are clear: (1) water for irrigation is priced to the farmer at a fraction of its total cost, the difference being paid by the taxpayer; (2) projects with costs exceeding benefits, some because costs were purposely underestimated and benefits inflated, are regularly undertaken; and (3) endangered species have been undervalued and even ignored altogether.

The process which produces these results is also clear. Water flows toward power and money. Members of Congress from states where water is a key issue secure appointments on relevant water committees. Powerful Congressional delegations trade projects off or authorize just enough projects to secure majority support for their projects. The branches of the executive concerned with water resources take an interest in their own appropriations and join ranks to promote projects even to the point of making cost/benefit analyses "come out right." Witness what happened to Erica's report in the case.

Conservatives who otherwise denounce socialism and government spending readily join the party. They know just as well as their more liberal colleagues that the costs will be paid by politically unaware outsiders and the benefits enjoyed by their knowing constituents.

The Colorado River basin is an excellent example of this phenomenon. After many years of nice and not so nice political give and take, portions of all the waters of the basin have been assigned to a variety of groups. Still the population of the region continues to expand. There are more endangered species in the basin than in any other region of the country. Traditional interests still compete for water. Impoverished native Americans press for their rightful share. Industry, agriculture, and municipalities vie for greater shares. Seven states tussle continually over relative allocations.

In all of this Arizonans have tended to get less than an equitable share of the water in the basin. Their response has been the Central Arizona Project, a mammoth project designed to bring water for irrigation to the

Phoenix and Tucson areas, which are rapidly exhausting their groundwater supplies. To give the project some semblance of cost effectiveness, high dams were originally proposed on the Colorado River. These dams would have flooded portions of the Grand Canyon outside national park boundaries. Eventually, after a long and bitter political battle led by environmentalists, the dams were rejected, but not the project itself, which continues to receive appropriations in spite of highly dubious cost effectiveness.

It is not clear whether the dam being considered in the case is part of the Central Arizona project, but it is important to remember that issues such as those raised in this case continually reappear in the charged political context in which decisions about water are made. Focusing on the data given in the case itself, it would seem that the combination of high costs, dubious benefits, endangerment of a rare species, and the need to come to terms with the realities of desert life, economic expansion, and a flawed political process adds up to a compelling case against the construction of the dam. Senator Elder may have the votes to carry it through, however, and a sympathetic judicial process may concur. It would be a mistake to think that rational analysis will automatically win the day.

To sum up, it would seem that in the short run the benefits of building the dam might outweigh the preservation of one species, but if the issue is viewed from a long-range perspective, the preservation of the Sonoran desert snake may well be much more important for human beings and the earth than the short-range benefits from the dam.

Nature in the Christian Tradition

The Christian basis for weighing the usefulness of the snake for humans over against the benefits of the dam comes from a distinctly utilitarian view of nature which has developed in Christianity. Thus in order to round out our discussion of usefulness it is important to consider this view of nature and the norm of stewardship which emerges from correctly interpreting it.

The authors of Genesis 1:26–28 state that God gave the first humans dominion over the earth and ordered them to subdue it. Out of this gift and demand has developed a perspective which sees nature as an "it" to be utilized for human benefit. This perspective has been especially strong in Western Christianity, and since the Industrial Revolution has dominated all other perspectives.

This view originally gained currency in Israel's competition with its neighbors. The Canaanites and others in the region worshiped nature gods. Although there were many variations, nature was generally seen as sacred in the worship of these neighbors. Nature had a life of its own and that life was divine. In contrast stood Israel with its faith based on history. God had made a covenant with Israel and continued to act in human history in accordance with the promises of this covenant. Nature was not sacred. It was a created good to be used, a thing with no divine status whatsoever.

Israel's neighbors were idolatrous in confusing nature and God.

To this view was later added a significant insight, the combination having tremendous consequences, according to historians. The insight was that since nature is a divine creation, it reflects the mind of God. Exploring it will increasingly remove the shroud of mystery which covers God's work in the world.

All the ideological ingredients for the rise of science and the unleashing of technology are there. Discovering the mind of God provides the motive and the encouragement. The utilitarian character of nature removes the restraint which comes from the fear of incurring the wrath of nature gods. All that is needed is for the fruits of modern science and technology to descend from heaven like manna. Senator Elder's dam is the last in a long train of such fruits, or so he would have his constituents believe.

The rise of modern science and technology is much more complex than this, of course, but the link to religious ideas is there. Judaism and Christianity contributed to this rise and generally both have supported or at least acquiesced in the rapid economic expansion which has resulted.

So as not to get carried away in celebration of science and technology, however, it is necessary to add that economic expansion and the philosophy of growth long ago shed their religious mantles. There is now considerable worry that dominion has come to mean unlimited exploitation. Indeed, if many of the goods of modern life are to be attributed to science, technology, and the ideology of growth, then so also must the detriments which go under the name of the environmental crisis. The combined effects of rapid population growth, depletion of natural resources, pollution, extinction of species, and the turning of people and nature into things to be exploited are producing a crisis which will not go away. The plight of the Sonoran desert snake is a microcosm of this crisis.

In light of this a return to the biblical texts is instructive. Dominion in Judaism and Christianity does not mean exploitation. Misuse of nature and people should be labeled with its true name, sin. Dominion in the Hebrew texts means careful and loving stewardship. In Genesis 1:26–28 dominion is given to humans as God's viceroys. The viceroys have authority, but the earth belongs to God, and the viceroys are to pattern dominion on God's loving and caring rule. This God of the covenant has declared nature good and works within it to redeem both humans and creatures. This God is concerned for the whole creation, not just for one part of it.

Stewardship is one key. Daughters and sons are to receive the earth from their fathers and mothers and pass it on in no worse and hopefully better shape than they received it. And as shepherds are accountable for the sheep in their care, so humans are accountable for their stewardship of nature. Misuse of nature is sin and will be judged as such.

The significance of the utilitarian view and its companion norm of stewardship is twofold. On the one hand, it gives warrant to calculations of utility in Christian ethics. The usefulness of the snake may be weighed against the usefulness of the dam. On the other hand, the norm of stewardship, when applied in the context of Western materialism and misuse of nature, encourages far better care of the earth, and, by implication, the Sonoran desert snake. The Christian understanding of sin adds weight to the position that advocates that humans must carefully scrutinize the consequences of the way in which they use nature. While nature may be used in a way that benefits all, humans will be prone to misuse, a sin which requires repentance.

The Goodness of the Snake

Beyond the norm of stewardship, which still places nature in the hands of humans, there is a muted but very important tradition which sees nature as a good in itself apart from humans. This is not nature worship, and the brutalities of nature are not ignored in it. It is rather a tradition which sees nature as personal, alive, and subjective. Examples of it are found in the Hebrew scriptures in Job 31:38–40, Exodus 23:10f., Leviticus 25:1ff., and Psalm 96:11f. St. Francis in his "Canticle of Brother Sun" is another example. And today the love of nature which is so strong in many Americans who are Christians is still another.

This tradition has one of its bases in God's gift of aesthetic sensitivity. Most humans are incapable of turning nature into an "it," and rightly so. An equally important basis is found in the declaration by the authors of Genesis that God created nature good. The Sonoran desert snake is good because the hand of God is somehow linked to its existence. Together these norms give warrant to the preservation of the Sonoran desert snake as a good in itself, not just as something which might be used by humans for their own good.

Are there degrees to this goodness? Is the preservation of the rhinoceros more important than that of a snake? Given the snake's "bad press" it would be a temptation not to care about it and maybe even to see extinction as good. But this is the same kind of thinking which can permit categorization of humans into classes and the oppression of so-called "inferiors" by their self-appointed "superiors." Goodness is goodness, even to the least of God's creatures.

ETHICAL CONCLUSION

In many ways this case is complementary to the cases "Rigor and Responsibility" in part 1 and "Power for Peace" in this part. What all three have in common is a new ethic of ecological justice. Prominent in this ethic are three norms: justice, sustainable sufficiency, and participation.

Justice means fairness. In the biblical witness the touchstone of justice is the welfare and liberation of the poor and the care of the land. In this case study justice calls for both the provision of a sufficient and sustainable energy and water supply to humans in the region and the preservation of the Sonoran desert snake.

Sustainable sufficiency means good stewardship. It refers to the long-range capacity of a system to supply energy and food for basic needs at a reasonable cost to society and the environment. This norm would certainly call into question the building of more dams in such an arid region. The costs are high and the sustainability of a large human population under such conditions is questionable.

Participation is having a say in decisions which affect one's life. In this case it leads to the mandating of an open political process where the needs of both people and the environment are heard and taken into account. The special interest politics which seem to be at work in this case should not go unchallenged. Finally, does this norm call for a statewide or regional referendum on the dam? If so, the snake would surely lose. But the answer to the question is "no" — the federal government with its environmental protection laws and power of appropriation for dams has made this a national issue, and in fact in many ways all environmental matters are international issues.

These three norms and the Christian views of nature are the basis for understanding and coming to grips with the decision of whether or not to build the dam. Beyond this, Erica Mann must make a personal decision. The case leaves her about to receive a phone call during which she will be asked where she stands. For Erica the decision involves a basic question of character. Will she stand on principle and resist efforts to eliminate the snake in the name of human progress, or will she seek to make compromises in hopes of future effectiveness in saving other species? Further, will she permit herself to be dehumanized by a bureaucracy which thinks so little of her professional integrity that it feels free to distort her report without even consulting her? The distortion of her report may only be a trivial matter; but at some point, always difficult to determine, the degree or frequency of compromise makes a mockery of principles. Some compromises so violate principles as to invalidate them. Instead of exceptions to principle, compromises can become the rule, and a person can lose direction as expediency becomes normative.

The case does not permit entry into Erica's conscience. How much a matter of principle the decision is to her is not clear. Nor are the total benefits of the dam to the people of the region known with precision. Erica might agree to the sacrifice of the snake and a little of her integrity if the benefits substantially outweigh the costs.

What is finally being weighed is the value to humans of the God-given goodness of the snake over against the value of the dam to humans. This is the ethical calculus. But tacked on, as it usually is, is a matter of character. Who Erica is as a person is as much a question as what to do about the dam.

ADDITIONAL RESOURCES

Brown, Lester. *State of the World 1985.* New York: W. W. Norton, 1985.

Bruggemann, Walter. *The Land.* Philadelphia: Fortress, 1977.

Hoage, R. J., ed. *Animal Extinctions.* Washington, D.C.: Smithsonian Institution Press, 1985.

Mather, John R. *Water Resources.* New York: John Wiley, 1984.

Reisner, Marc. *Cadillac Desert.* New York: Viking Penguin, 1986.

White, Lynn, Jr. "The Historical Roots of Our Ecological Crisis." *Science* 155, no. 3767 (March 10, 1967).

Case

Power for Peace

The job offer with important new management responsibilities at a significantly higher salary was not unexpected. Carl Knight had been working in his present position with Easton Industries' Nuclear Energy Division for some time. His annual performance evaluations had been excellent, and he was highly respected in the energy industry.

By accepting the offer Carl would have achieved about all he could have hoped for at this stage in his career. Acceptance would also put him in line for further promotions. By declining the offer all this might be jeopardized. Certainly his path up the management ladder would not be helped. Easton stressed company loyalty and support for the work of its various divisions.

The rub was the production of plutonium for nuclear weapons. Easton wanted Carl to move from his present position in nuclear energy research in Cincinnati to the N reactor on the Hanford Reservation near Richland, Washington. The new position involved the processing of weapons grade material from the reactor, the only nuclear facility in the United States which produced both electrical energy for a power grid and plutonium for weapons.

The long conversation the night before with his wife, Barbara, had given him the chance to vent his feelings and to get her reaction. Barbara had many of the same qualms he did about being part of the bomb-making process. She, like Carl, was a child of the nuclear age and knew how destructive nuclear weapons could be. She also knew about the so-called nuclear winter and the possibility that all life might be extinguished in an all-out exchange between the Soviet Union and the United States.

Still, she supported his association with the military. After all, Carl had done a tour in the Navy, and her two brothers were career army. And while she didn't have any solution to the nuclear arms race or alternatives to the strategy of deterrence, she did feel it was better for Christians like Carl to be in charge. That way, she felt, there would be some restraint. She had concluded by saying, "I'll go where you go."

As for Carl's continuing work with nuclear energy, she had few if any qualms. She trusted Carl's expertise in his field and knew he wouldn't expose his family to something he didn't feel was safe. "There is a difference," she told him, "between nuclear power and nuclear weapons. Nuclear power is a necessity in this energy-hungry world; and when you consider it against its alternatives, nuclear isn't threatening to me."

Now, almost twenty-four hours later Carl was mulling all this over as he climbed the stairs to the third floor meeting room in his church where his men's group met every Tuesday afternoon. He had come to appreciate the sharing and support of this small group. He intended to present his dilemma and seek advice.

The advice was not long in coming. Larry Mize, a former employee of the Southern Ohio Electric Company, unexpectedly launched into Carl's involvement with nuclear power rather than Carl's immediate dilemma. He related the difficulties of Southern Ohio Electric with its nuclear plant on the Ohio River. Larry had left Southern Ohio over these difficulties and had become increasingly opposed to nuclear energy.

"It's a bad bargain," he insisted. "Those reactors aren't safe, and the radiation spewed out in an accident can be devastating. You just can't make those reactors safe enough, and if you try, you will only run the cost up and make nuclear power less competitive than it already is. You're in a risky business, Carl.

"That's not all," he went on. "Uranium is a depletable resource and will eventually run out. Miners are lost in extracting it, although not so many as in the mining of coal. Nuclear power is a complex system — milling, enriching, fabricating, generating, reprocessing, and disposing of wastes — each step involving a set of risks.

"The waste disposal problem has not been solved, and as you know, Carl, Hanford is one of the sites considered for that stuff. There are fears out there that radioactive material could eventually find its way into the groundwater through the basalt formations along the Columbia River. Can you imagine a radioactive river all the way to the Pacific? Think about your grandchildren, Carl!"

Larry then reviewed the problems associated with the decommissioning of old nuclear plants and weapons proliferation. He seemed really worried about the social implications of a nuclear society. He caricatured such a society, or so it seemed to Carl, as one dominated by numbers and machines and repressed by the large police forces which would be needed to keep terrorists away from the nuclear plants. He concluded that conservation, concentration on renewable resources, and simpler lifestyles would eliminate the need for nuclear power. "If only we could learn to share and think of dominion of the earth in terms of sufficiency instead of growth," he said, "everything would be OK."

Carl had heard all this from Larry before. But he wasn't so sure things were so simple, and he certainly didn't agree with Larry's assessment of the nuclear industry. Granted one has to take extra precautions with nuclear reactors, but he had worked with them all his adult life, first in college, then in the Navy, and since with Easton Industries. "Radioactivity, like air and water," he explained, "is not inherently dangerous. The misuse or mishandling of radioactive material can be dangerous, but so can the mistreatment of the air we breathe and the water we drink. Our reactors are safe," he reiterated to Larry and the others for the umpteenth time. "The industry continues to mature and I believe the risks associated with nuclear power are acceptable."

Sometimes he felt it was like hitting his head against the wall on this safety matter. So many people failed to make the distinction between bombs and power stations. You mention nuclear energy and they see mushroom clouds over Hiroshima. He often wondered to himself how nuclear energy would have been received had it come before the bomb.

Satisfied on the safety question, what worried him most were the energy needs of coming generations. "Even if energy demand per capita leveled off," he explained to them, "the total demand for energy will grow as a result of population increase and rising material expectations. Our future is in the hands of politicians, and what politicians have the courage these days to restrain sexual habits and material desires? To be against growth jeopardizes re-election," he added.

"As for stewardship and dominion," he assured them, "nuclear is safer, cleaner, and more efficient than coal, and on par with nonrenewables such as oil and gas. If the safety precautions pressed on the nuclear industry were also pressed on other forms of energy, they would be just as expensive. Why is it we insist that our reactors be super safe when we do little to stop acid rain which results from the combustion of coal?"

He addressed the waste storage and decommissioning problems by saying both were capable of being solved with current technology. He wasn't sure geologic repositories were needed, but if they were and if scientific tests indicated the Hanford basalt formations were too risky, then that location should not be used.

He summed it up by saying that we need power from nuclear fission until we reach the point where technology really gets us into cheap, sustainable forms. He ended by painting a less than rosy picture for fusion power and solar energy.

He then abruptly shifted focus. "We've hashed all this over before," he said. "I have an immediate problem with involvement in nuclear weapons on my mind and I need your advice." He explained about his new job, careful not to reveal classified information. He did make clear, however, that he would be working in the plutonium production side of things at the N reactor. "What puzzles and troubles me," he told them, "is how to square being a servant of Jesus Christ with making nuclear weapons. When my daughter asks me, 'Daddy, what do you do?' how do I tell her I am a bomb maker? How do I teach her to be a peacemaker when I myself am a maker of mass destruction weapons?"

George Chambers, a frequent golfing partner and fellow engineer who had lived for a number of years in Richland near Hanford, quickly jumped in with what he thought were the missing pieces to Carl's puzzle. "You have to see the big picture," he explained. "We are locked in a struggle with the Russians, and if we are to stand for freedom, we must stand up to them.

"We don't live in a perfect world," he continued. "You have to be realistic about human sin, especially the sin of atheistic communists who are masters of deceit. The only way to peace and justice is to be prepared for war. Jesus' ethic of turning the other cheek is for a world which is free of sin. The great banquet in the realm of God will come in the future. Here and now we must salvage the only peace which is possible, that which comes from the threat of retaliation. Look what happened at Hiroshima and Nagasaki. By dropping those bombs we ended that war and saved the millions of lives which would have been lost in an invasion of Japan. Violence sometimes brings peace, and the threat of violence maintains it. I repeat, we don't live in a perfect world."

Carl had frequently heard George out on his hawkish views. He certainly agreed with the need for an adequate defense. He was no pacifist. Yet George's passionate embrace of violence and especially his tendency to view things in terms of good guys and bad guys bothered him. But rather than engaging George in what would be an endless argument, he returned to his own problem.

"When I was in the Navy," he told them, "I fueled the power plants of nuclear subs. I had nothing to do with weapons. I felt I was part of a team providing for the defense of my country. But this nuclear weapons business is another matter. It has made me think about where I stand. For me the question has become: Who do I say that I am? Where do I stand? Standing up to the Russians and standing with God are not so easily reconciled."

Now he was really into it. "God," he said, "gives us freedom of choice. God doesn't tell me to do this or do that. I make those choices. My wife tells me I need to rely on both God and my own sense of the issue, that my sensitivity in these matters will help keep things from getting out of hand. But I don't know. I am not comfortable in applying my energies to weapons. God of course will be with me wherever I go. God will be present with me if I decide to make those things. But what does it mean to be a servant of Jesus Christ? How can I be a servant of the great peacemaker Jesus Christ who tells us to love our enemies and to serve him in everything we do? I can't just mouth the words of servanthood. My practice must somehow follow what I preach.

"What's worse, when I finally received the invitation to interview for the job, I immediately started to rationalize my involvement with those weapons. They need Christians in responsible positions, I said to myself. I can't know George's big picture since I don't have all the pieces. Someone needs to defend the country. All those things ran through my head. But where does it all stop? Who is responsible? The reality is, I can't serve two masters. I don't think I can give 100 percent to this job. I am the one who is responsible."

They all sat in silence for a moment. George made a stab at bringing his reality back into the discussion. "I see how you feel, Carl, but you just don't have the information to make decisions on matters of vital national defense. And do you know what will happen economically in places like Richland if your conscience gets loose? The place will become a ghost town over night. I know. I lived there. At last count 14,000 workers were employed on the Hanford reservation, and the Department of Energy pumps about $800 million a year into its operations there.

"If nothing else, keep all this to yourself," he went on. "Remember that priest in Richland I told you about, the one who spoke out about nuclear weapons and immediately lost rapport with his congregation? You don't want that sort of thing to happen, do you?"

"I don't know," Carl quietly responded. "I just don't know! I guess the the question for me is the one Barbara raised last night. Will it be plutonium for peace or plutonium for war? I can't get over that question. Can I really in good conscience take that job?"

Commentary

Power for Peace

The shifting fortunes of the nuclear energy industry since its beginnings in the 1950s have occupied the nation's press as few other stories. Launched with phenomenal optimism, the industry peaked in the mid-1970s with an avalanche of orders, then went into decline. Although over one hundred nuclear plants are now on line in the United States, no new orders have been placed since 1978, and every order between 1974 and 1978 has been canceled. Political opposition jelled by concerns over costs and safety has hardened, and few months pass without new announcements of abandoned projects and financially troubled utilities.

The N reactor on the government reservation at Hanford, Washington, has been a unique nuclear plant throughout this period of shifting fortunes. As the case notes, it is the only reactor which produces both electrical power and weapons grade plutonium. It has done neither as efficiently as other plants because of compromises in design taken to make it serve two quite different functions. Completed in 1963 with an expected life of thirty plus years, in early 1988 came the announcement of its closure for budgetary reasons. As many as 6,500 workers will eventually lose their jobs as a result of the closure. Age, the high cost of safety modifications, real and perceived dangers, and a surplus of weapons grade plutonium finally caught up with the plant, which thus becomes another casualty in a declining industry.

The closure in no way simplifies this case. In fact it deepens and complicates it by adding the problem of plant closures to its list of issues. At the heart of the case, of course, are the two issues of nuclear energy and nuclear weapons raised coincidentally by the design of the reactor. The two issues are alive and well whatever the fate of the N reactor; and Carl Knight could just as well be two persons, the one deciding on a job in the nuclear power industry, the other in nuclear weapons production.

Carl's Christian qualms about participating in the production of nuclear weapons may be the more compelling issue in this case. The placement of the case in this section, however, indicates an intention to give the discussion between Larry Mize and Carl Knight over nuclear power prior consideration.

NUCLEAR ENERGY

The era of cheap and abundant energy is almost over. The oil and natural gas currently supporting industrial societies are being depleted rapidly and are not renewable. Both will be in short supply and very expensive sometime in the next century. Coal reserves are sufficient to last several hundred years even with increased consumption. Of great concern, however, are the serious drawbacks to the use of coal, notably the environmental degradation of strip mining, the costs of transportation, and the severe air and water pollution caused by combustion. From an environmental standpoint coal is no bargain, and its use should be kept to a minimum unless strict environmental safeguards are enacted.

Eventually nations must develop means of meeting their energy needs from sources that are sustainable over a long term, essentially renewable resources. Solar power is frequently mentioned in this regard. From wind and hydroelectric to passive absorbers and giant reflector farms, solar energy has an important future although at present it is competitive with fossil fuels in only a few places.

Conservation will also be essential. Conservation is the name given efforts to save energy either by cutting back on its use or by producing it more efficiently.

The realm in which renewable sources of energy and conservation reign will be markedly different from the present realm where economic growth governs. Sustainability and sufficiency will necessarily guide energy decisions, not growth, at least not the growth of energy- and resource-intensive production and consumption.

Between this realm and the one to come there will be a difficult period of transition which may have already begun and whose duration is difficult to predict largely because the rate of technological innovation cannot be known. The realm to come can be delayed if limits to growth are attacked with the so-called technology fix, that is, a commitment to find technological solutions to all constraints. Certainly new technology will have a role to play, but if the shape of human communities and the distribution of costs and benefits are disregarded in the rush for technical solutions, the new realm will hardly be worth inhabiting.

Finding a way through this transition will be a matter of great urgency because modern societies have become so dependent on energy. The way will entail fundamental and simultaneous changes in the way nations conceive and use technology, the economic and political structures they design to carry them through, and the basic values which guide them.

Nuclear energy is and will continue to be an important player in the transition in spite of its present state of decline. It offers the potential for a huge supply of energy and continuing support for the technical sector. But the debate over nuclear will continue to be acrimonious because nuclear energy is both risky and symbolic of deeper divisions.

As a form of energy it has two configurations: fission and fusion. In brief, fission energy comes from the heat generated by splitting heavy atoms, usually uranium or plutonium; and fusion energy comes from the heat resulting from forcing together or fusing two isotopes of hydrogen under great temperature and pressure. Fission is the atomic bomb, fusion the hydrogen.

Fission energy has been commercially available since the 1950s. Today there are over two hundred commercial reactors worldwide. Uranium supplies for fission are depletable although they can be extended considerably at high cost by using breeder reactors.

Fusion energy is not commercially available and may never be due to the difficulties and dangers of containing the great temperatures and pressures which are required for the reaction to take place. If fusion energy were harnessed, however, it would provide an almost unlimited source of power since the hydrogen bound up in the world's oceans is its supply. Indeed, were fusion energy to come on line at a reasonable cost, it would probably stifle all talk of limits, obviate any need for a transition, and set nations on the path of the technological fix. The sky would be the limit, although heat pollution and the complexity of the technology would still remain problems.

Another reason fusion seems so attractive—this goes for coal as well—is the well documented problems with fission. Uranium reserves are limited. In spite of a good safety record, accidents like Three Mile Island and Chernobyl do happen, and more can be expected. Such accidents are given so much attention by the media and so linked in the collective imagination to nuclear weapons, that fact and fancy are difficult to unravel. That commercial reactors cannot explode like a bomb is hardly appreciated as the risks of fission are magnified out of proportion. Still the dangers of radioactive fallout and core meltdowns are considerable and give adequate ground for added safety precautions and concerns about liability for accidents. Building in safety precautions is expensive, and liability could be astronomical. Concern for safety has been a major cause of the skyrocketing price tag for new plants and for the delays in licensing which have taken nuclear momentarily out of the competition. Carl Knight alludes to this when he asks why we require nuclear reactors to be super safe and do little to stop the acid rain caused by the combustion of coal. His point is well taken and should probably be understood as a plea to stop acid rain.

Nuclear waste also remains a problem. Hanford was one of the final three sites considered for long-term storage and is not yet out of the running. Some scientists worry that the basalt rock formations in the Hanford area would allow eventual leakage of long-lived radioactivity into the Columbia River. Nevada has apparently won the dubious right to store nuclear waste. At least it appears as if it will be the only site tested for storage by the Department of Energy. The costs of storage have not been calculated but will be considerable and will add to the already high price of nuclear.

In addition, nuclear plants require large security forces, up to 20 percent of those employed, because they are vulnerable to sabotage. The proliferation of nuclear weapons is a constant worry. While the plants themselves do not produce weapons grade material, they do provide waste material which can be used in weapons if it is processed further.

Even with these drawbacks, proponents of nuclear energy like Carl still see it as a major transitional fuel. Mouths must be fed, and basic needs met, Carl points out. As for the risks, Carl is quick to point out that nothing is without risk; but just as quickly he adds that the risks are acceptable. Unfortunately the accuracy of his assessment cannot be determined. Like his opponents, Carl can only speculate about the future.

In addition, his discussion with Larry is confined narrowly to technical problems and economic costs. Larry Mize does raise a very significant question, however, near the end of his disputation against nuclear energy. It is a question that can be easily overlooked in a preoccupation with technology and economics. Larry mentions the social implications of a nuclear society and goes on to caricature it, or so Carl thought, as one dominated by numbers and machines and repressed by large police forces.

His Orwellian caricature should not obscure a critical insight. Technical choices, here about energy, are social and value choices. Put differently, the choices we make today about energy will go a long way to determine the shape of future social institutions and values. Until this significance of energy choices sinks in, the momentous nature of the discussion between Larry and Carl cannot be fully understood.

To repeat, energy choices are social and value choices. If North Americans decide on lives which consume large amounts of energy and natural resources, they will simultaneously choose the economic and political structures to organize and sustain such a decision and a value system to support it. The question of nuclear energy is much larger than meets the eye when only technical and economic calculations are taken. In its largest dimensions the question is what kind of society do present stewards of the earth want for themselves and their children, even to the fourth and fifth generations. And beneath this lurks basic questions of social identity and character. Who are we as a people? And what should be the center of our common life?

While crystal ball gazing is not an exact science, a commitment to nuclear will probably bring with it pressures for continuous economic growth and maximization of output. A nuclear society will be large in scale with complex technology and centralized, probably hierarchical, administration. Materialism will carry the day.

Alternatively, a society geared to renewables and conservation will bring pressures to live sustainably and to be satisfied with basics. It will be a society where appropriate scale, simplicity, a greater degree of decentralization, and greater equality will prevail.

Given the current tendency to let technological innovation set the social course, it is unlikely that a conscious choice will be made about future directions, particularly if abundant energy resources are available. Nations will drift into their futures, more or less unconsciously letting thousands of technical decisions, each made on grounds of efficiency and control, set the course. The impact of the automobile on North American society and culture is just one illustration of this tendency. Who chose the society oriented to the automobile?

Concern about this tendency and the shape it will give future society plus the awesome power and importance of nuclear technology make the nuclear question a lightning rod for all sorts of apprehensions. Its destructive potential, witnessed by nearly everyone in film footage of Hiroshima and Nagasaki, raises anxieties about total annihilation. The difficulties of understanding its complexities result in fears of technology running out of control and lead to such phenomena as people envisioning the growing concentration of power in the hands of a few ruthless persons in control of nuclear sources. The potential nuclear power has for spawning a new round of materialism worries those who lament decreasing spirituality. Real concerns about safety and costs trouble even some of its proponents.

The nuclear debate will not go away any time soon. It is more than scientists and technicians calculating total costs and degrees of risk. What is at stake is the very social fabric of modern culture. And while the tendency will be to drift into the future, communities do have choices. Christians need to be clear about the values which will guide their choices and to have the will to bring these values to bear on social direction. It is not outside the realm of imagination to think that modern technology can be directed, if not restrained.

GUIDELINES

The ethic of ecological justice, developed at greater length and theologically grounded in the discussion of "Rigor and Responsibility," applies to energy choices as well. Justice, sustainable sufficiency, and participation are the relevant norms to guide public policy and the centerpiece for social identity from a Christian perspective.

Stated in normative terms, the goal for energy policy in the transition to renewable sources of energy should be the provision of an equitable distribution of sufficient and sustainable energy to support basic needs in an environment conducive to widespread political participation. The process of determining energy policy should be as open as possible, limited only by the necessity to make timely decisions.

On the one hand the provision of basic needs, the availability of long-lasting supplies, and the drawbacks of coal—all concerns of Carl Knight— make nuclear an obvious alternative, especially in the transition period.

On the other hand there are a number of factors which combine to make nuclear fission incongruent with the ethics of ecological justice. Among these are the risks, real and perceived, associated with nuclear power; the cost of making nuclear reasonably safe and environmentally sound; the likely shape a nuclear decision will give to future social institutions and values; the tying up of large amounts of capital which could be alternatively invested; and the threat of nuclear proliferation. In addition, a highly charged political context makes participatory decision making and timely resolution of disagreements almost impossible.

Given these incongruities, nuclear fission should be seen as a source of last resort with the burden of proof resting on the demonstration of a threat to energy sufficiency defined in terms of basic human needs. Its use should be constrained by strict environmental and human safeguards. The ultimate goal should be reduced dependence on fission power with eventual phase out as conservation measures and renewable sources are developed.

Fusion power is still an unknown quantity. It offers a potentially huge source of energy. It eliminates some of the risks of fission, but will probably add some of its own associated with the extremely high temperatures and pressures required. Its effects on social structures and values would be similar to a commitment to fission. Research should probably continue but with a careful assessment of social and environmental impacts.

The high cost of nuclear and popular perceptions about risks currently give the edge to Larry Mize in his debate with Carl. The prospects of oil and gas shortages and continuing high demand, which will result from the present lack of restraint, may well shift the balance to Carl in the not too distant future. The nuclear industry is currently banking on such an out-come. Political opposition should not be discounted, however, and may be the determining factor. The passion generated by antinuclear forces has stopped more than a few projects in their tracks.

Whatever the short run produces, the longer range should be kept in view. The goal should be the phase out of nuclear energy, a scaling down of energy consumption by the rich, and reliance on renewable sources. That at least is a social policy consistent with an ethic of ecological justice.

CARL KNIGHT AND NUCLEAR WEAPONS

Given what has been gleaned from a brief slice of his life, Carl Knight seems content in the American mainstream. Moving up the ladder in his company, relatively comfortable within the hierarchical structures of the Navy and Easton Industries, happy with his traditional family, supportive of the defense establishment, and self-assured about the progressive nature of economic growth and technological innovation, Carl would seem to be an excellent candidate for promotion into the weapons business. Yet he combines this essentially conventional and conservative outlook with in-trospection and a moral sensitivity not always found in mainstream Americans. The difference is worth exploring because its apparent foundation is Carl's Christian faith.

From what Carl says in the case a few things can be inferred about his religious outlook. He sees God as an active force in his life standing beside him in whatever decision he makes. Although he does not make clear how God will stand beside him—whether as guide, judge, or ratifier of his decision—Carl sees God as acting in a way which leaves people like him free to make moral choices and to be accountable for them. In his support for the military and his participation on a Navy team providing for what he calls "the defense of my country," Carl appears to agree with George Chambers that sin persists and a future act of God will be necessary to bring in the realm of Christ.

Yet he disagrees with George in a significant respect. George apparently gives full reign to sin and sees God's decisive act in Jesus Christ as primarily in the future. Jesus Christ makes no apparent difference now, so nations are left to their own defense, and the way to peace is to balance power against power.

Alternatively, George might say that God's decisive act in Jesus Christ relates only to the life of individuals. God brings salvation now and life in heaven after death to those who accept Jesus Christ as their personal savior. Groups, such as modern nation-states, are provisional vehicles for order and have little bearing on an individual's personal relation to Jesus Christ. Their function is to restrain sin.

Either way for George, the life and teachings of Jesus Christ have little relation to the affairs of nations. But for Carl God's power is not totally in the future or unrelated to the behavior of groups. Jesus Christ is lord of all realms. God has acted decisively in Jesus Christ and continues to work in the world through the Holy Spirit in a way which is consistent with the central revelation of God's love in the cross and resurrection. This decisive act makes a difference which is relevant to the way nations arrange their affairs and conduct their defense.

For Carl one point of relevance is found in the inconsistency between the image of Jesus Christ as peacemaker and the production of weapons of mass destruction. Carl is not being simplistic and naive in highlighting this inconsistency. For him conventional weapons are still required in a world where sin hangs on in spite of God's decisive act. This probably puts him in the Christian realist and justifiable war camp discussed in the case "Vietnam's Children."

But there is about nuclear as opposed to conventional weapons something basically different, which Carl has latched on to but not expressed. While nuclear weapons change nothing we do, they make possible the end of all we do. International relations continue to be conducted with the old balance of power rules. Carl's work routine is not interrupted. The children go to school. The movies play at the local theater. Nothing changes, yet everything can change at the flick of a switch. For the first time in history humans have the capacity to destroy all life. This is a mind-boggling reality which is beginning to sink in with folks like Carl. If even a portion of the more than fifty thousand weapons held in U.S. and Soviet arsenals were unleashed, the resulting "nuclear winter" would produce climatic catastrophe. There can be no justifiable nuclear war.

Here a Stangelovian logic enters. As Christian ethicist Larry Rasmussen glibly but gravely points out: "You can't live with 'em and you can't live without 'em." To live with nuclear weapons courts the disaster of annihilation through accident, misperception, or the desire to beat the enemy to the punch. But to disarm unilaterally is to court annihilation from another quarter. What national leader would not be tempted to make the world safe for capitalism, or communism, or some other -ism if he or she had a nuclear monopoly? Unbalanced power has always been a temptation to the ruthless and the cunning. So either way the human race courts disaster. That is the nuclear dilemma.

And to top it off, short of an immediate transformation of all people, this dilemma will be with the human race as long as it survives. There is no getting rid of nuclear weapons. The weapons themselves may be dismantled, of course, but not the knowledge of how to make them. Nuclear weapons are the ultimate symbol of the ambivalent nature of modern technology. Nuclear technology gives the capacity of both unlimited power for peace and unlimited power for destruction. It is no wonder that nuclear power and nuclear weapons are linked in the popular imagination, and it is not surprising that for that reason Carl keeps hitting his head against the wall on the safety issue. Nuclear power and nuclear weapons have a common denominator not just in Hiroshima, but more importantly in the fear that technology is out of control and that communities have little to say in the way they will live.

Carl Knight appreciates all this and is troubled. As with everyone else, however, he does not know what to do about it. The arms race, like modern technology, has a certain inexorable logic to it which seems to defy individual and community initiative. He may refuse to take the job. He may do what he can within Easton Industries to reverse the arms race. Just the same, he knows Easton will have no difficulty filling the job. He knows there are powerful financial interests who are well served by weapons production. He knows about the pressures to toe the line in places like Hanford. He knows what the economic impact of closing the N reactor will be. He knows the gross rationalizations—"it is better to the let the experts in Washington, D.C., decide because they alone have the whole picture"—which make participation in the nuclear process so easy to digest morally. He even knows the subtle justifications—"it is better to have Christians in charge"—which wrongly assume that Christians are immune to the inexorable logic of the arms race.

Carl is not alone as he agonizes over the nuclear dilemma. Christian churches in the United States, especially those in the justifiable war tradition, have been agonizing with him. The central issue for these churches has been the ideology of deterrence, the current thinking about strategy which holds that peace is best attained by balancing nuclear weapons against nuclear weapons. As former President Reagan was so fond of saying, "If you want peace, prepare for war."

The problem for the churches stems from their own understanding of the justifiable war tradition. Following the lead of American Catholic bishops in their 1983 pastoral, "The Challenge of Peace," these churches agree that there can be no justifiable nuclear war. It is immoral and even unthinkable. They also agree that threatening nuclear war, a threat which is at least implied in the possession of nuclear weapons and the strategy of deterrence, is also immoral. The conclusion would seem to follow from these agreements that possession of the weapons and the strategy of deterrence would be immoral as well, and unilateral disarmament the only ethical option.

Here the churches take different courses, however. The Catholic bishops held that possession of nuclear weapons for deterrence is immoral as a long-range policy for peace, but deemed deterrence, as a short-term policy on the way to disarmament and not an end in itself, morally acceptable.

The bishops of the United Methodist Church in their statement, "In Defense of Creation," took a stronger stand in 1986 rejecting deterrence and declaring: "The ideology of deterrence must not receive the church's blessing, even as a temporary warrant for holding on to nuclear weapons." But the door they apparently slammed shut was left ajar when they went on to reject unilateral disarmament and allow for "the lingering possession of [nuclear] weapons for a strictly limited time." Their quarrel, it seems, is with the ideology of deterrence, not with the possession of nuclear weapons.

In contrast the Lutheran Church in America in a 1984 statement, "Peace and Politics," is much more supportive of a deterrence strategy, maintaining that "insofar as aggression . . . is restrained by the possession of nuclear weapons (which includes the threat to use them in retaliation), nuclear deterrence remains at the present time as the lesser of evils. Yet evil it is and remains."

Why all this fuss about deterrence? Because the ideology of deterrence is the primary moral justification for Carl Knight as he considers promotion into the weapons business. The logic of this ideology would have him build weapons to restrain sin and sustain peace. The ideology has it that deterrence is the best available option in a sinful world, or, looking at the other side of the coin, the lesser of evils.

The Catholic and Methodist bishops go a long way to close the door to this justification. They are particularly upset at the use of deterrence ideology to justify any and all nuclear weapons. They see the ideology as the primary fuel of the arms race. Yes, they do leave the door open a crack on the way to disarmament, but in reality give Carl little moral justification for taking the promotion.

The statement of the Lutheran Church in America is much more supportive, and if Carl is looking for justification, he can also find Christians who have no moral qualms about deterrence or participation in the production of nuclear weapons. Pat Robertson and Jerry Falwell come immediately to mind.

Finally, Carl must decide for himself. Others cannot decide for him, even if they are bishops or popular preachers. Perhaps the question really does boil down to faith in Jesus Christ. Has God indeed acted decisively in Jesus Christ so that God's peacemaking powers are released in the world and make a difference? Or does sin still reign to such a degree that nations do not experience God's power and thus need to thwart each other with a balance of terror?

PLANT CLOSURES

The announcement that the N reactor would shut down before the end of its useful life came as a rude shock to the Hanford Reservation. Long accustomed to the vagaries of federal spending on defense and energy, the Tri-Cities of Richland, Kennewick, and Pasco, Washington, adjacent to Hanford, will be harder hit than ever before. If none of the laid-off workers is hired to convert a new but mothballed energy reactor on the reservation to weapons production or to clean up defense wastes, 6,500 of the current 14,000 government jobs will be lost. The ripple effect will push the total considerably higher in the community. This will add substantially to the unemployment rate, which at the time of closure stood at about 11 percent, four percentage points higher than the state of Washington as a whole. The closure will have a devastating effect because Hanford's 14,000 workers account for 27 percent of all nonfarm jobs in the Tri-Cities area and 45 percent of nonfarm payroll.

The fate of the Tri-Cities is not shocking news to many American towns and cities that have undergone similar circumstances. Plant closures, for example, in the auto and steel industries, have already produced tremendous hardships in the so-called rust belt of Michigan, Ohio, and Pennsylvania. The unemployment rate in Michigan has been considerably higher than the nation as a whole for some time now.

One response to plant closures is to chalk them up to the normal operation of an efficient market system. Employers in this view have no social responsibility other than making a profit. The responsibility for picking up the pieces belongs to institutions of the community and to the initiative of individual workers who are told in so many words, "tough luck," and urged to take the initiative and relocate.

This cavalier approach to plant closures can have no place in a Christian perspective. Employers do not have the responsibility in a capitalistic system to keep obsolete and uncompetitive plants open. But they should be responsible for such things as making timely capital investments to keep potentially competitive plants going, adequate advance warning of closure, a willingness to shift control to worker-based initiatives, liberal termination benefits, and assistance to faithful employees in retraining, relocation, and weathering through the psychological trauma of unemployment.

The closure of the N reactor will be a great hardship to the Tri-Cities region. Unemployment will rise and the fallout will be accompanied by increased mental illness, alcohol consumption, and family abuse.

Fortunately many of the unemployed are skilled technical workers and will find new employment far easier than a laid-off auto or steel worker. The Tri-Cities region has known for some time that the N reactor would soon be on the chopping block. A callous "tough luck" is not a sufficient response, however. Federal and state governments have a responsibility to smooth the transition from dependency on nuclear energy and weapons to new alternatives.

ADDITIONAL RESOURCES

Geyer, Alan. *The Idea of Disarmament: Rethinking the Unthinkable.* Elgin, Il.: Brethren, 1982.

Hollenbach, David. *Nuclear Ethics: A Christian Moral Argument.* New York: Paulist, 1983.

Kaku, Michio, and Jennifer Trainer. *Nuclear Power, Both Sides: The Best Arguments for and against the Most Controversial Technology.* New York: W. W. Norton, 1982.

The Lutheran Church in America. "Peace and Politics." Adopted July 1984. Division for Mission in North America, 231 Madison Avenue, New York, N.Y. 10016.

Rasmussen, Larry R. "The Nuclear Dilemma." In Beverly W. Harrison, et al., eds., *The Public Vocation of Christian Ethics.* New York: Pilgrim, 1986.

Shell, Jonathan. *The Fate of the Earth.* New York: Knopf, 1982.

Shrader-Frechette, K. S. *Nuclear Power and Public Policy: The Social and Ethical Problems of Fission Technology.* Dorrecht, Holland/Boston: D. Reidel Publishing Co., 1983.

United Methodist Council of Bishops. "In Defense of Creation: The Nuclear Crisis and a Just Peace." In *The United Methodist Reporter*, May 9, 1986.

United States Catholic Conference. "The Challenge of Peace: God's Promise and Our Response." Washington, D.C.: USCC, 1983.

PART V

BUSINESS

Case

10/9

Big Business and the Boys' Club

Pastor Dave Hopkins stepped off the elevator and through the carved mahogany door into the quiet elegance of the Chicago Men's Club. He was struck by the contrast between this environment and the recent images of the Jamaican slums which prompted his request for this luncheon meeting. After giving his name to the club's host, Dave was courteously informed that he was several minutes early; he was welcome to wait in the bar until Mr. Palmer and the rest of his party arrived.

Dave Hopkins's mind sifted through the events of the past four weeks as he considered how he would share his Jamaican experience with Frank Palmer and George Delaney, executives in transnational corporations with interests in the Caribbean as well as members of his affluent North Shore congregation, and Harold Atkins, a management consultant to the travel industry and a good friend of George. The previous month while Dave and his wife, Carol, were vacationing in Jamaica, they unexpectedly ran into Anthony Robinson, a Jamaican pastor who had done his seminary "field education" in the United States under Dave's direction. When Dave and Carol saw Tony for the first time in four years, he was playing the piano in their hotel's cocktail lounge. They spoke briefly during Tony's break; he invited them to come with him the following morning to his new "parish."

After serving as associate pastor — in Tony's terms "unsuccessfully" — in a large Jamaican congregation, Tony had requested and been granted by his conference an unsalaried, three-year leave from regular pastoral duties to work in the slums of Montego Bay. Tony worked primarily with a boys' club during the day and supported himself and his ministry by playing the piano at night in the lounge of a fashionable tourist hotel.

This case was written by Alice Frazer Evans and Robert A. Evans. Copyright © The Case Study Institute under the original title "A Matter of Pride — Part B." Revised 1988. All names are disguised to protect the privacy of the persons involved in this situation.

Dave remembered vividly the events of the next morning as they drove through Montego in the Hopkinses' rented car. At the time Dave expressed his astonishment at the contrast between the extreme poverty of the great mass of people in the area and the plush tourist zone and the homes of affluent business and government leaders. In Tony's "parish" Dave and Carol saw hundreds of crude palm shanties, many with seven and eight occupants. There were no plumbing facilities, and the only available water, as much as a half mile away from some huts, came from a single faucet put in by the city. Tony explained that most of the adult population was uneducated with little or no hope for employment in an increasingly urban-oriented nation.

In his words, Tony was convinced that "the very presence of the concentrated wealth—the fruits of an economy largely based on the tourist industry, where those fruits are not shared with the nation although they are primarily the products of the natural tropical setting of our island—is essentially destructive and explosive." Tony continued, "The young people with whom I work have virtually no public education available. They see the contrast between the haves and have-nots and are understandably bitter and frustrated. My boys turn to gangs, drugs, and stealing out of desperation and a lack of self-worth. The human tragedy in this slum is a crime against God's good creation and is contrary to Christ's mandate to love our neighbors as ourselves. In Luke 4:18 Jesus declares his mission as 'good news to the poor and liberty for the oppressed.' We are called by Christ to be in solidarity with the poor and oppressed of our world. This is not only my parish, but as a Christian it is also yours."

In his spare time while with his former congregation and now full time, Tony worked with a gang of young boys. He used his gifts as a musician to teach them to play the few instruments he could gather. They had slowly formed a band. Now Tony felt there was real competition among the boys to belong to the band. "For most of these boys playing an instrument gives them the first feeling of accomplishment they have ever experienced. It is only with a concept of pride and self-worth that these young men can even begin to hope for a different life."

Tony's plea to Dave Hopkins still rang in his ears. "Reverend Hopkins, I've got over a hundred boys and twelve instruments. My church is struggling in Jamaica; it simply has no funds to work in the slums, and most of the church members place no priority on this kind of ministry. Through your congregation and your contacts in the U.S., can you get support for my club? God has empowered these boys to fight for human dignity. Join us in this struggle for liberation. I know from my time with your congregation that you have influential and powerful businessmen who could help us.

"Bauxite, exported to the U.S., is Jamaica's primary source of foreign exchange. But the U.S.-based tourist industry is second and more directly affects our economy. Tourism annually grosses millions of dollars through the exploitation of our beaches and the cheap labor of our people. Yet virtually no Jamaicans are in management positions. Day laborers, with visions of North American dollars, come from coastal villages and small farms up in the mountains to work in the hotels. With limited skills and no job security, they are at the mercy of fluctuating tourism trends and more often than not end up homeless and unemployed. Whole families try to survive by begging tourists to buy shells, fruit, or straw hats. These factors directly contribute to the growth of the slums. Tourism has also corrupted our culture by its presence, producing assembly line handicrafts and phony festivals. Don't your Christian executives who benefit from the social structures which have been created by their businesses here have some real responsibility for their brothers and sisters in Jamaica who are negatively affected by those structures?"

Dave Hopkins snapped back to the present as Frank Palmer put his hand on Dave's shoulder and said, "Welcome to the club again. Our table is waiting." After the men had ordered lunch, Dave sketched the essence of his morning in Kingston and put Anthony Robinson's questions to his friends.

Frank Palmer, now sixty-six, recently retired from the vice-presidency of Consolidated International Beverage Company, turned to Dave with a grin. "When the church urged you and Carol to take that vacation, I should have known you couldn't just go and escape for a week! Well, to deal with the issues Tony put to us, we may first need to sort out why we have any responsibility. I personally believe that I *am* my brother's keeper. As a Christian, I find it impossible to observe conditions such as you describe and not seek a responsible way to help. Revolting conditions of hunger and health address not only company executives but boards of directors and stockholders. There is a minimal but increasing sense of corporate responsibility in many companies. Tony is right. We get a profit—we must give in return. As the Bible says, 'Those to whom much has been given, much will be required.' The issue then goes from rationale to strategy."

At this point George Delaney cut in, "Frank, as corporations we do give already in terms of salaries for individuals, opportunities for small local businesses, and taxes to the government which provide funds that country had no access to prior to our arrival. As you know, I am in the hotel business and Tony has got to face some realities. He speaks of U.S. companies grossing millions in the Caribbean. This is true, but he has a superficial view of gross operating profit. The return on investment is frequently very poor. The initial risk of building a hotel is increased by political instability and even the danger of eventual expropriation of property. For weeks following recent political unrest, the Jamaican tourist industry lost revenue of over a million dollars a day from cancelled reservations. After the tremendous expense of building in a developing country, the management then has to continue to import at great expense the luxuries our customers expect. Most tourists really want to feel at home with familiar cuisine, in the air-conditioned comfort of their hotel which provides a secure base for a controlled exposure to an alien culture in the streets and markets.

"To provide that U.S.-like retreat center in another culture is expensive. In fact the percentage of operating profit in the Caribbean is the lowest of any major overseas operation as reflected in the studies for Worldwide Hotel Operations which I brought along for your reference. In addition Horwath and Horwath's statistics show the Caribbean to have some of the highest employee salaries and benefits. We return a tremendous amount of income to those people. Good Calvinists like us acknowledge we're all sinners, but a significant number of Jamaicans benefit from U.S. corporate presence.

"Look, Frank, for me to say I'm against helping the less fortunate is like saying I'm against motherhood. But as you have said in the past, you don't sell a moral attitude on its own merits. You've got to convince a company that it's in its own self-interest to create a good working environment in order for its business to prosper. That's not only good business, it's sound policy based on human nature. Frank, while we may disagree on the rationale, we seem to agree on the conclusion. The long-term view of stability and profitability call for a controlled, careful strategy for corporate involvement in international issues."

"But George," Dave Hopkins responded, "aren't we called as Christians to 'serve the world' and not to attempt first to maximize our own benefits? I've seen you personally take a strong stand in the community on issues you felt were morally correct, even when this might jeopardize your image or result in a personal loss in the view of some people. Why must the assuming of social responsibility for a corporation always be based on self-interest in contrast to the individual's responsibility? And as Tony has indicated, what about the self-interest of the vast majority of Jamaicans who don't benefit from those statistically high employee salaries? While acknowledging our own sin, don't we also have to see the sin of an elite group of Jamaicans who link their self-interest to U.S. corporate profit?"

Harold Atkins, thirty-eight, who headed one of the largest consultant firms in the Midwest, had been silent up to this point. Harold now spoke clearly and firmly. "Self-interest or not, I frankly don't think there is *any* premise for a business to become involved in the social concerns of a host country. Just as our country is based on a clear separation of church and state, so should our economic institutions function independently. Our Lutheran friends got it right when they speak of two realms, one secular and one religious.

"A corporation is not an individual. A business has one responsibility — to create customers. If it does this well, there's profit which benefits host and guest. If not, both are out of business. An individual can afford to act responsibly in relation to his or her moral commitments. There is no corporate moral commitment in a business. Corporations do not have the luxury of being responsible in the same way. I may personally give money or time to some world social agency, but I'm not about to counsel my client to do the same thing. My client's primary responsibility is to his or her stockholders who have invested in a business, not in a philanthropic organization."

Frank Palmer slowly turned to Harold. "I used to operate with a similar logic in executive decisions, although I don't think I was ever asked to articulate it. Now, I am less persuaded. That logic appears, so my children argue, to divide one's life into neat compartments that don't correlate with one another. Why should a company be released from moral responsibility simply because it's a corporate institution? A business has several levels of obligation, only one of which is to its stockholders. True, you can't sell being a 'do-gooder,' but I am accountable for my employees because they are my employees, and I am accountable for those in need because they are in need. Somehow I must assume responsibility for my influence in my private and corporate life—even for my sins. This is at the heart of any sense of stewardship for the natural and human resources of the world. I'm not thinking simply about myself; I'm worried about the world my grandchildren and Jamaicans' grandchildren will be living in."

As the lunch arrived, Dave Hopkins joked that judging by the intensity of the conversation, he certainly didn't need to encourage his friends to express their opinions. Dave indicated that he was struck by the genuine ambiguity and complexity of the problem and needed to focus the concern he felt. "If we all agree that *some* moral responsibility exists—be that personal or corporate—how, for example, could an influential individual or hotel chain in the Caribbean go about effecting change for those in need? How can we respond, if at all, to Tony's request for help?"

"I've learned from experience," responded George Delaney, "that it is a mistake to sidestep the established channels. Governments, even of developing nations, tend to thrive on the status quo. We must convince them that economic stability depends on a solid middle class. It's in both our best interests to establish technical training programs. We should also seek to support, through supervised grants which use the resources of our money and our people, health and education projects as well as indigenous crafts and music. This helps maintain the original culture; it also protects the reasons the tourists go to places like Jamaica. Mutual self-interest is the key."

Harold Atkins retorted, "But how do you justify any immediate return to your stockholders? The hotels I advise pay fair wages by local standards; this is income for people who wouldn't otherwise have jobs. These people appear content with their lives. You're making paternalistic assumptions that it is in the best self-interest of Jamaicans for their country to become a copy of our society. My hotels pay high taxes. It's the local government's responsibility to channel the taxes into social programs *if* they see fit. But the ultimate use of taxes is not my client's business. Personally, however, I would be willing to give Dave, here, money to be sent to Tony's boys' club."

"Now here's where I have to back off," interposed George. "Tony is not working through channels. It is my understanding that he was given that leave of absence from the church after a dispute with his conference over priorities. Lack of local support for his program also seems to indicate alienation from his former congregation. I remember Tony as a responsible young man, but to give him money without some form of control is another matter. To ask a hotel or corporation to sponsor such a charitable project could jeopardize their relationship to the established middle class and possibly to the government. If these boys reach a point of 'self-realization' in which they put on pressure to evict my hotels, or worse, expropriate the investment, a project without supervision would be self-destructive. We must face the realization that our businesses are parasites on another culture. We need to work for the most symbiotic relationship possible between a parasite and its host. We don't seek the death of the host or the extermination of the parasite. Both organisms can survive and flourish through negotiated mutual interest and respect."

Frank Palmer shook his head. "Our lives, our corporations are involved in risks every day. We must respond in a way which is not demeaning. We can't offer assistance to Tony and then show him we have no confidence in his vision for his own people. A semi-paternalistic attitude is perhaps inevitable, but the over-paternalistic style of the 'company mill' will corrupt our humanity and theirs. We need more than bigger mission gifts — strings or no strings attached. The request from Tony, our former pastor and student, is to assume some responsibility for those who are in need based on Christian concern. I'm reminded of Christ's repeated call to Peter to 'feed my sheep.' Tony points us to children who are hungry for human dignity. A strategy for development ought to involve business, government, and church interests in Kingston and Chicago. Our church never touched me in this area, or perhaps I never listened. I feel called — I just don't know where."

George Delaney responded, "Frank, this is the vision of a retired corporation executive who has leisure and security. I wish you luck. Project-oriented, mutual-interest programs are what Tony really needs and if my competition will concur, we could make some headway here. A low-profit region like the Caribbean may be a place to try out such an approach. We have less to lose by the risk."

Harold Atkins countered, "As a consultant I don't think you have weighed properly the pressures of profit and growth at home or of instability and corruption in Jamaica. Are you willing to make the necessary payoffs? A corporation advisor would counsel, 'don't exceed your corporate responsibilities for involvement.' However, as an individual I will make a pledge and write a check to Tony for his work. I always wanted to play a flute; this way I can at least buy one."

"The meal is almost over," Dave said. "We seem to have gone in so many different directions I'm wondering if there is any way we can consolidate our efforts in response to Tony."

Commentary

Big Business and the Boys' Club

Jesus Christ ministered to the poor and the politically powerless and lived within their midst. For centuries this man and his ministry have confronted his rich and powerful followers with the scandal of relating poverty and powerlessness to the wealth, might, and indifference of Caesar in his various ecclesiastical, political, and military configurations. In this case the destitution and muted desperation of Jamaican youth joined in a boys' club confront the confidence born of power of businessmen gathered in the quiet elegance of the Chicago Men's Club. Are these two all-male clubs destined to remain alienated from each other and the women of the world until the Lord returns in glory? Or has the power of Jesus Christ trickled down to all the clubs of this world?

This is a case first about corporate responsibility and second about Third World economies and the place of transnational corporations (TNCs) within them. Since the latter is more appropriately the subject of the case "Prophets from Brazil," this commentary will focus on corporate responsibility.

The surface questions in the case are whether and how to assist Tony Robinson and the boys in his club. The deeper question is whether corporations have social responsibility beyond their economic responsibilities to produce goods and services, hire workers, and realize a profit.

This is a complex case. The characters may at first glance seem easy to understand, but their positions are a maze of assumptions, strategies, and theological understandings. Exploring this maze is the primary order of business. Four routes through the maze are offered by Tony Robinson, Frank Palmer, George Delaney, and Harold Atkins. Each route provides a way to assist Tony and thereby to exercise corporate responsibility. Each has theological foundations. And each is open to criticism.

TONY ROBINSON

Tony is the first of the four to make an appearance. Dave Hopkins and his wife run into him in the cocktail lounge of their Jamaican hotel where Tony is playing the piano at night to support his work in a Montego Bay slum during the day. Tony recounts the ups and downs of his ministry in the four years since their last meeting. The term "unsuccessful" is used to describe his service in a large Jamaican congregation. Later George Delaney reveals that Tony was given a leave of absence from the congregation after a dispute over priorities. George adds that Tony does not work through channels. Almost unnoticed is the further information that Tony worked with a gang of young boys in his spare time at this former congregation. Apparently this gang and its slum environment are Tony's new parish.

From this sketchy information and his obvious sympathies, it is safe to assume that Tony feels squeezed between rich and poor worlds inside Jamaica, and North and South global perspectives outside. He is not playing the game according to the "rules" and as a result finds himself isolated and without resources except for his music.

Tony is outraged at the conditions in the slums of Montego Bay and blames the tourist industry and its confederates in the Jamaican government, whose generosity has meant the slum has all of one water spigot. Tony clearly takes the liberation perspective developed at some length in other cases in this volume, for example, "Vietnam's Children" and "Prophets from Brazil." His approach to relief of the poor is to jump into the thick of the fray and to empower the poor to provide their own relief. Specifically he is using the vehicle of a band to drive the boys to a new and liberated consciousness based on an awareness of their own self-worth. He seeks the support of TNCs in order to empower the boys. This is explosive stuff, and George Delaney is correct to recognize it as such.

Tony seems ambivalent about TNCs. He lays at their feet the ills of Jamaican society. The conclusion would seem to follow that they should get out and take along their "phony festivals" and "controlled exposure to an alien culture." But Tony does not follow through to this conclusion. Furthermore, he draws pay from his adversaries and even asks them through Dave to support his work with the boys. He apparently believes that corporations have a responsibility to help pick up the pieces of the shattered Jamaican culture.

Liberation theology is the foundation of Tony's perspective. He cites Luke 4:18, a favorite text of liberationists. He makes use of liberation themes and methods as he tries to create a new awareness among the boys. His criticism of TNCs echoes liberation theologians. He explicitly urges Dave Hopkins to join the struggle for liberation.

George Delaney insinuates that Tony is a dangerous radical. This is understandable, for however much Tony actually deserves this label, his ideas and actions are clear threats to TNCs and to George as an executive in the tourist business. "Who knows," George must be thinking, "those kids might rise up and burn the hotels. And if they stop short of that and just cause local riots, Jamaica will be dead to tourism overnight." To the supporters of TNCs and the form of development they bring to Third World countries, George's insinuation and thoughts will be well founded. To supporters of liberation they will seem self-serving.

FRANK PALMER

On the surface of things Frank seems to be the good guy in the discussion at the men's club. He is so willing to help. A retired executive of a beverage company, Frank leads off the discussion with his versions of helping the poor and corporate responsibility.

According to Frank the way to help the poor is to involve business, government, and church interests in a coordinated development effort. He seems to assume that such a coordinated development plan is on the drawing boards and that the interests he mentions can be harmoniously drawn into such an effort on behalf of the poor. Unfortunately, there is no plan, harmony is nonexistent, and he admits a lack of direction.

On the matter of corporate responsibility, however, Frank is clearer and more direct. The wretched conditions of Montego's poor cry out for correction. TNCs have been among the forces which have generated these conditions and profited from them. TNCs have a social responsibility beyond making a profit which in no way differs from that of an individual. They are called to respond to Tony's request.

Theologically Frank anchors his position in the biblical concern for the poor, repentance, stewardship, and the integration of all life under the lordship of Jesus Christ. He cites Jesus' summons to "feed my sheep." He mentions Cain's response, "Am I my brother's keeper?" to God's query regarding the whereabouts of Abel, Cain's slain brother, and thus Frank emphatically rejects Cain's implication that he is not responsible for his neighbor. Frank insists that a corporation is responsible on several levels for its acts, and especially for its sins, suggesting that TNCs have been short-sighted in Third World countries and need to change their ways. He links this responsibility to the grand theme of stewardship. Individuals and corporations are God's stewards and are responsible for passing on to future generations what they have inherited in no worse—and preferably in better—shape than they received it. Finally, he rejects Harold Atkins's separation of reality into individual and social spheres with different moralities. For Frank there is one world in Christ. Corporations cannot claim release from social responsibility just because they have characteristics and functions which distinguish them from individuals.

Several criticisms are directed at Frank's position. George calls him paternalistic, a charge which has some foundation. Frank advocates corporate responsibility but links it neither to substantive social change nor to the participation of the poor. His coordinated development effort is not coordinated with the poor he would coordinate! Business, government, and church leaders will presumably do all the work, then descend on the poor with their grand schemes. He also appears satisfied with responding to the symptoms of poverty with repentance and charity.

Harold Atkins refuses to budge from his distinction between individual and social realms and its implied rejection of Frank's argument for corporate social responsibility. In so doing he follows a long and honorable tradition in Christianity which makes this distinction. This tradition holds that groups have different functions and less moral resources than individuals and sometimes must act in ways which cannot be justified on ideal grounds. Violence and the justifiable war response to it is only one instance of this.

Left unmentioned is Frank's optimism that responsibility can be exercised easily, and a harmony of interests established. His sense of sin is almost nonexistent or at least not explicit.

GEORGE DELANEY

George is engaging because of his hard-headed realism. An executive in a TNC with interests in the Caribbean, he looks at corporate responsibility in dollars and cents terms and with a careful calculation of interests. His position may not be as hard-boiled as it at first seems, however. He does not subscribe to an unvarnished version of Adam Smith's "invisible hand," which guides the pursuit of self-interest toward the social good. He does not agree with Harold Atkins that corporations discharge all their social responsibilities in making a profit. His dogged pursuit of mutual self-interest is hard-headed in its understanding of sin, but leaves the door open for TNCs to do more than just pursue profit.

For obvious reasons George is very cautious about helping the poor. He argues that Dave and Frank are overlooking the many ways in which TNCs already assist the poor through salaries, purchases in local markets, and taxes to governments. He assumes that these expenditures represent new money for Jamaica, an assumption which may be true in the case of his firm, but which is not generally true in the Third World, where TNC investment funds often come from local sources.

George goes on to give details about the Caribbean region and its travel industry, which he depicts as being on the brink of disaster. The purpose of all his realism about social unrest and costs is probably to persuade his colleagues that the travel industry can afford neither social change nor social responsibility.

To Jamaicans of Tony Robinson's persuasion, however, George's other details about luxury, familiar cuisine, air-conditioned comfort, controlled exposure, and alien cultures send a different message. These Jamaicans will automatically compare these details to their experience of poverty and conclude that George is arrogant and insensitive. Dave Hopkins softens this conclusion a bit when he points out George's involvement on moral issues in his own community.

The essence of George's position on assistance to the poor and the role of TNCs can be summarized in the words "mutual self-interest through established channels." What he appears to be advocating is a TNC-led model of development which stresses rapid economic growth. Eventually, or so the logic of this perspective goes, the poor will be best served by a careful strategy of corporate involvement with local governments which slowly lets the gains of economic growth trickle down to the poor. Stability and a solid middle class are essential ingredients.

George understands self-interest to be the motivating force in economic decisions and reasons from this to an accommodation of interests in mutually beneficial projects. He is not naive about harmonious accommodation, however. He recognizes that Tony's view cannot be included. Negotiations should go on between established powers with radicals such as Tony excluded.

Theologically, George's perspective rests on his view of sin. More precisely, it rests on the good which results from containing sin, especially the sin of those who threaten the established order. He refers to the tradition of Protestant reformer John Calvin and its heavy stress on sin. He returns again and again to self-interest as the primary motivator. He speaks of a "sound policy based on human nature." Finally, his anxiety about instability and revolution suggests a strong fear of anarchy. Order must be maintained even if it means a measure of repression.

George has historical evidence to support his case. The tortured course of human history offers ample grounds for realism. But for his colleagues Frank Palmer and Dave Hopkins, George's realism must be too thoroughgoing. For them, mutual accommodation of self-interest, particularly when it refuses to accommodate a majority of the population, cannot be the limit of human creativity and morality. Dave even protests George's realism by citing his involvement in the community. Still George makes reference to no positive norms. Jesus Christ does not seem to make a difference for him in social affairs. Corporate social responsibility for its own sake is apparently too much to expect.

For all his consistency on sin, George is not particularly consistent in apportioning it. While he assumes corporations are motivated by self-interest, he is not nearly as worried about their sin as about Tony's. He overlooks entirely the well-documented evidence of TNC contributions to oppressive conditions in the Third World. He is oblivious to the failure of TNC-led development to decrease Third World poverty. He ignores altogether the sin of the "solid middle class," which partially controls most Third World governments. Indeed, in most Third World countries the middle class George refers to is a small, wealthy elite protecting its own interests. Witness the one water spigot in the Montego Bay slum. In short, George's prescription is to protect the rich and constrain the poor.

HAROLD ATKINS

Harold is the youngest of the trio of businessmen and head of the largest travel consulting firm in the Midwest. The strength of his conviction that corporations have no place in the social welfare business or interfering in Jamaican internal politics may suggest an uncaring attitude. Such a suggestion would be wide of the mark, for Harold makes quite clear his willingness to give as an individual.

The division of individuals and corporations into separate spheres is the driving conception in Harold's scheme of things. Harold, unlike George Delaney, expresses no reluctance to assist Tony. He almost writes a check on the spot out of his personal account. He would not, however, approve a request from the treasurer of his company to issue a check on the corporate account. Individuals may give, but corporations may not.

This division of things into separate spheres is deeply ingrained in Western ways of thinking. It stems among other places from ancient Greek thought with its dualisms of light and dark, mind and body, and good and evil. It informs the U.S. Constitution with its separation of powers and its distinction between church and state. In religious terms it is expressed in the "two-realms" understanding to which Harold himself refers.

Harold argues that corporations have one and only one social responsibility, to make a profit. Profits are the lifeblood of any business enterprise. Without them a business must shut its doors, and when it does, it fails in its ancillary responsibilities to shareholders, employees, customers, and even the public through its incapacity to pay taxes. Profits are also an important signaling device. They tell investors where to put their money so that resources will be efficiently allocated. Harold is certainly correct in one respect. There is little room for romanticism about profits and their link to the production of goods and services. Profits are the first priority of any business in a market economy.

The question, however, is not really about the priority of profits. No one at the lunch table would disagree. Even the absent Tony would probably concur. The question is whether corporations have other social responsibilities. Harold seems to think not.

His full argument, were he to make it, would probably go something like this. The moral responsibility of corporate executives is to produce goods and services and in so doing to serve the interests of the owners. Investors entrust their funds to executives and become owners or shareholders with the expectation of a return. Executives are stewards of these funds and break trust with the owners when they use corporate profits for their own self-selected causes. In effect they levy a tax on the shareholders without giving them representation in the decision. Morally, executives must respect the wishes of shareholders and abstain from trying to do good for them. It is the owners who should be the ones to exercise moral responsibility as they allocate their corporate dividends among competing claims.

Harold might also argue on pragmatic grounds. Using hard won earnings on extraneous social concerns not only reduces profits directly and makes a company less attractive as an investment, but also can indirectly necessitate higher prices to cover higher costs, as with a company taking solitary action to clean up its pollution while competitors continue to pass pollution costs on to the public in dirty air and water. Either way a competitive disadvantage results and with it inefficiency.

On pragmatic grounds Harold might also question Frank Palmer's knee-jerk advocacy of corporate social responsibility. Would Frank really want powerful corporations paternalistically mucking around in the affairs of nations and individuals? The days of the company town are over. Corporations are not well situated to set priorities for governments or to decide complex moral and social issues. More than likely they will set directions in their own narrow self-interest and bungle tasks they have assigned themselves.

Thus for a host of philosophical, moral, and pragmatic reasons Harold would urge corporations to stick to production and money making and let individuals and governments set social priorities.

Theologically, Harold bases his perspective on the call to give, which he would answer individually with personal good deeds and socially with government activity. He also cites the "two-realms" understanding first articulated by Augustine and later developed by Luther. This perspective divides reality into sacred and secular spheres which respectively are governed by God's right and left hands. The right hand of God, exercised in the church, is the hand of faith, hope, and love. Grace, forgiveness, charity, and nonviolence abound in this realm. The left hand of God, exercised by governments and other social institutions, is the hand of order, pragmatic calculation, and justice. Punishment, coercion, and even justifiable violence (the so-called "sword" as a symbol of the ordering function) have important roles to play. These two spheres are distinct, if not separate, and should not be confused. They are held together by the two hands of one God and by individuals who are free to live in both spheres while recognizing their differences.

Corporations as economic institutions are part of the secular realm and are governed by different norms than individuals. The function of corporations is not to love people, which it cannot do anyway, but to order economic life so there are sufficient resources for basic necessities. For corporations to get mixed up in charity or noneconomic social concerns is to confuse the way God has ordered human life. This confusion will lead to disorder and in the end accomplish little. Charity is the province of individuals and groups organized to provide it.

This perspective is well established in the tradition. Yet a too rigid separation of realms, which Harold may be guilty of, misses the subtleties of the traditional two-realms formulation. The realms are not separate. To repeat, they are held together by God and by individuals who carry motives of love and intentions to serve ethically from their personal faith into the social realm. Faith, hope, love, grace, forgiveness, charity, and nonviolence are not irrelevant to the primary economic function of corporations. At the very least corporations can act justly, obey the law, and refrain from causing injury.

Frank Palmer counters Harold's tendency to separate by distinguishing levels of responsibility. He makes a good point. Corporations have different functions and priorities, but God's realm of love, though distinct, is relevant to every level of Harold's work and to the business of his firm. The thorny issue is discerning relevance from distinction and deciding what is the appropriate exercise of corporate social responsibility.

CORPORATE RESPONSIBILITY

Actually a number of mediating possibilities stand between Frank's "either" of full social responsibility and Harold's "or" of limited responsibility. George Delaney articulates one position in spite of its problems. He advocates social responsibility as long as it is consistent with the overall interests of the company, with long-term profit presumably high on his list of interests. Another position would allow for social responsibility if it enhances profitability and would give managerial discretion if it does not.

Harold Atkins's perspective shorn of its theological wraps is usually associated with economist Milton Friedman. In a now classic essay, "The Social Responsibility of Business Is to Increase Its Profits" (*The New York Times Sunday Magazine*, September 13, 1970), Friedman set the case for profits as the exclusive responsibility of corporations. Friedman made many of the same arguments as Harold Atkins. Corporations are not persons. Managers have a moral responsibility to serve stockholders with profits. Individuals and social institutions other than corporations are better situated to set and carry out social priorities.

But even Friedman stepped back from an extreme interpretation of this view. In a little-noticed sentence of his essay, Friedman spoke of profit seeking "while conforming to the basic rules of society, both those embodied in law and those embodied in social custom." Conforming to the law does not substantially change his position, but his openness to social custom certainly makes a difference.

The fact is that most North Americans expect corporations to be ethical. The best run and most profitable firms, as ethicist Charles McCoy points out, are often ones in which values and social responsibility are woven deeply into the corporate fabric. In other words, there is such a thing as corporate character, and ethics flow out of character.

McCoy and others go on to observe that corporations cannot avoid social responsibility. They are so large and powerful that their activities inevitably spill over into noneconomic realms. It is really not so much a matter of "yes" or "no" to social responsibility as it is of being responsible or irresponsible.

Corporations being responsible does not mean they should become flag-waving social activists out front on each and every social cause. Profits are primary in a market system. Corporations cannot meet all the claims placed on them and certainly should not fool themselves about moral purity. Harold Atkins is correct about the exercise of corporate social responsibility.

It can cause competitive disadvantage and injustice and lead to the setting of wrong priorities and to poor execution. All these are considerations which constrain the capacity, if not the imperative, to be moral.

How managers should act in pursuing corporate responsibility is open to debate. At very least there are two moral minimums: to act according to the law and to avoid and correct injury. To follow the law is self-explanatory, however ambiguous it may be at times. To avoid causing injury and to rectify past injuries caused may be as simple as adequate on-the-job safety precautions or as complex as pulling investments out of South Africa. Included in this second minimum is certainly the just treatment of employees and customers.

Beyond this minimum the debate begins. The call to charity and the obligation to lend assistance are strong parts of the Christian tradition, more so when there is a critical need, proximity, capability, and no one present who is better able. The distinctions encountered in the two-realms understanding give pause and to a degree constrain, but do not finally limit this obligation. Jesus Christ is the lord of both realms, and the Christian is called to live ethically as an individual and as a member of social institutions. Life is of a piece, not separated into exclusive spheres.

The forms that corporate responsibility can take are infinite, but four general categories stand out:

1. Self-regulation to avoid or to correct injury.
2. Affirmative action to correct internal corporate abuses and to improve conditions internal and external to the corporation.
3. Leadership in moral causes.
4. Developing corporate character and managing values so that morality permeates the corporation.

In particular the fourth should receive greater attention than it has.

Should Tony then be assisted? It would be a small matter and generous for the three businessmen to open their pockets and give individually. As for a corporate gift, that would also be in order, easily accomplished, and a matter for objection only to those purists who deny any social responsibility for corporations.

In the larger context, however, this apparently simple question raises fundamental and perplexing dilemmas. In terms of the Christian tradition the dilemma is how to connect the poverty and powerlessness of Jesus and his followers to the wealth and might of the modern corporation. In terms of the Third World the dilemma is how to bring poor peasants and urban slum dwellers into a just relationship with TNCs and local elites. The three solutions proposed in the men's club in typical power-broker fashion all rely on charity, although Frank talks vaguely about a coordinated development effort and George about mutual assistance projects. None includes a shift of power and privilege. Tony's overall orientation has seeds for fundamental change, but little is said about power.

Is charity all rich Christians can do to link the worlds of poor and rich? Perhaps corporate responsibility, at least in the Third World, means something more daring: either to take the poor as the point of departure or get out. To take the world's poor as a point of departure would be difficult for TNCs. They have little expertise in meeting the needs of the poor, and, with self-interest as a given, little inclination. The poor have no money to buy their products, and TNCs make high profits with things as they are.

To pull out of Third World situations might then be the responsible path. Jamaica might be better off without the tourist industry. But try to tell Jamaicans that. A few might listen, but whatever else they do, TNCs provide jobs and thereby infuse or at least generate income. They may not be the right kind of jobs, and taking them may mean serving the status quo, but Jamaicans have few alternatives. No institutions are waiting in the wings to infuse large amounts of capital while taking the poor as their point of departure.

This more daring either/or of corporate responsibility is an indictment of TNCs. It is not, however, an indictment of TNC executives as mean-spirited and uncharitable. They are part of a system which has been tremendously productive and meets the material needs of many people. They must be self-interested. The problems they face are systemic. At present, TNC-led market capitalism is not adequately meeting the needs of the world's poor. Sensitive executives feel squeezed between the forces at work. Perhaps one thing they could do is to pay Tony a visit and learn firsthand about conditions in the Third World and the view from the vantage point of the poor.

For the time being, anyway, the two worlds of poor and rich remain alienated and apart. The power of Jesus Christ has not been allowed to trickle down. This leaves Christians themselves squeezed between conflicting perspectives and wondering which alternative is the best to act on in an imperfect world.

ADDITIONAL RESOURCES

Beauchamp, Thomas L., and Norman E. Bowie, eds. *Ethical Theory and Business.* 2nd ed. Englewood Cliffs: Prentice-Hall, 1983.

Friedman, Milton. *Capitalism and Freedom.* Chicago: University of Chicago Press, 1962.

———. "The Social Responsibility of Business Is to Increase Its Profits." *The New York Times Sunday Magazine* (September 13, 1970).

McCoy, Charles S. *Management of Values.* Boston: Pitman, 1985.

Niebuhr, Reinhold. *Moral Man and Immoral Society.* New York: Charles Scribner's Sons, 1932.

Simon, John G., Charles W. Powers, and Jon P. Gunneman. *The Ethical Investor.* New Haven: Yale University Press, 1972.

Case

/o/ll

Foreclosure on the Future

"I just don't know how much more I can take at work, John." Ruth sighed deeply as she sank into the rocker next to her husband. She got no response from John. She looked at him intently. When she left the house that morning, he said he thought he would be able to finish the last of the corn harvest before nightfall. He seemed unusually quiet tonight. She watched him as he read the newspaper.

Ruth had worked for twenty years with the Rural Loan Association in a small Midwestern town. She was a county supervisor responsible for processing loan requests. She had always enjoyed her work and knew all her clients personally. She would get caught up in the excitement of young couples who were just beginning a life together on the farm. She would plan to spend a little extra time when she visited a client's farm. Then she could find out how their children were doing in school, or talk about the recent changes in the grain market, or simply banter about the unpredictable weather. Her clients often invited her and John to the family weddings, baptisms, and graduations. She lived and worked in a very close and supportive community.

BACKGROUND TO THE CRISIS

The mid- to late-1970s were economic boom years for the farmers: market prices were fair and futures looked promising. The government had encouraged farmers to expand and increase their productivity, not only for the sake of the farmers, but also because many thought that rising agricultural exports signaled the answer to worsening balance of trade rates for the United States. As industrial production shifted from the United States to other countries, the United States would counter by exporting food. The Soviets had made several large grain purchases. And food sales to Third

World nations were up as a result of development loans from Middle Eastern nations with excess petroleum dollars. The dollar was weak; thus American exports were cheap abroad. So farmers borrowed heavily to buy better equipment and to increase the size of their livestock herds.

But the boom years were short-lived. Afraid of the effects of continuing inflation, the government had instituted a tight monetary policy which dealt farmers a double blow. It raised the value of the dollar abroad, making American food exports expensive, and it created high interest rates. High interest rates hurt farmers because they not only borrow for capital improvements, but also to fund operations until stored harvests can be sold when the price is highest. The drop in inflation further hurt many farmers by lowering the value of the land they had used as collateral for expansion.

But the major problem for farmers in the 1980s was the drop in market prices. Ruth was convinced that one reason for low prices was overproduction in the absence of sales abroad. But Ruth found out that government farm policy hurt the farmers. Congress set a very low loan price on farm goods. (The loan price is the price per bushel the government guarantees to farmers who participate in the government's set-aside program for curtailing overproduction.) The stated logic was that lower prices would increase foreign sales. The low loan price forced market prices down. In addition Congress gave the administration permission to release government reserves of agricultural goods onto the market. This further lowered prices. At the same time, production costs were soaring and taxes increased. With prices so low, it had cost many farmers more to grow each bushel than they could hope to make by selling. They went deeper into debt with each harvest.

Since 1985 the market price had gone up some, so that more farmers were breaking even, but for many it seemed impossible to escape from the burden of accumulated debt. One after another, farmers were forced to auction their equipment and livestock just to be able to pay the interest on their loans. A few farmers resorted to restoring old horse-drawn implements if they were lucky enough to own a team of horses. From morning to night they walked their fields behind the teams, but in the end, they were just too far in debt to break even.

Homes and property had to be repossessed. Ruth's agency alone held the deeds to eighty houses. With the economy so poor, businesses in town were closing. When farmers in a farming community had no money to buy, the farm equipment dealers, auto dealers, clothing stores, and even grocery stores had few customers and many unpaid bills. Even though some of the repossessed houses could be purchased with little more than the price of the unpaid back taxes, there were no buyers.

FORECLOSING ON OTHERS?

John looked up from his paper. "You know Cy Burke, down at the bank? The paper says he shot himself last night."

Cy Burke had worked at the local bank for seventeen years. Recently he had become more and more withdrawn.

John continued, "They say he had to make so many foreclosures on friends and even family that the pressure finally got to him."

Ruth heard the sadness in John's voice. He and Cy had been friends for a long time. Ruth could well understand the pain and sorrow Cy must have been feeling these last few months. She thought back to her own feelings that very afternoon at her office when Joe Farley came in to discuss his financial situation. Together they had painstakingly gone over the figures again and again. There was just no way he could afford to make the payments that were so long overdue. His wife had recently lost her job in town and there was nothing left to sell, except the land and the home. When he finished signing the repossession forms, he sat back in his chair and began to cry. Ruth choked back her own tears. She had known Joe for a long time. He had a reputation for being an independent man — always able to provide for his family.

"What am I going to do now?" he sobbed. "All your life you give and give and give to the land — believing you'll reap what you sow! Now it's all gone — all gone. I'm fifty-seven years old and all I know how to do is farm. What am I going to do now?"

Ruth was speechless. Her faith had taught her to always trust in the Lord. She had often found comfort in the words from Matthew: "Do not worry about your livelihood, what you are to eat or drink or use for clothing." Yet today there had been little comfort in those words as she watched Joe Farley wipe his eyes on his sleeve, reach out to shake her hand, and then slowly walk out the door.

As Ruth sat silently beside her husband, she reflected on the demands of her job. She worked many hours of overtime just to keep up with the paperwork. It had been that way for years and she was accustomed to it. From time to time, there had been an inevitable foreclosure or bankruptcy. Often it was because a young farmer had tried to get too much too fast and had exceeded the limits of what the land could produce. Luckily, for them, there was always the hope that they could start over again — somewhere. But where could the Joe Farleys of this world go? What hope could anyone offer them?

Ruth had once talked to her pastor about her feelings of hopelessness. "Pastor, what can I say to these people to give them some hope?" He had just shaken his head, bewildered by the complexity of the situation. He said he didn't know the answer. All he could do was pray, and he assured her he would pray for her.

Ruth turned again toward her husband, who looked drawn and ashen tonight. She asked, "Did you finish the corn?" John slowly lifted his head and replied, "Yep. And it's a good crop. With the income from your job we can just make it another year. Isn't it ironic — we can stave off foreclosure because we have a job foreclosing on others? And in the end, it's all for nothing, because we're killing the land to survive, and you can't do that long. All the years of conservation to preserve and improve the land, wasted in just a few years of trying to wring the last dollar out of the land." He leaned back in the recliner and closed his eyes.

That decided it for Ruth. John had his own burdens to bear, and usually wasn't one to talk much about his feelings or his problems. Tonight was not the time to share those from her job with him. She sighed again, gathered her strength to get up, and went to the kitchen to prepare their supper.

Commentary

Foreclosure on the Future

This case presents some very complex problems at a number of different levels. The basic question concerns the structure of U.S. agriculture. Should U.S. farm policy encourage large-scale agribusiness or medium-scale family farms? The answer to this question will involve a great many other policy questions. Should the United States produce more food than it needs, hoping to balance its trade deficits with agricultural exports? What policies are acceptable for promoting foreign markets for food exports? If farmers are made dependent upon government export policies, what obligations does government have to farmers, if any?

Regardless of how we decide these practical issues, this case also presents us with profound theological questions about the nature of Christian community. What obligations do we as individuals, churches, communities, and governments have to those who suffer from shifts in social policy? How do we best minimize pain and suffering to those harmed by such shifts? And last, but certainly not least, where do we as Christians find hope in the midst of disruption and alienation?

STRUCTURING AGRICULTURAL POLICY

Scripture and theology offer a vision of the just community which details the relationships between persons and between land and persons. The Mosaic law offered a vision of human community structured around three concerns, which were echoed in Jesus' words and actions and in Christian theology.

First, the land was understood to belong to God, who entrusted it to Israel for the good of all its people. This understanding of the Israelites as stewards of God's land was remembered in practical ways, and this recognition of land as under God's ownership and human stewardship was basic to Jesus' ministry. When Rome conquered Israel and Judah, Caesar claimed to own the land by conquest, and ordered Jews to pay taxes to Caesar to use it. Jews understood their first-fruits offerings in the Temple as the legitimate form of taxation to the real owner, God. During Jesus' boyhood the Romans had first held a census and then instituted taxation based on the census rolls, despite Jewish opposition and periodic rebellion. When Jesus was asked whether or not Jews should pay taxes to Caesar, he was faced with the most dangerous politico-religious question of his day. He first disarmed his hearers by asking his questioner for a Roman coin, demonstrating that he did not carry such coins and therefore was not a part of Caesar's economy. His ultimate answer, to give to Caesar what was Caesar's and to God what was God's, was not simply clever. For Jewish farmers whose taxes were to be paid in the fruit of the land, his answer confirmed their religious belief that if the land were God's, paying the fruit of the land to Caesar in taxes was idolatrous.

In this case study Farley expresses something of an understanding of stewardship. He understood his farming as a vocation in the religious sense, as his choice of a way in which to devote himself to the activity of God in the world. It was an all-consuming vocation; that was a part of its satisfaction. Part of his pain comes from an inability to understand how such a vocation can be lost. How can a life of stewarding God's earth, undertaken with relative sacrifices of time, energy, and wealth, be found unworthy?

A second aspect of the scriptural vision of community is an overriding concern for justice. Justice is more than merely obeying law; it is to participate in God's intentions. Justice therefore encompasses not only equity between individuals, but also compassion for the needy and a concern for the quality of communal life. The law demanded a basic equity: the courts and officials were to treat the rich and poor alike, and merchants were to use the same scales for everyone, not robbing the weak. The oath of a poor person was to be as respected as that of a rich person. And yet there were special protections for the poor and the weak. God's law for Israelite society insisted that there was to be no permanent underclass. Not only was enslavement for debt limited to seven years regardless of the size of the debt, but the law provided that every fifty years, in the Jubilee year, debts were to be cancelled, slaves were to be freed, and land was to be returned to the original owners. If the Jubilee law were carried out, no single family or group of families would ever control vast holdings to the detriment of the rest.

On farms the entire crop was never to be harvested, so that the poor could glean the edges of the fields and the last of the vineyards lest they go hungry in winter. The law gave hope for surviving misfortune on a day-to-day basis, as well as hope for a new start free of slavery and debt. The law implemented this vision not only by demanding that individuals treat each other with justice and compassion, but also by demanding that social institutions and the authorities which controlled them enforce these provisions.

A third insistence of Mosaic law was that the welfare of the community rested not only on just access to resources, but on the cultivation and conservation of resources. The law enjoined farmers to let fields lie fallow every seven years so that the land would regain its fertility. Fruit trees and vineyards were not to be harvested until they were mature, lest their strength be sapped. According to the law, land is the basis of community prosperity; it must be treated with respect, not used up and drained of its life-giving power. Land is a gift for all generations. In this case, John is disturbed that in the present crisis farming techniques are using up the land rather than conserving its fruitfulness out of recognition of its integrity. Theological reflection in the Judeo-Christian community has often joined the understanding of stewardship with that of land conservation. This is especially true in the modern treatment of private property, where private property is understood as a provisional right only, which could possibly be revoked if the land is not used to meet serious needs of the community now and in the future.

ANALYZING PRESENT REALITY

The process now at work in U.S. agriculture bears some remarkable similarities to that in Jesus' time. Two aspects in particular are striking: that of consolidation of farms under absentee owners, and that of large-scale displacement of farmers. Galilee, where Jesus lived, was dominated by farming. It was a rich agricultural area but high Roman taxes were accelerating the displacement of small subsistence farmers in favor of large estates producing cash crops for export, a process begun in the eighth century B.C. The large estates were owned by wealthy absentee Romans and Jews, who hired stewards to manage the estates. The small-scale farmers who once owned the land could either remain in the area as itinerant day laborers or swell the ranks of unemployed beggars in the cities. Many dispossessed farmers and descendants of displaced farmers were attracted to the anti-Roman guerrillas, the Zealots, who were strong in Galilee.

Today family farms which are lost to unpaid debt are not being bought by other families breaking into farming, but by corporations or wealthy individuals who hire managers to run large farms on which the owners do not live. Such ownership patterns undermine local communities. Town businesses—groceries, hardware stores, insurance agencies, drugstores, local newspapers—suffer from the lower numbers of farmers who patronize them, and absentee owners have little interest in supporting local communities.

Land conservation practices also suffer under corporate farming whether in poor nations or rich ones. The corporate motivation for farming is profit. The owners are not committed to a particular farm or local community; they do not intend to live there, raise their children there, make local friends, and pass on the farm as a legacy to their children. Because the farm unit, however large, is usually only one small part of the corporation's holdings, the emphasis is often on short-term profit. When the farm unit loses money, those losses can be used to lower taxes on high profits elsewhere, and ultimately the land is sold, with the capital transferred to some other high-profit enterprise. Land conservation limits high short-term profit, and is seldom a concern to businesspeople, who are accustomed to dealing with nonrenewable resources which are replaced when they wear out.

Today farming requires huge capital investment, tremendous acreage, and high levels of mechanization. Family farmers seem to lack economy of scale. Many people believe that corporate farming patterns are inevitable because family farms are not equally efficient. In this view, the displacement of farmers is regrettable, but necessary for progress, from which all will benefit. If one accepts this view, then the real issues are how to minimize the suffering of those caught in the transition between these patterns of agriculture.

But before one can reach such a conclusion one must analyze whether we can ever say that such a transition is inevitable. As the case made clear, the government has been a major actor in this drama, and has acted in many ways as the indirect employer of the farmer by setting the conditions under which farming has occurred: prices, interest rates, export policies, reserve policies. That is to say, the crisis occurred in a situation structured by a series of direct government decisions. Upon examination, it is doubtful that these decisions were undertaken with adequate understanding of the consequences and risks involved.

Government policy in agriculture has focused for many years on controlling overproduction. U.S. farmers produce far more food than the U.S. population can consume. This constitutes a problem for government because it complicates its dual goals of seeing that farmers get a market price which makes farming attractive, at the same time that consumers pay the lowest possible price for food. Overproduction suits consumers because it lowers prices, but if the prices get too low, producers will stop producing. Managing overproduction has been the government's role. This is how the government got into the set-aside program and setting loan prices for stored crops. It is also how the government came to own the largest grain reserves in the world. These reserves represent hope for hungry victims of disaster around the world, but as we have seen already, in poor nations their existence and use can be problematic. In particular, care must be taken in the construction of reserve policy to see that farmers in the United States get adequate prices.

One basic issue for government policy is whether U.S. farmers should only produce what the people of the country could foreseeably need, or whether they should produce for export also. If the decision is to export, the government needs to ask some hard questions about stimulating export sales. Since P.L. 480, sometimes called the Food for Peace program, became law in 1954, U.S. policy has aimed at disposing of dangerous overproduction by providing gifts, low-cost sales, and trades of U.S. food products to food-needy nations. Some small part of the resources governed by P.L. 480 has gone to disaster relief, but most of those resources have gone to bolster foreign policy objectives in nations such as Korea, Vietnam, Cambodia, and El Salvador. Regardless of the identity of the receiver nation, the effect of P.L. 480, Title 1—by which 80 percent of the commodities have been disposed—has been to undermine local farmers in receiver nations.

The displacement of family farmers by large corporate farms in Third World nations is connected to U.S. concessional food sales, and together they cause an increase of hunger in the world. When land in poor nations moves to corporate farming, it is often used not to raise food for farmers and local consumers, but put to cash crops for export, a decision often endorsed by local governments who are starved for the necessary foreign exchange earned by export. Governments in poor nations often keep the cost of staple foods for the urban poor, many of whom are displaced farmers, low by controlling the price; U.S. policies of selling farm surplus to foreign nations at prices well below market aid many poor nations in supplying cheap food. The overall effect of such policies, however, is to discourage farmers, especially small farmers in poor nations, from growing food crops for local consumption because they cannot make a living selling food at the discount price set by U.S. concessional sales programs. Small farmers are then forced to either sell out or turn to cash crops, too. As this process continues, poor nations become ever more food dependent on foreign sources. Hunger increases because there are limits to the amount of bargain food from the United States, and imported food from other sources to supply the additional need is so expensive as to be beyond the ability of most people to pay. In some places the result is tragically ironic: small farmers who used to raise a variety of foods for their own and local consumption now become malnourished because the cost of food has risen beyond the limits of the income they earn from selling their cash crop. Such food-dependency of Third World nations on the United States was considered the answer to U.S. overproduction and a boon to U.S. economic and diplomatic power until the debt crisis of the last two decades left few poor countries able to buy food at any price.

CRITERIA FOR CHOOSING SOCIAL POLICY

The United States needs a food policy which encourages itself and all its trading partners to attempt general food self-sufficiency. No nation should export food when its own people are hungry, as is currently occurring all over the world. This violates stewardship and justice. The United States needs to continue to hold a thirty-day grain reserve for famine relief at the same time it encourages other nations to establish reserves as they are able.

Since the international goal of the United States should be general food self-sufficiency, it should not aim at *creating* new markets abroad, and therefore needs to cut down production. This could be done in a variety of ways, but whatever is decided, land conservation should be a high priority. Increased rates of erosion, the cutting of trees which provide windbreaks and hold soil in place, disastrous lowering of the water table in many areas, and chemical pollution of water, soil, and air should be stopped. Attention must also be paid to the processing of food products which often adds more to the cost of food than does the price paid the farmer, while cutting the nutritive value and taste of food.

Within these overall constraints, we need to decide as a society whether the medium-scale family farm or large-scale agribusiness is more compatible with our long-term interests. There are many other areas of long-range planning which will impact farming in the years to come. Some cities, especially in the Southwest, worried about water availability in the decades to come, are buying large tracts of farmland with a view to siphoning off their water resources in the future. Food processing and retail sales are increasingly becoming monopolized by large firms, as are agricultural supply businesses. What dangers for consumers lie in the prospect of food production also moving into the hands of a few powerful corporations? Are there ways of preventing such monopolies or of controlling their power? Where is the size limit between family farming and corporate farming? Is it measured in numbers of owners, numbers of acres/square miles, or numbers of farm workers on a farm?

HOPE AMIDST DISASTER

Regardless of the decision about the overall direction of U.S. farm policy, there needs to be immediate action to help those caught in the present disaster. Local, state, and federal agencies of all kinds must coordinate aid. Farmers who lose their farms in bankruptcy proceedings must be allowed to retain a stake that will allow them to start again, even if outside farming. Special priority should be given to those who with minimal financial assistance could maintain their farms and be self-sufficient. Retraining should be available for the displaced, and coalitions between different levels of government, agriculture-based businesses, social service agencies, churches, and local groups should seek ways of minimizing the need for relocation, especially for older farmers.

Churches, especially, must cooperate with local social service agencies to provide spiritual and psychological support to victims and to be alert for depression and suicidal drift within the community. One of the most appalling points of this case is the inability of the minister to respond to Mary's appeal for some words of hope.

It is very striking that in this case all the individuals seem to be facing their crises alone, without human solidarity. Even Mary and John do not share their concerns with each other. Mary cannot talk to her tragedy-stricken neighbors as she works with them. The anguish expressed by Farley is repeated all over the community, and yet we see no one able to respond, no programs to attempt to help people respond to their own pain and that of their neighbors. The minister can only offer private prayer. It is almost unbelievable that John has to read in the newspaper that his friend killed himself the day before. In a small community such failures of communication occur only when the natural communication system has been shut down. This happens when people have retreated inside themselves because they do not know how to express or respond to their own pain or the painful situations of others that the communication system presents. John seems to have withdrawn not only from his friends, but from Mary as well. And she decides not to disturb him, but to leave him withdrawn.

In dealing with the potential for despair in this case a major task of the church is to free farmers of paralyzing guilt. Because the consequences of the situation fall on the farmers, it is natural for them to wonder if they brought the disaster on themselves and are being punished for their sins. They need to see that they played only a part in this disaster, and must forgive themselves that part if they are to save themselves from the paralysis of guilt and be able to act together as a community to secure the best possible outcome. Like Job, they are called to hold fast to both their convictions of their own righteousness and their faith that God is with them in their time of trial.

Jesus agreed with Job that misfortune was not proof of having sinned. This was why he insisted that neither the blind young man of John 9 nor his parents had caused his blindness through sin. Jesus himself was a sign of hope to his followers. Through him they were put in touch with the love and forgiveness of God. Jesus' resurrection is the symbol of Christian hope, a sign that God can overcome sin and death. They are not yet overcome, but the possibility is there. The times in our lives when we see little resurrections, signs of God at work in the world through people coming together to act in love against sin and suffering—these are the sources of Christian hope.

We do not often understand this. Too often we look to the far horizon for signs of hope rather than to our own lives. We look for signs that the world is making clear and rapid progress toward the reign of God. We look for proof that such progress is continuing and inevitable, and when such proof is not forthcoming, we despair of hope. In this case we might be tempted to look for hope in a comprehensive overhaul of U.S. farm policy. This would certainly be welcome. But Christians cannot demand such riches as a precondition for hope.

Truly Christian hope is tentative. It is based, not in certainty that sin is about to be vanquished, but in the small victories over sin. Christian hope needs to be constantly renewed. This is its strength, not its weakness. Our need for hope to keep us going in love should drive us to recognize and celebrate the small victories and to participate in action which creates more of those victories. In this case the community must begin to act as a community, to reach out to one another, to listen to each other's grief, and be with the suffering. Out of this experience of shared suffering the community must begin to respond to the crisis, to organize, to involve organizations and institutions at the local, state, and national levels. Christian hope encourages not passive waiting for God's reign, but active involvement. This is where Mary needs to look for hope.

In many ways it is in situations of disaster that we uncover and examine our faith and its basis. Too often it takes a crisis to demonstrate that the faith of humans is as self-interested as Satan in the book of Job insisted it was. We offer worship and belief to God as the price for keeping us safe and protected from suffering, as if we can bribe God with our faithfulness. In fact, faith does not keep us from suffering; the faithful are just as prone to disease and death, bankruptcy and injustice. What faith offers is a way to live through suffering with the support of God and neighbor, a way to resist suffering and not be destroyed by it.

ADDITIONAL RESOURCES

Echegaray, Hugo. *The Practice of Jesus.* Maryknoll, N.Y.: Orbis, 1984.

Nelson, Jack A. *Hunger for Justice: The Politics of Food and Faith.* Maryknoll, N.Y.: Orbis, 1981.

Platt, Lavonne Godwin, ed. *Hope for the Family Farm: Trust God and Care for the Land.* Newton, Kans.: Faith and Life Press, 1987.

Reeves, Don. "Responding to the Farm Crisis." Bread for the World Background Paper no. 98, June 1987. Available from: Bread for the World, 802 Rhode Island Ave., NE, Washington, DC 20018.

PART VI

MEDICINE

Case

Baby Boy Hernandez

Mary Flemming closed her office door trying to shut out any more interruptions to her morning. She had a difficult staff meeting in thirty minutes and wanted to finish the outline for a paper she was presenting as an incoming officer of the State Hospital Administrators Association.

As the Associate Administrator for Medical Care at Oglethorpe Memorial Hospital, Mary's responsibilities included oversight of one of the five regional neonatal intensive care units in the state. In light of increasing fiscal problems, Mary had been asked to address issues of funding for neonatal care.

Mary glanced through her notes, aware of the dramatic changes in care for newborns over the past four years after the hospital had been designated as a regional neonatal center. As a matter of fact, the excellent neonatal program at Memorial had been a significant factor in luring Mary from her previous position. The State Department of Human Resources in collaboration with the Council on Maternal and Infant Health had identified and awarded federal funds to select hospitals for renovations, equipment, staff, and newborn transport vehicles. Mary was convinced that under the direction of Dr. Sam McBride, Memorial had one of the best neonatal units in the South.

The effects of the program had been dramatic. Although it was still the state's number one health problem, infant mortality had dropped 25 percent after the system was established. There was a parallel drop in the number of premature infants with permanent mental and physical handicaps. When Mary had first come to Memorial, it was a thrill for her to see those little babies survive. The whole unit rejoiced with the families, and Mary remembered the heartwarming letters she and members of the staff had received from grateful parents. Memorial was saving an average of

This case was prepared by William P. Bristol and Alice Frazer Evans. Copyright © The Case Study Institute. The names of all places and persons have been disguised to protect the privacy of the individuals involved in this situation.

seventy-five babies a year who would have died without specialized care.

But in the past few years Mary felt that problems with the unit had begun to outweigh the benefits. As the technology had improved, smaller and smaller babies began to survive. And as the birth weight went down, the incidence of long-term complications and the cost of care went up. Mary checked back over her files for the previous year. During that year Memorial had admitted over fifty infants weighing less than one thousand grams (slightly over two pounds). The cost of care for some ran as high as $90,000 per infant, with an average cost of $12,000. The real squeeze came because a disproportionate number of mothers with SGA (small for gestational age) babies sent to Memorial from Comstock and other county hospitals were indigent with no medical insurance whatever. In the early years of the program, the $5,000 per infant state subsidy for these babies was significant; today it hardly seemed to make a dent. On top of that the state funds available to Memorial ran out completely a little more than halfway into the fiscal year. With the present state budget squeeze, Mary had little hope that additional funds would be allotted to neonatal care. With the skyrocketing cost per infant, the end result was a cut in state funds.

In the past Mary could have charged some indigent cases off to the Department of Child Services. She knew her predecessor had even charged some to the old migrant worker program that the state ran during the seventies. When she had first come to Memorial, Mary had been able to elevate costs in some areas to absorb the losses, but both federal and insurance programs were now designing regulations to prevent cost shifts. Increasingly, patients of independent means were going to the smaller, private hospitals for maternal care. Last year, counting overhead costs, Memorial's Neonatal Intensive Care Unit lost over a million dollars. Mary knew the hospital, specifically her department, was faced with some serious decisions. And, she ruefully realized, she had been dumb enough to agree to address the issue before her colleagues at next week's association meeting. They were all aware of the problem; she had to come up with some answers.

Mary glanced at her watch and realized she was due at the neonatology staff meeting. Twice a week various members of the staff gathered for what was called "the patient planning meeting." More often, Mary mused, it could be described as a battle royal. Baby Boy Hernandez was today's topic. Mary muttered to herself as she hurried down the hall, silently swearing at Comstock County Hospital for dumping another nonpaying obstetric case on Memorial. This Hernandez baby alone had run up a bill approaching $40,000, and Sam McBride still didn't have the kid off the respirator. Migrant workers like Anita Hernandez had always been a problem in this part of the state. They had no money, no insurance, and rarely spoke English.

Most of the staff showed up on time although two nurse representatives had just been called away to a "code." As they gathered around the coffee table in the small lounge next to the nursery, Mary nodded to Sam McBride, young Corey Blake, Mrs. Darden—the chief ward clerk of the neonatal unit—and several house staff Mary was sure Sam had dragged along to the meeting. Mary watched Sam as he joked with the pediatric interns he was supervising. Corey sat alone at the edge of the group.

Corey Blake was the midwifery student who had delivered Baby Hernandez in the ambulance on the way from County Hospital. She spoke Spanish fluently. Blake had pulled some minor miracle in just getting the baby from Comstock to the unit. A Furman graduate, she had earned her RN and then spent time as a nurse in the Southwest with a missionary group. Her parents lived in Atlanta, and she had returned to Emory to enter their two-year midwifery program which was now receiving state funding. Mary knew Corey had originally intended to return to New Mexico, but her field supervisor at Memorial was encouraging her to stay. In a private personnel review with Corey's supervisor, Mary remembered her saying that there were certainly enough poor, pregnant women in the surrounding counties to keep Blake happy for all of her days. Everybody in the county seemed poor since the recession hit and the textile mill closed in Comstock.

When Mary had encouraged the hospital board to accept the midwife supervision program at Memorial, she wasn't averse to the income or the promise of more if additional state funding came through. She also saw the logic of programs directed to low-cost preventative medicine that the midwives were being trained to deliver. Mary was aware of a major Institute of Medicine study in process. Early findings were clear. Low birth weight babies (2500 grams or less) were forty times more likely to die than normal weight babies and had increased risk of long-term handicaps. Inadequate prenatal care appeared to be directly linked to low birth weight. Corey's program focused on this kind of care, especially for poor, nonwhite women. Studies indicated there were as many as two thousand indigent, high-risk pregnant women in the six counties surrounding Memorial. Mary saw the long-term logic of putting state funds here. But she wasn't sure yet that midwives were the answer.

Mary knew that in spite of her skill, Corey Blake had a hard time being accepted by the medical staff. She recalled a conversation she had overheard between two interns about "those damn midwives." It wasn't that they disliked Corey—"she was pretty enough"—but all she preached was "feeding the poor" and "vitamins." And in spite of her license, she would never be able to handle any "real emergencies."

Mary shifted her attention to Sam McBride as Sam called the group together. In Mary's estimation, Sam was a fine doctor. An Emory graduate, he had taken his pediatric training in Pennsylvania before returning to the state university as a fellow in neonatology. He had been hired by Memorial nine years ago to head the neonatology staff. Late one night over coffee Sam had shared with Mary some "war stories" of his first years at the hospital. Those were the heydays in the development of neonatal care. New techniques coming out every day, survival rates of the mid-weight babies were excellent, and the neonatologists were a fun, swashbuckling group. No one complained that the annual meetings were held at Aspen; they were all good skiers. Underneath that jovial exterior, Mary knew Sam had not only the skill but a driving passion for saving the babies.

Sam opened the meeting with a frank discussion of the Hernandez baby's current and future problems. The infant, barely thirty-two weeks, was small for gestational age, SGA. He had developed a refractory hypoglycemia and respiratory distress syndrome (RDS) necessitating a respirator. Then as the baby's RDS got better, he went into heart failure due to lack of closure of the ductus arteriosis. Sam added that even five years ago most kids didn't live long enough to be troubled with a patent ductus arteriosis (PDA). As of this morning, his hypoglycemia and hyperbilirubinemia were under control and the RDS was getting better. But the boy was not weaning well from the respirator and Sam feared long-term respiratory complications. The PDA showed no sign of closing despite aggressive medical therapy, but Sam was not yet willing to call in the cardiac surgeons. Most importantly, the baby's nutrition was lousy and the only weight he seemed to be gaining was water weight. Hyperalimentation was plagued with complications, but it seemed the only reasonable route to get the child through this nutritional crisis. Sam wished his mother had eaten better.

During this long discourse, Mary Flemming had become increasingly upset. She struggled to keep her voice under control. "Dr. McBride, do you have any idea what this gift from the county is costing us—not only in terms of dollars, but staff time and energy? We've got to consider the broad picture. Many more cases like this one and you ultimately threaten the very survival of the hospital. Is there any possibility you can transfer him back to Comstock County Hospital?"

Sam McBride did not respond to Mary's question. Instead, he turned to Corey and asked her to tell the staff what she knew about Anita Hernandez. Corey glanced quickly at both Mary and Sam McBride. Her initial hesitancy soon turned to confidence as she began to share her observations. Ms. Hernandez should have gone home long ago, wherever home would be for her now, but she had not done well following her delivery. Although Anita told Corey that she was twenty-two, she looked more like sixteen and was really very frail and underweight. She also smoked constantly, a habit that Corey was obviously not going to change since the woman had no reason to trust her judgment.

Corey continued: "As you all know, following delivery, Anita developed a pelvic infection; it was pretty rough for a few days until we brought the sepsis under control. But this did give me a chance to talk to Anita about her life. She had been born down around Harlingen, Texas, and had been making the trek north and east following the sun. She ended up here weeding peanuts and processing peaches. This was her second pregnancy. Her first baby, a girl, lives with her grandmother just south of Harlingen. The baby was very pretty in the picture, a chubby three-year-old with gorgeous eyes. Quite a contrast to Anita right now."

Corey paused a minute and then added that there was one thing that particularly bothered her. Anita didn't go down to the nursery to see her son very often and she hadn't named him yet. She paused again briefly and then continued: "I guess I need to say too that I don't know where she'll go when she leaves the hospital. She won't be strong enough to work for several weeks. There's a good possibility this baby will be physically handicapped as long as he lives. This will be a tremendous burden for Anita." Corey's voice became stronger. "I know you all realize that in our surrounding counties there are hundreds of women in worse shape than Anita. I spend most of my days in the county clinics and in the shacks where our rural poor people live. Between the mill closings and the crop failures, there are people out there starving to death."

Before Mary or other members of the staff could respond, a nurse hurried into the lounge to call Dr. McBride. In the nursery the cardiac arrest alert sounded shrill in contrast to the monotonous beeps of the other monitors. There was a flurry of surgical green as the nurses went to work on Baby Boy Hernandez.

The staff meeting was postponed until further notice. Mary Flemming walked slowly back to her office.

Commentary

Baby Boy Hernandez

From Mary Flemming's perspective there are two questions posed in this case. One is what kind of care Baby Boy Hernandez should receive. The other is how to make the neonatal unit financially secure. In Flemming's mind, these two questions are closely connected. Both of these questions in turn provoke other questions. Who should decide the fate of this child and others like him? On what criteria should the decision be based? Should the financial security of the neonatal unit, and perhaps the hospital, be secured by limiting access to the unit to those who can pay? These latter questions raise an issue that Flemming does not consider, but which underlies all the others: Is the overall health care delivery system, of which this neonatal unit forms a small part, one which is just and equitable?

SCRIPTURAL AND THEOLOGICAL RESOURCES

Scripture can be a powerful source of Christian values relevant to this case. Though it does not directly address issues in medical technology, scripture has a great deal to say about the value of life and the place of death in life. For scripture, life is more than existence alone. When Deuteronomy 30:19 says "choose life," it explains the choice of life over death as a choice for goodness, for loving God, for keeping God's laws, for community, for prosperity and achieving fullness of life. Physical life is not the ultimate value. Stories in the Old Testament make clear that individual life, while valuable, can be sacrificed in the interest of the quality of life of the community; war and capital punishment are taken for granted in the stories of the patriarchs, the Exodus, and in the Mosaic law. Within Israel the Mosaic law was to ensure that the life of the poor and powerless was respected by the rich and powerful. This included provisions such as one that stated that the poor be allowed to glean the edges of the fields of the rich (Lev. 19:9–10) and one that declared that the cloak of the poor man not be taken overnight as security for loans (Deut. 24:10–13). David's killing of Uriah in order to hide his adultery with Bathsheba was a scandal not merely because he shed blood, but because he abused the power entrusted in him by Yahweh by killing another in his charge (2 Sam. 11–12).

Many of Israel's laws were based in prohibitions on idolatry. One such command was that the Israelites not sacrifice children (Deut. 18:10), as their pagan neighbors did in the dedication of their public buildings in order to appease the gods who threatened earthquake, winds, and lightning. If we interpret this prohibition literally, as merely forbidding the killing of children on altars to pagan gods, we fail to understand scripture as relevant to our lives. The purpose of the prohibition was to remind us that social institutions are not to be secured by the sacrifice of innocent life. Rather, for the law, the purpose of social institutions was to safeguard the life of persons and community.

According to the Gospels, Jesus, too, understood life in broader terms than mere individual existence, or he would never have risked — deliberately and repeatedly — his own death in order to carry out his mission of announcing the reign of God (Mark 9:30–32; Luke 9:43–45; Matt. 17:22–23, 20:17–19). Furthermore, he clearly calls his apostles, in the name of fullness of life, to risk death (Luke 21:12–18; Matt. 10:34–39; Mark 13:9–13). Though each of us is also called to discipleship, we can only make the decision to risk ourselves. Thus, while life is not for the follower of Jesus the ultimate value, Jesus gives no support for deciding to end the life of *another* person in the name of a higher value. The decision that one should die in the interests of the many was that of Caiaphas, the high priest responsible for the death of Jesus (John 18:14).

Though the Gospels detail Jesus' many warnings of the judgment to come for groups who exploit or mislead the poor and weak (such as the scribes and Pharisees, or the moneychangers in the Temple), he himself refused to judge and condemn individuals. He not only refused to condemn the adulterous woman, but he intervened to stop the crowd from stoning her as the law prescribed (John 8:11). He refrained from condemning his own betrayer (John 13:18–30), and promised salvation to the thief crucified beside him (Luke 23:43). If Jesus was not willing to condemn the guilty, can it be legitimate to condemn the innocent?

The theological traditions of Christianity reflect scriptural traditions concerning the value of life and the need to protect the life and welfare of the weak. From early times Christianity condemned infanticide. Furthermore, in the development of the just war teaching, the church placed both women and children in the protected category of noncombatants who were to have total immunity from war. The theological and moral teachings most directly relevant to this case are twentieth-century teachings in medical ethics. Among Roman Catholics, the 1952 distinction made by Pope Pius XII between ordinary and extraordinary means of preserving life gave what seemed to be helpful criteria to the debate about euthanasia. Pius maintained that there are extraordinary measures of preserving life which are not morally required. For many in medical ethics even outside of Catholicism there followed two decades where this was the standard often used — that ordinary means of preserving life, such as food, water, oxygen, and common medications could not be denied to the sick/dying, but that extraordinary measures, such as mechanical respirators, food tubes, radiation, and surgery, or experimental techniques in general, were not required.

This teaching was easily applied at both ends of the treatment spectrum. It supported standard medical practice, which insisted that the poor, the retarded, and the otherwise defenseless had moral rights to ordinary medical care which could not be denied. On the other hand, for seriously ill patients who wanted to be allowed to die without painful or intrusive interventions which could only possibly or minimally extend their lives, the teaching made clear to what extent families and medical personnel could accommodate their wishes. The teaching was understood as objective, as concentrated on means of preserving life, rather than on complicated subjective judgments of quality and length of life.

There were always problems with this teaching. One which became obvious in succeeding decades is that advances in medical science tremendously alter what medical personnel understand as ordinary and extraordinary measures of preserving life. What was extraordinary a decade ago is standard today. At any given time, it may be difficult to judge whether a particular treatment is ordinary or not. Innumerable surgeries and mechanical techniques which used to be experimental are now routine.

Some analysts of our health care system point out that another problem with the ordinary/extraordinary teaching is that it functions to justify the provision of a higher quality of health care to the rich than to the poor. Everyone is to have access to ordinary measures of preserving life, but within a capitalist society, the voluntary nature of extraordinary measures serves to make them dependent upon the ability to pay. This is certainly the case with Baby Boy Hernandez. The infant unit is understood to provide extraordinary measures of care, far above the standard care of other hospitals. The child whose right to the care is questioned is the one who cannot pay.

Recognition of both these problems with the ordinary/extraordinary teaching has led to an unwillingness on the part of the medical profession in the last twenty years to decide treatment on the basis of means alone. Instead, there has been a shift toward joining the means issue with an evaluation of the possible benefits of treatments weighed against the counter-indications for the treatment. Sometimes this consequential evaluation is done on medical grounds alone; more recently medical ethics has moved toward incorporating more perspectives in this evaluation, as we see by the varied personnel involved in the conference described in our case. Chancy or experimental treatments are more likely to be morally required when they offer the possibility of restoring full life and health with minimum pain and risk.

RIGHT TO DECIDE

Also of great interest in the theological/moral literature on preserving threatened life is the question of who makes the decision. Cases where patients are not competent to choose for themselves are the most difficult. In such cases, treatment is usually decided by the parents or close relatives in conjunction with the medical staff. In this case Anita Hernandez, the mother and natural guardian, may be either uninterested in or incapable of representing the best interests of the child. The decision may have been shifted to the hospital team by default. This is a difficult position for medical personnel, for the presumption in their training is that they deal with a competent patient or relative whom they can expect to represent the psychological, relational, and personal values of the patient, while the medical staff represents the medical interests of the patient. Only relatively recently has it been recognized that medical personnel also inevitably represent their own interests and the interests of the institution as well as the medical interests of the patient. These interests can sometimes conflict.

In this case Corey Blake, a member of the hospital staff, is the spokesperson for the relational situation of the child. As she presents the situation, the mother does not seem interested in the child and is hard-pressed to care for herself. The child will probably have serious long-term medical problems. It would be easy to be swayed by the fact that the person who presents this grim analysis is the member of the staff who has dedicated herself to medical care for the poor and who was earliest involved with the mother and child. There is temptation to see Corey as the natural advocate of the child. If even she cannot make a good case for continuing care, then who could? But Corey also represents a midwife program, a primary care health program which is here appended to a major institution devoted to emergency medical intervention. From the perspective of primary health care, priority funding should be aimed at ensuring that all have basic nutrition, vitamins, vaccinations, sanitation, and health monitoring, so that the need for emergency intervention is greatly reduced. In this case, Corey's program is now funded largely by the university and the state, with hope for additional state funding. Midwifery is understood by the staff as unequal in the real work of emergency intervention, and more or less peripherally valuable. Corey, more than anyone else, may feel threatened by the financial burden this baby poses, since hers may be one of the programs most vulnerable to state financial cuts.

Even if Corey were to become an advocate for the child, there are other factors undermining such advocacy. By reason of both her sex and her professional credentials Corey is not accepted as the equal of some of the other members of the professional staff. Even if she were strongly to advocate prolonging the life of the child, the description of her relationship with male medical personnel—who describe her as "pretty enough"—suggests that she might not be taken seriously unless she were to resort to stereotypical feminine attempts at persuasion, i.e., flirtation or seduction. While such an attempt may or may not be effective in the short run, it would threaten not only her dignity and self-respect, but make it impossible for her to earn professional respect from the male staff in the future.

Is there an advocate for this child? And if there were, on what criteria should advocacy be based? On an absolute right to life, whatever the social and medical conditions? On an equal right to the quality of care given children who can pay? Or only on a strictly medical evaluation that this child has a good chance to live and grow in a normal life?

SOCIAL ANALYSIS

If we apply social analysis to this case the issue which immediately emerges is that the question of whether to allow this child to die would not have arisen if the parents were able to pay for his care. Within a health care system designed, as ours is, around centers which specialize in emergency intervention, treatment is both therapeutic and experimental. That is, the treatment of newborns is designed not only to save this particular child but to thereby develop new techniques which save future newborns. Specialized units such as this one have greater success than ordinary hospitals precisely because they can call on greater experience in experimenting with technique. Such experimental systems, however, have no internal brake. They are inherently inflationary, as the number of possible interventions is exponentially increased over time, and it becomes difficult to discover *medical* reasons not to expand treatment constantly. The only brakes are financial, so that treatment expands until there is no more money to support its maintenance or expansion. Preservation of such units is often understood to be essential because of their proven success in saving babies, so financial limits often press administrators to see the problem in terms of limiting access. Since the threat is financial, the most obvious criterion for limiting access is ability to pay.

Critics maintain that such a system ensures that public monies support centers from which the disadvantaged end up being excluded, thus perpetuating their disadvantaged status. Our health care system, because it is organized around such specialized intervention centers, tends to neglect basic health care and to support high levels of care for only part of the population. This is why we have the ironic situation of being the nation which represents the apex of sophisticated techniques for saving newborns at the same time that we have one of the highest infant mortality rates in the developed world; sixteen nations have lower rates than ours. If the purpose of our system were to save as many lives as possible and to ensure the health of the greatest numbers, the available funds would be spent on relatively inexpensive diagnosis and treatment of the most common health problems, rather than on high technology interventions for the few.

When we understand that present medical personnel are trained and employed in the high-tech system, which also supports employment in high-tech equipment industries and the construction and insurance industries, we can see a large interest group supporting the present system. In our case, the medical conferences held in skiing resorts across the country illustrate this point. Those elements which are best rewarded by the present system — doctors, administrators, and industrial and insurance executives — are those who are best organized to wield political power and are recognized by media and government as the experts in the field of medicine. But support for the present system is not merely a matter of self-interest on the part of those employed within it.

The present system is also the one geared to produce astounding breakthroughs in medical science. The quest for new knowledge and techniques which will save lives is a major attraction of the present system for researchers and inventors, as Mary Flemming makes clear in speaking of Sam McBride, the head of the neonatal unit. Such people are willing to work long hours, expend great energy, and often dedicate themselves to their work. The work is exciting, it is fast evolving, and the gratification that comes from saving frail underweight babies is both immense and immediate. The system is set up to support this scientific quest, which has far outstripped the ability of the system to distribute the products of the quest to the entire population.

REACHING A DECISION

What seems to be happening in this case is that the question of how to treat the Hernandez baby is being conflated with the question of how to balance the neonatal unit's budget. This seems to be a mistake. What kind of treatment the Hernandez baby should receive should not be determined on the basis of the financial health of the neonatal unit. Treatment should be decided using the same criteria which are used for all the other infants in the neonatal unit. The criteria which should be applied to all the infants will certainly be influenced by the financial resources of the neonatal unit. This seems necessary and appropriate.

Furthermore, the resources available to the neonatal unit should not represent the sum of the funds available for maternal and infant care. The basic needs of some should not be neglected in favor of the extraordinary needs of others. This is not a matter of equalizing spending for all infants; the most threatened have a primary claim on our care and resources. But among those infants who are threatened, spending should be allocated so as to save the largest possible number in the fullest manner possible.

It is not possible to completely equalize medical care for the poor and the non-poor, just as it is impossible to equalize education or housing for the poor and the non-poor, for none of these services exists in a vacuum; they are all interrelated. Even if the neonatal unit is able to keep this child alive in the short term, because it is so underweight and underdeveloped for its age its long-term recovery will depend upon the level of food and housing, not to mention health monitoring, that Ms. Hernandez provides. A major issue for Christian ethics is whether in such situations we apply the norm of equity to the means or to the end. Do we give the same care to the poor and the non-poor, or do we give to the poor whatever is necessary to allow them future equity with the non-poor? If the Hernandez baby were continued at levels of extraordinary care, should he be released at the weight at which middle-class babies are released, or should he be allowed an extra margin due to the fact that his food and housing and overall care will likely be less than theirs after his release? If we insist on the same degree of care for the same medical condition regardless of class, then in marginal cases the extraordinary care will have been wasted on the poor child, for the resources to sustain long-term recovery are lacking. And yet while we attempt to reform the very structures of our nation in the direction of greater justice, we must also work to see that existing structures do not exacerbate or reinforce existing discrimination and injustice by excluding the poor from basic opportunities such as life-saving medical care.

ADDITIONAL RESOURCES

Fletcher, John. "Abortion, Euthanasia and Care of Defective Newborns." In Thomas A. Shannon, ed., *Bioethics*, 3rd ed. New York: Paulist, 1987.
Maguire, Daniel C. *Death by Choice.* Garden City, N.Y.: Doubleday, 1974.
Nelson, James B. *Rediscovering the Person in Medical Care.* Minneapolis: Augsburg, 1976. Chapters 5–6.
Outka, Gene. "Social Justice and Equal Access to Health Care." In Shannon, ed., *Bioethics*.
Ramsey, Paul. *The Patient as Person.* New Haven: Yale University Press, 1970.
Thurow, Lester C. "Medicine Versus Economics." In Shannon, ed., *Bioethics*.

Case

AIDS Protection — For Whom?

The urgency in the nurse's voice rang in Sarah Cochran's ears as she hurried down the university clinic hallway to the central foyer. As the only medic on duty in the emergency room, she had been called to attend to someone who had fallen on the stairs.

Sarah entered the foyer and pushed through the crowd of onlookers to find a young man lying on the floor. He was bleeding profusely from what appeared to be a deep gash on his forehead. He seemed to have fainted and was slowly reviving. Sarah lifted his hand to take his pulse. Because he was dressed in street clothes, she was startled to find he wore a hospital I.D. bracelet. She asked softly, "Are you a patient here?"

The young man looked up at Sarah and saw the sea of faces surrounding them. The young man nodded. "What are you being treated for?" asked Sarah. He hesitated only a moment, then said, "You need to take body fluid precautions. I'm an AIDS patient."

There was an audible gasp as the crowd backed away. Sarah's most immediate reactions were of anger at the crowd and of compassion for the distress she saw in the man's eyes. She then realized her next thoughts were for her own safety. It was with real discomfort that she reached for the plastic gloves in her case before she began to apply pressure to the wound and wipe away some of the blood.

The patient, Donald Hughes, was taken to the emergency room. Sarah had some concern that the cut would scar his face. She consulted the plastic surgeon on duty to ask if he needed to suture the wound. Following a brief examination, the physician indicated the cut was "not deep enough to require two layers of suturing." Sarah then proceeded to suture and bandage the laceration herself. In the course of her conversation with Donald Hughes, Sarah learned that he was an outpatient being treated for an

This case was written by Alice Frazer Evans. Copyright © The Case Study Institute. The names and places in this case have been disguised to protect the privacy of the individuals involved.

AIDS-related infection. He had come into the infirmary to get an intra-venous injection of antibiotics and to have routine blood samples taken. He suggested that being in too great a hurry to get to a class and not sitting long enough after the blood work precipitated his fainting. He must have hit his head on the stair railing as he fell.

The following day Sarah learned from Janice Adams, an infirmary staff nurse, that Dr. Donald Hughes was an assistant professor in the university. His illness was not far advanced. Beyond the medical staff who worked with him directly, Jan thought that very few people outside of his immediate family had known of his illness. After the accident in the hallway this would certainly no longer be the case. Jan also expressed concern for Hughes's teaching position. "You and I know that there is absolutely no way Dr. Hughes can infect any of his students through casual contact in the class-room, but 'hyper' parents will probably bring pressure on the university. He has enough grief without losing his job."

Sarah also learned from one of the orderlies that leaders of the union to which over one hundred of the clinic's technical and clerical employees belonged were "hopping mad." No one had told the workers who cleaned up the blood on the stairs that the patient had AIDS, so no precautions were taken. One of the women had badly chapped hands, and there was a possibility that she had been infected. The orderly cited an article that had been in the paper only two days before. The article was clear that most cases of AIDS were contracted through sexual intercourse and sharing of needles by intravenous drug users. But there were now documented cases of lab technicians and other hospital workers who had been infected with HIV (human immunodeficiency virus, the virus that causes AIDS) through their work because of "needlesticks" and other open skin lacerations.

These conversations and others Sarah had during the day increased her unhappiness with the way the clinic administration handled identification of PWAs (Persons with AIDS). As a physician's assistant, Sarah was in-volved in primary care of emergency patients who came into the clinic. She was fully aware that she didn't have the same kind of "clout" the physicians did. Nevertheless, Sarah made an appointment to speak with Tom Ander-son, the chief administrator of the university clinic.

As she voiced her strong concern for the safety of the hospital staff, Sarah could hear the agitation in her own voice. "What if Dr. Hughes had been unconscious? What if he had chosen not to tell me? The burden shouldn't be on him to announce his condition to the world." She concluded by urging that some form of notification for body fluid precautions be placed on charts and wrist bands of patients with active cases of AIDS.

Sarah was assured by Mr. Anderson that all necessary precautions were being taken. A manual, available to all employees, had clear guidelines for dealing with AIDS patients. In addition, it was the clinic's policy to put the information in the "in-patient" charts for those personnel who came di-rectly and regularly into contact with the patient. In response to Sarah's challenge on this point, he acknowledged his awareness that some members of the staff refused to place this information on the charts. He reminded her that whether intended or not, charts and bracelets were open to public view. Because of the ignorance and irrational reactions of the general public, confidentiality was even more important in AIDS cases. "We have other AIDS patients besides Dr. Hughes. For all these patients the right to privacy comes first. I realize that the emergency room protocol has not previously been one of automatically wearing protective gloves for all cases, but perhaps you personally should take this precaution. True health care professionals take these kinds of risks every day and put the welfare of the patient first. That's what the Hippocratic oath is all about."

During lunch Sarah visited with Rebecca Andrews, a young physician who had recently joined the staff. Rebecca spoke carefully but with strong conviction: "I don't agree with Tom Anderson. Historically the risk went with the territory, and many physicians died from diseases they contracted from their patients. This includes 15 percent of the physicians who treated tuberculosis patients in the early 1900s. AIDS is unique. It is uniformly fatal. During my internship, I watched emaciated AIDS patients in severe pain, with no control of their minds and bodies. For two years I had nightmares about dying like this.

"I overheard your conversation with the plastic surgeon and Hughes. In spite of assurances from the Center for Disease Control [CDC] of minimal risk, there are surgeons who resist operating on an AIDS patient unless it's an extreme emergency. First, we're dealing with a terminal patient. Second, no matter how well a surgeon is protected, when there's a lot of blood, there's an increase in the risk of infection through nicked gloves, errant suture needles, and spurting blood. I disagree with the American Medical Association's directive on AIDS. It says, and I quote, 'When an epidemic prevails, a physician must continue his labors without regard to the risk to his own health.' I say, no. There are limits to professional responsibility."

A week passed. In spite of Sarah's meeting with Tom Anderson and growing dissent by the union officials, no announcements on AIDS policies were made by the administration. Sarah called the union steward and volunteered to attend a union meeting and to express her concerns. The steward's reception seemed cool; he told Sarah that he would contact her if he thought this would help their grievance against the university's handling of infectious diseases. After she hung up the phone, Sarah had the uneasy feeling that as part of the professional staff, she was perceived as one of the "enemy." She wouldn't hold her breath for that call.

Sarah also spoke with several of the nurses and physicians in the clinic, some of whom had become close friends during her two years on the staff. She was surprised that their reactions to her press for identifying patients who necessitated body fluid precautions were so mixed. Some were angry — "These people are dying in a horrible way. Don't add to their agony by going out and tatooing their foreheads!"

Others seemed to be wrestling with the issues as much as Sarah. Carol Simmons, a nurse in the emergency department, took a strong position in support of identifying AIDS patients within the university clinic. "I have to admit that I know physicians who have refused to help AIDS patients, but this isn't the case with anyone on our staff. There are hospitals that refuse to identify AIDS patients out of fear of patients losing their insurance. And others where terminal patients are evicted as soon as their insurance runs out. Again, that hasn't been the case here within our university system. We are considered a 'liberal' university, with basic commitments to the 'common good.' But is it always in the common good to protect the rights of individuals?

"In our greater metropolitan area there are over two hundred documented cases of AIDS. Five years from now there will be over two thousand. These are people already infected, and we have no way of preventing the progress of the disease. Our present community health care facilities aren't able to care for patients now, and the number of cases doubles every year. The specialized care needed for AIDS patients—disinfecting procedures, slower, more careful handling, expensive trial drugs, counseling for patients and family—will dramatically affect medical costs in the future. I'm convinced this care is more costly and time-consuming when it is covert. We're hiding our heads in the sand. Until institutions openly acknowledge *and* support AIDS patients, the archaic denial of this vicious disease is going to continue. The university clinic is in a unique position to take a stand on this."

Though Carol was clearly supporting her position, Sarah was conscious of her own reservations about public declaration of PWAs or of individuals who had been exposed to the HIV but might never fully develop AIDS. She knew of a family whose baby had been given a blood transfusion shortly after birth, before the present intensive blood screening had begun. They were recently notified that Tim's blood now tested HIV positive. Though he had no trace of AIDS, and there was a chance he would never contract the disease, the parents felt they couldn't tell friends or family members or even the family physician. They were afraid even grandparents would stop hugging and holding the baby, though there was no chance he would infect them.

If the information was in Tim's medical history, he could never be insured. Suppose Tim did develop AIDS. Sarah knew that often hospital costs for an AIDS patient exceeded $150,000, and families are faced with bankruptcy. Sarah was acutely aware of the loneliness, depression, fear, and helplessness of these families. She was also aware that some states were considering legislation to make it a felony not to reveal HIV positive results. This was directed toward adults who deliberately withheld information from sexual partners or when donating blood, but the legislation could have much broader implications. Maybe Will Jackson was on the right track, after all.

Will, an intern on the staff, took a position quite different from Carol Simmons. "As I see it, one of the main problems is that the American public is just not ready to deal with knowing who has AIDS. Rather than listen to the facts about infection and respond rationally to PWAs, we fire them from their jobs, evict them from their apartments, make them eat from paper plates, and even keep them *and* their children out of public schools. AIDS is so associated with homosexuals and intravenous drug users — both seen by most people in terms of voluntary choice — that the basic tendency is to blame PWAs for having brought this onto themselves. I'm convinced that beyond ignorance, the source of our violent reaction is fear, not only fear of death but fear of our own sexuality. Until the public gets beyond that point, we must keep the AIDS records strictly confidential. As medical professionals we have to continue to take the risks and assume the primary responsibility for our own health."

Sarah was impressed with Will's sincerity and his analysis, but not with his conclusion. Assuming primary responsibility implied that the staff assumed all the precautions. The Center for Disease Control in Atlanta had published a guide warning that "any time contact with blood or other body fluids of any patient is anticipated," health care workers should take precautions. "Contact with blood" involved a significant number of patients seen in the emergency room. In a recent publication the CDC not only recommended wearing disposable gloves but also stated that "masks and protective eyewear or face shields should be worn" during procedures that would expose the health care worker's mouth, nose, and eyes to blood or other body fluids. This approach was totally alien to Sarah's training and her deep sense of compassion for others. If the emergency room moved to adopt radical precautions, she could just imagine the anxiety of injured children or even adults greeted by masks and goggles! Not only would patients be alienated, but such obvious precautions by hospital personnel could only add to the public hysteria about contracting AIDS. She was convinced that many of the staff would resist these suggestions.

It wasn't possible to know for sure which patients were infected, but the chance of infection of staff was significantly reduced if they could identify the ambulatory patients who definitely required body fluid precautions. She was still convinced that there was some way that confidentiality could be preserved without medical personnel having to take greater risks than necessary.

Several other friends were sympathetic, urging Sarah to continue to press the administration — "The institution should care as much about us as it does about its patients."

With encouragement from her friends, coupled with her own frustration with no response, Sarah decided to write a letter to the university board of directors responsible for administering the clinic. She was struck, however, by the fact than not a single one of her supporters was willing to cosign the letter. In her letter Sarah related the incident of emergency care of the AIDS patient. She acknowledged that there was established protocol for identifying patients with AIDS on their medical charts. However, once the infirmary accepts such a patient, "it is by extension committing all departments to caring for them."

Sarah's letter continued: "I was asked by three clinical staff members if the patient had promptly identified himself as having AIDS, implying that the onus was on him to inform me. I believe this line of question directs attention away from the central issue: the burden of identification should not rest solely with the patient. The clinic must assume primary responsibility for implementing a system that identifies ambulatory patients with this risk factor. The patient himself told me how embarrassing it was for him to state publicly that he has AIDS."

In the letter Sarah then made two specific proposals:

1. A special wrist bracelet identifying the patient's blood/secretion precaution by either a color or code differentiation. All staff would be informed of the code.
2. A list of ambulatory patients with blood/secretion precautions. The list could be kept in an accessible yet private area in the emergency department. This is the most likely department to have a patient brought in under emergency conditions without benefit of a chart.

Sarah concluded the letter with a number of other suggestions, including the need to post AIDS protocols clearly in the nursing stations with information about how to disinfect contaminated instruments and how to dispose of contaminated paper products.

Though Sarah received a brief acknowledgment of receipt of her letter, she received no further word from the administration. Two weeks later there were notices that union and clinic administrators were meeting to discuss the union demands. Officials later announced that there would be mandatory training sessions on infectious diseases in addition to the short-term workshops for employees initiated shortly after the Hughes incident. However, no mention was made of patient identification for body fluid precautions.

Sarah Cochran felt determined to get some kind of response from the administration. Her sister had always joked that her determination doubled when she was confronted by a stone wall. Maybe the present policy was right, and a patient's confidentiality should be protected at all costs. It seemed pretty clear that was the direction the university was going to take. Then where did the legitimate rights of caregivers begin? Sarah was convinced that the issues needed at least to be openly discussed. She glanced down and saw the newspaper articles in which the union's grievances had been aired. Sarah picked up a copy of her unanswered letter to the board, wondering if the publicity which would come if she released it to the media would bring in fresh air or completely destroy the possibility of future changes. She also glanced at the wastebasket. Maybe she had taken her concerns as far as she could.

Commentary

AIDS Protection — For Whom?

All the subjects in this case seem to recognize that a tension exists between the interests of health care workers and those of PWAs (Persons with AIDS, the term preferred by PWAs). The PWA has a right to confidentiality, which is especially important given the hysteria and prejudice surrounding AIDS. Health care workers have a right to be protected as thoroughly as possible from contracting this deadly disease. A public policy effective in stemming the rising tide of AIDS cases requires that both sets of rights be protected. If the confidentiality of PWAs is not respected, persons at risk will be much less motivated to seek testing that will identify them and help prevent inadvertent spread of AIDS. If health care workers are not protected it will become more difficult to recruit workers willing to treat PWAs and possibly any patients. Health care in general could be greatly affected.

SCRIPTURAL AND THEOLOGICAL RESOURCES

What scriptural and theological teachings are relevant for issues involving AIDS? We have some scriptural analogies, especially around treatment of leprosy, which was a relatively common, degenerative, deadly, and communicable disease. In the Old Testament, the Mosaic law refers to leprosy extensively (e.g., Lev. 13–14). Lepers were largely excluded from the community and forced to live apart. They were obliged to cry "unclean" as a warning to anyone who approached them (Lev. 13). They were often the victims of abuse; their lives were blighted by their disease. This is especially tragic to note since primitive diagnostic skills often resulted in the priests, who were charged with diagnosis, confusing leprosy with many nonserious, noncommunicable diseases. In general, the Old Testament treatment of leprosy was designed to protect the community at the expense of the afflicted individual.

In the New Testament we find Jesus active in healing lepers, whom he allowed to approach him in defiance of law and custom. He usually healed through the laying on of hands, and made no exception for lepers, even though this contact contained a risk of contamination (Mark 1:40–44). Jesus presented his healing miracles as a sign of the love of God available to all, and as a call to his followers to imitate him in communicating God's love to all through similar outreach.

All followers of Jesus should recognize the shared mission of embodying God's love to all, especially those most in need. This mission mandates a pastoral attitude toward those suffering from communicable disease, despite the risks. Though we are to minister to the needy in spite of the risks, this does not prohibit the use of precautions. In fact, we have an obligation to use all available precautions. Jesus calls us to love our neighbor as ourselves, and love of self requires that we safeguard our health while we minister to the neighbor. If we did not, we threaten our ability to love other needy neighbors in the future.

The need to extend ourselves in love to neighbors in need does not mean that the needs of the patient with communicable disease take precedence over the need to protect the entire community of neighbors, whom we are also called to love as ourselves. Biblical teachings do not solve the dilemma of choosing between the needs of the afflicted individual and the well-being of the community, but only give us criteria which set the limits on our decisions. Biblical teachings, for example, could not justify a doctor's decision to refuse to treat all PWAs. Similarly, there is no Christian warrant for PWAs to protect their confidentiality and rights by refusing to inform a fiancé, spouse, sexual partner, or medical worker who could be infected by contact with them. Neither action is compatible with Christian love.

The real problems in this case revolve around public policy making, not around personal moral decisions. Public policy questions are often the more difficult aspect of AIDS. Although many personal decisions around AIDS entail great suffering, it is somewhat easier to decide what the moral action should be, if not to carry it out, than it is in public policy questions. Many personal decisions—telling a fiancé that one is HIV positive, deciding not to fire or expel employees or students who have AIDS, deciding to get tested because one is a member of a high risk group—seem to require more courage and suffering from us than seems possible to endure. In this case the cost of personal decisions around AIDS is very high. Dr. Hughes has risked his future to protect Sarah and others from danger in handling his blood. Sarah herself was willing to put herself on the line in writing the university board when none of her co-workers were willing to go public with their concerns. She risked not only the disapproval of her employers on the job, but the uncomfortable notoriety which can accompany such stands. However painful to ourselves and others, we cannot morally destroy lives either by allowing others to be infected or by rejecting and discriminating against PWAs who are not a threat to others.

Public policy, on the other hand, must deal with the problem of how to treat those who are not acting in morally responsible ways. Should we force members of high risk groups to be tested? Should we compel health workers to treat PWAs? Should we forbid discrimination against PWAs by employers, hospitals, insurance companies, landlords, and morticians? In making such decisions we must balance as best we can the interests and needs of all.

There are no simple formulas. Attempts to protect at all costs the needs of the majority—a kind of utilitarianism—can backfire in two ways. If the limitations and suffering in the situation are not distributed, but attributed to only one individual group, then we have unjust scapegoating of the minority, which in turn endangers the majority. For future situations could find groups within the present majority selected as scapegoats. On the other hand, insistence on the rights of the individual needy, here PWAs, can lead to the misuse of rights in ways that spread the disease and engender backlash against the infected minority.

RESPONSIBILITY FOR PROTECTING THE COMMON GOOD

Sarah is concerned that the responsibility for precautions against the spread of the AIDS epidemic not be placed solely on PWAs. Dr. Donald Hughes should not have had to announce publicly that he had AIDS, because of the serious effects this would have on his life: the probable loss of employment, and possible loss of housing and friends. Sarah is also concerned because Dr. Hughes could have been unconscious from his fall and therefore unable to give the warning. These are legitimate concerns; she wants to protect both PWAs and health care workers. The real issue is how this is best done.

Sarah wants body fluid precaution notices placed on charts and on wrist bracelets for all inpatients and outpatients to protect all hospital personnel. Such notices would not only cover PWAs, but other types of illness communicated through body fluids as well, for example, hepatitis, which claimed the lives of two hundred hospital workers last year in the United States.

There are a number of possible problems with her suggestions. First, there is the very real probability that the wearing of such identification bracelets, especially for outpatients, would increase acts of discrimination and abuse against PWAs as the community came to identify the bracelet with the rising numbers of PWAs. (Hepatitis is usually treated on an inpatient basis.) The fear and hatred around AIDS in the United States, which seems to be far worse than in other parts of the world where AIDS is not so identified with homosexuality, might find ready targets in outpatients. This in turn would almost certainly result in a refusal of PWAs to wear the identification.

In addition, the nature of AIDS itself works against the adequacy of such a system. AIDS may take five to ten years, perhaps even longer, to develop in exposed persons. This means that there are many exposed persons who do not know they carry the disease, and yet are capable of passing it on. Any person who enters the emergency room may carry the AIDS virus, not just those who have been tested HIV positive.

Sarah's suggestion in itself might not have prevented the spread of infection in the very case which gave rise to it. For the persons who were not protected by Dr. Hughes's warning—the housekeeping staff—would not necessarily know that the blood on the stairs came from a person wearing body fluid precaution identification. Housekeeping is not generally done until the patient and medical staff have moved away from the scene of an incident.

The hospital's decision seems to be an adoption of general procedures which will, if followed, reduce risk to health workers. If precautions in handling body fluids become routine and are taken with all patients, then workers will be protected not only from already diagnosed PWAs, but also from as yet undiagnosed AIDS carriers. The greatest obstacle to such a policy is compliance. It takes a great deal of effort to make the donning of masks, gloves, and other precautions routine, even when we know the risks. The effort might be compared to convincing people to stop smoking or begin wearing seatbelts. We know that quitting smoking and wearing seatbelts greatly reduce the chances of early death. But we also know that the dangers of smoking this one cigarette, or driving on this one errand without seatbelts, are relatively low. We take our chances. If we knew which cigarette would begin lung cancer, or which trip would involve us in an accident, we would be sure to use precautions. But we don't, just as health workers don't know which patients have AIDS.

This difficulty of making caution routine seems to be a major reason for preferring identification of PWAs over making body fluids precautions routine. The role of habit in the moral life is greatly undervalued. If we are consistently to act lovingly and responsibly toward all, we must make many kinds of action habitual. This is what we mean when we speak of character formation as a moral task of humans. For the most part we form our character through first discerning responsible reactions and then over time making them habitual.

Another problem with Sarah's suggestions is that it assumes that PWAs are a small minority. This is true in most areas of the country now. But in some major metropolitan areas AIDS cases already represent a significant percentage of the ill, and the projected increases in cases are likely to make that a common occurrence. As that happens, "special" precautions with identified patients would become more and more routine anyway. Understanding AIDS cases as minority, as an unusual occurrence, is a major problem in coming to grips with this disease not only in the United States, but in the world as a whole. It is estimated that between a million and a million and a half people in the United States have been exposed to the virus—that is, have antitoxins present in their bodies. The vast majority of those exposed will contract the disease (some scientists insist that all will), and, barring some unexpected new cure, everyone who contracts the disease dies from it. In some African nations whole villages and even regions are decimated by the disease, which is spread in Africa predominantly through heterosexual sex and childbirth. Predictions are that as many as one-third of the populations of Uganda and Zaire will die from AIDS in the next decade or so.

AIDS is a worldwide threat which will be around for the long haul. We need to take our heads out of the sand and institute international cooperative procedures and structures to succor the dying and protect the still healthy. In the United States we need to stop blaming homosexuals for the disease as if by pinning the blame on them we become safe from the ravages of AIDS.

Sarah had two objections to the hospital's response. First, she felt the hospital was refusing to accept any institutional responsibility for the protection of its workers, but was instead making them responsible as individuals for their protection. Second, she objected to routine donning of protective equipment as an intrusion between health care providers and patients. She feels that such protection distances care providers from patients and prevents patient trust in care providers.

It would certainly be wrong for the hospital merely to adopt guidelines which throw total responsibility on the workers. But if the hospital administrators were not only to provide workshops for employees in all areas of the hospital to explain necessary precautions, but also provide the needed equipment, post guidelines, and monitor compliance with the guidelines, this would indicate their willingness to share responsibility with workers. If all supervisors were charged with enforcing the use of protective equipment, if all training programs for new employees included instructions about the precautions, then the precautions could quickly become routine. In an earlier age of medicine before antisepsis was fully accepted, frequent washing of hands by doctors was regarded as annoying, unnecessary, and insulting to patients. But it did become routine, and within a generation maternal mortality rates in hospitals plummeted to a fraction of their earlier rate.

As for such precautions as gloves and masks intruding between care providers and patients, this may be so. Jesus himself in the healing of lepers eschewed precautions and the strictures of the law. But even Jesus sometimes changed his mind when he became convinced that his intentions could be carried out in a better way (Mark 7:24–30). Our actions must not only be lovingly intended, but they must appear loving if we are effectively to mediate God's love to our neighbor. Because patients are not accustomed to them and do not understand the need for them, gloves and masks could easily be resented. This problem, however, is not insurmountable. Patients accept the need for such precautions in all types of surgical procedures already. In some ways gloves and masks could free care providers to be *more* compassionate with patients, to reach out to touch them or hold their hand during feared or painful procedures, with less fear of contracting anything from or transmitting anything to patients. It is not as if hospitals were disease-free before AIDS. Hospitals have always been one of the highest disease-producing environments both for patients and workers. Such garb could lower risks for both, and would in time become routine.

AIDS AS A SPECIAL CASE

In some ways AIDS is a special case among diseases. There are other fatal diseases, but they are either fatal only sometimes or are not communicable except genetically. As an always fatal communicable disease without a cure, AIDS stands alone. The fear it engenders is enhanced by its connections with sexuality. In the United States, unlike many other countries, the most common method of contracting AIDS has been homosexual sexual activity, although shared needles among drug users now account for over a quarter of the cases, with birth, heterosexual contact, laboratory accidents, and blood transfusions all accounting for small percentages. Ours is a homophobic community; we fear homosexuality and often shun and discriminate against homosexuals, as Will Jackson pointed out in the case. We also fear and have disdain for drug users. The public understands the vast majority of PWAs to belong to two groups considered dangerously deviant, and therefore treats them as pariahs. Many respond to the threat of AIDS not with reasonable precautions, but irrationally, by blaming all PWAs for their situation and assuming they are enemies of society.

There are no grounds for such a response. Any of us have run the risk of contracting AIDS if we have had unprotected sexual contact with either sex, have received a blood transfusion, handled human blood without protection, shared a syringe with anyone, or been born of a parent who did any of these. Anyone can turn out to have been born of an infected parent, had sex with a spouse who had other sexual partners before us, or handled contaminated blood with exposed skin lacerations. We can choose to abstain from intravenous drug use and homosexuality, but we have little or no control over the many other ways that AIDS can be contracted.

One of the reasons that such strong fears and hysteria prevail around AIDS is that we are socialized to see ourselves as being in control of our lives, and to demand such control as normal. We are strongly attracted to the idea that we control our own fate. This attitude is largely a product of the phenomenal economic and scientific success our society has experienced. Our ability to control our world and to conquer many of the destructive illnesses and natural disasters which have victimized societies of the past has created the illusion that we are invulnerable, or at least on the verge of being invulnerable. AIDS is also more threatening to large segments of our population because it is a disease that attacks the young, often in the prime of life.

There are some very positive aspects to our attitude that we control our fate. People *should* realize that they have responsibility for their lives, that they irresponsibly raise the risk of serious medical problems when they smoke, fail to exercise, or eat poorly balanced or high cholesterol diets. We do control many of the behaviors which influence our health. We need to accept such responsibility in many different areas of our lives.

But we are not ultimately in control of our lives, even of our health. So that while my guilt feelings at being a smoker may be appropriate, it would be wrong to assume that all lung cancer patients are responsible for their illness. Some have never smoked, others were put at risk by smog or conditions of their work, or by an inherited predisposition. We often do not make this distinction. We move from the assumption of individual responsibility and control to blaming those who are unfortunate enough to be needy and suffering.

We do this because we are uncomfortable acknowledging our lack of ultimate control. Such an acknowledgment means that we are constantly at risk, in danger, vulnerable. In the past, Christian theology understood the assumption that we are in control of our lives as atheism, a failure to acknowledge that God controls all. Many theologians and ethicists today deny that God causes things like AIDS and cancer or other evils, and would rather say that when we insist that we are in control, we deny the reality of our finitude. This has implications for our relationship with God, for if we believe we can prevent ourselves from being needy, from falling victim to suffering and disaster, we do not need God, and cut ourselves off from God who offers us solace and strength. This same process which leads us to cut ourselves off from God leads to cutting ourselves off from others, and thus we sever ties that bind the human community together. We especially cut ourselves off from those who suffer and cultivate an ignorance about them. For they represent a special threat to our desire to believe in our own omnipotence: if these are innocent and are nevertheless afflicted, why not us? It is this desire to protect our own sense of safety that makes us shun the diseased, the raped, the poor, and other sufferers. We *want* to believe they are to blame. This is not only un-Christian, but it is an ultimately ineffective strategy, for we are not in full control of our lives. Suffering and death fall on the just and the unjust.

In making effective public policy around AIDS, we must all claim some responsibility for stopping the spread of the disease and supporting the needs of those who have contracted it. In order to do that we must understand AIDS as another in a long series of epidemics which have arisen in history to scourge humanity: bubonic plague, tuberculosis, small pox, and venereal disease, to name just a few. The danger of AIDS is a part of the human condition which we all share. Only when we accept the danger can we accept the responsibility. To do this is both a practical need and a moral challenge. Rising to meet this challenge will demand both courage and solidarity. We can hope that science can come up with treatments and ultimately a cure, but there is no guarantee of that. Even if there were some certainty that a cure existed in the future, there would be no excuse to ignore the challenge which AIDS represents today.

The practice of Christian ethics is not only about choosing action which promotes the coming of God's reign, but about making ourselves into moral persons modeled on Jesus Christ, persons who in some ways embody that reign. We are called to model the hope, the love, the justice, and the community that God intends for us. Part of that task is making responsible action habitual. Another part is acquiring the habit of understanding ourselves as part of the human community, sharing its dangers and successes, its temptations and failings. The temptation to evade responsibility by blaming those we regard as sinners has a long history in the annals of Christianity and other religions. Committing ourselves to follow Jesus does not make us righteous, as opposed to others who are sinners. Rather it calls us to root out of ourselves this temptation to understand ourselves as other than sinners.

CONCLUSION

Sarah Cochran's insistence both that the hospital take responsibility for protecting workers from AIDS, and that such responsibility should not be left to PWAs like Donald Hughes, is well grounded. Whether her suggestions for chart coding and coded wrist identification for inpatients and outpatients are the most effective ways both to protect workers and meet the needs of PWAs is not clear. Whatever the final decision, and that decision may well be a combination of her suggestions and the hospital's guidelines, that decision should involve a sharing of responsibility by all involved. Everyone is potentially vulnerable to AIDS; therefore the task of preventing its spread belongs to all. We cannot expect that our employer, or our government, or any other institution, can or should relieve us of the responsibility to protect ourselves or our neighbors. Nor can we expect that our own actions can make us invulnerable to AIDS. We have no source of total immunity.

It often happens that it is only when we come to accept that we are all endangered by a common threat that we can come together in solidarity. This is what has happened in many areas of the homosexual community in the cities of our nation. Countless individuals in the homosexual community, transformed by their witness to the devastation caused by AIDS in that community, have committed their lives to practical and pastoral work for AIDS patients, and in that work have found profound community. It is tragic that so often we only find such solidarity in the face of disaster. But regardless of our feelings about homosexuality or the homosexual community, such examples of solidarity should be understood as a model for all of us of what the Christian community is called to be. We are not called to avoid the evil of death and suffering, but to struggle against it in solidarity with the suffering.

ADDITIONAL RESOURCES

Center for Disease Control. *Morbidity and Mortality Weekly Reports (MMWR) Supplement.* September 1985. The reports are available from the Epidemiology Program Office, Center for Disease Control, Public Health Service, U.S. Dept. of Health and Human Services, Atlanta, GA 30333. See also *MMWR,* 1987, 36, no. 25.

Center for Disease Control. *1985 STD [Sexually Transmitted Disease] Treatment Guidelines.* Available from above address.

Flynn, Eileen P. *AIDS: A Catholic Call for Compassion.* Kansas City: Sheed and Ward, 1986.

Gallagher, Joseph. *Voices of Strength and Hope for a Friend with AIDS.* Kansas City: Sheed and Ward, 1987.

Nelson, James. "Responding to and Learning from AIDS." In *Moral Issues and Christian Response,* Paul T. Jersild and Dale A. Johnson, eds. 4th ed. New York: Holt, Rinehart and Winston, 1987.

Patton, Cindy. *Sex and Germs: The Politics of AIDS.* Boston: South End Press, 1985.

Shilts, Randy. *And the Band Played On: Politics, People and the AIDS Epidemic.* New York: St. Martin's Press, 1987.

PART VII

SEXUALITY

Case

Getting Away from It All

"I wish you would have died in that fire and not my father!" The apartment door slammed as Alicia stormed out. Helen Edwards grimaced as another piece of plaster fell in the narrow hallway. She walked to the front window and peered out to see Alicia emerge from the stairwell and run across the littered cement courtyard to the next housing block where her friend Mae lived. Would it do any good to drag her fourteen-year-old daughter back to the Mid-Town Teen Clinic?

Rock music blared from Alicia's portable radio. As Helen went to turn it off, she looked at the clock and hurried to get her handbag. She could not stop now to find Alicia or she would be late to work again. Helen did not cry very often. It was not her way. But she was as close to tears as she had been in a long time.

She tried to imagine what Alicia was feeling, to remember what it was like to be so young. Helen's hands felt cold as she maneuvered her old car through the heavy morning traffic. Helen felt like she had never been young. Her eldest, Joe, had been born when she was fifteen. Then Sam came along a year later. If she had known what she knew now... When Alicia was born, Helen swore she would never let her become a teenage mother and fall into the same trap she had gotten herself into. Daniel Moore, Alicia's father, had had some problems, but he was a good man. They had struggled to raise their three children, but then their life together had ended when Daniel died in a fire at the factory where he had worked.

Six months after Daniel died, Helen married Jim Edwards. She remembered the arguments with Jim about a baby. Helen had said there was no way they could afford another child. Jim was employed temporarily with odd jobs. Hers was the only steady salary. Jim was insistent and eventually won out. Jackie, their baby, was now nearly a year old and looked just like Jim.

It had not worked out too badly. Jackie was a good baby and everybody loved her, especially Jim. Helen clenched the wheel when she remembered that Jim had spent nearly a week's salary, over $180, on baby clothes that Jackie outgrew in less than a month.

Helen had worked for the Andersons for about six years. Although she started as a domestic, she increasingly took over the care of their four children. Mrs. Anderson had said that Helen should think about going to the vocational school and getting her child care certificate. She could even start her own center. But there were too many nights she stayed late, sometimes overnight. Helen remembered feeling proud that Alicia, even at ten, could put together a supper for her brothers.

The Andersons had given Helen a month's leave to have Jackie and welcomed her back afterwards. Some days she could even bring Jackie to work. Usually she left the baby with Mrs. Morris, an older neighbor in their apartment block. Alicia was supposed to pick her up after school. That was happening less and less.

Helen's mind went back over the past few months trying to piece together the changes she saw in Alicia. Even though Jim had been with them for nearly two years, Alicia still did not get along with him. Close friends did not help much when they kept commenting on how much Alicia looked like her father. Then when Jim was drunk, sometimes on weekends, he would shout at Alicia. Alicia would stay away from the apartment for hours at a time. Helen learned she was running around with a much older group of teens in the project. Some of them were dropouts. Several had police records. Helen's oldest boy told her it was a rough crowd. A lot of them were into drugs.

Helen became determined to move her family out of the project. She spent hours reading newspaper ads, looking for anything they could afford. Because Mrs. Anderson did not make her fool with social security, Helen's take-home, including overtime, was sometimes over $800 per month. They needed at least three bedrooms, and most rents started at $600 per month. Helen had found a two bedroom she thought they could afford, but the manager refused to show it to her when he found out she had four children.

Several weeks later in September Helen learned that Alicia, then thirteen, had a boyfriend who was seventeen. Not long after he gave Alicia two tapes and a bracelet. Helen made an appointment for Alicia at the Mid-Town Teen Clinic. Helen tried to talk to her about not getting pregnant. She was still a little girl. For her own sake as well as that of a child she might have, she needed to wait until she was older. Helen hoped Alicia would listen to someone at the clinic.

When Alicia came out of the interview with Ms. Wilson, she showed Helen a six-month supply of birth control pills and promised her mother she would take them. Alicia made an appointment to come back again in six months. Helen continued to search for a new place to live. Less than three months after the visit to the teen clinic, Alicia told her mother she thought she was pregnant. Helen talked to Mrs. Anderson the next afternoon. Mrs. Anderson made arrangements for Alicia to see her own gynecologist. Helen would have to pay $80 for the visit. Helen took the day off to take Alicia to the doctor's office. She sat and waited for over an hour in the lounge while Alicia saw the nurses and then the doctor. Alicia was very quiet when she came out. She cried on the way home. She told her mother the doctor had been very straight about the options, and that if the tests were positive, she had to decide what to do. She said that she wanted to talk to her boyfriend first.

The doctor's office called Helen at the Anderson's the next day. The blood test was negative. They were sure Alicia was not pregnant. That night Alicia said she would go back to the clinic. She had thrown the pills away when she thought she was pregnant. Helen took another afternoon off to drive Alicia back to the teen clinic. Alicia promised again she would be careful.

Over the next two months Alicia drew further and further away from the family. She began spending every afternoon with her friend Mae. Helen learned from her oldest boy that Mae was eighteen and had dropped out of school when she had a baby. She lived with her mother and got $135 a month from welfare.

Helen had not worried too much about her boys. Joe and Sam seemed to manage all right in high school. They tried odd jobs when they could. Helen remembered seeing on television that unemployment for teens in the city was over 75 percent. But just keeping Alicia in school was a problem. Her truancy had gotten so bad that Helen had taken to driving Alicia to school to make sure she got there. Then pressure at work made this impossible. If Helen could not make it to the Andersons' by 8:30, they would have to get someone else.

Things at home seemed to get worse. It was a bitter cold winter and the heat bills were high. By the end of January Helen hardly had enough money to buy groceries. The phone company had come and taken out the phones again. Jim still had not found anything steady. He was going on weekend binges more often. One night after he hit Helen and swore at Alicia, Helen decided that Alicia needed to go and live with her cousin in Atlanta. Alicia was back home in three weeks. Her aunt refused to keep her. Helen never found out what happened.

Jim left the first week in March. A week later Alicia's school counselor called Helen at the Andersons'. Alicia was being suspended for fighting with another girl in school. Helen told the Andersons she needed to quit work and stay at home with her daughter. She made arrangements for a good friend at church who was unemployed to work temporarily for her.

Two weeks later Helen went back to work for the Andersons. She had hoped staying at home with Alicia would help, but Helen found Alicia almost impossible to handle. Several days she did not come home at all. Helen remembered one night she was so mad at Alicia that she told her she would turn her over to the juvenile court. When the period of suspension was over, there were days when Alicia left school soon after she got there. The school counselor told Helen she had a case load of over four hundred children. She did not know what to suggest for Alicia. Had Helen tried taking her to the Mid-Town Teen Clinic?

For the month Helen had been back at the Andersons', Alicia seemed a bit more responsible and was coming more regularly to pick up Jackie from 'Mrs. Morris. Helen knew that Alicia had another boyfriend, but she had refused to talk about him.

Then this morning when she was taking off the bed sheets to do laundry, Helen found Alicia's unused container of birth control pills under her mattress. Helen shooed the boys off to school early and told Alicia to stay. "What do you think you are up to, girl? Why aren't you taking these things? I know your cycle. You still have time to start this month. Has this fancy new boyfriend of yours put ideas into your head? There's no way I'll believe that boy is using any protection." Helen tried to keep her voice under control, but knew she was shouting at Alicia.

Alicia glared back at her mother. "My boyfriend gave me that blouse you wouldn't buy me for my birthday. He treats me like a woman. He thinks it would be cool to have a baby. You can't make me take those things. I'm old enough to make my own decisions. Besides, my boyfriend doesn't want me to take them. You're always picking on me. I wish you had died in that fire. . . ."

As Helen pulled her car into the Andersons' long driveway, she saw Mrs. Anderson waiting with the two-year-old. She smiled as Helen got out of the car. "Helen, I have a wonderful surprise. This next week when the children's private school has spring break, Mr. Anderson and I plan to take the family to St. Simon's Island. We learned yesterday we can have one of the larger houses, and there would be just enough room for you and Jackie. I've heard you say you have never been on a trip and that you have never seen the ocean. With so much for them to do, the children should be easy for you to watch on the beach. And Mr. Anderson and I would be around most evenings. Helen, you really look tired and need to get away from it all. Why not come along with us?"

Commentary

Getting Away from It All

It is important to note at the outset that the case does not state the ethnic background of the Edwards. As 70 to 80 percent of the population of most urban housing projects are black or Hispanic, it would be understandable if one assumed the Edwards are members of an ethnic minority. However, using statistics as an entry point for this case may be a trap into stereotypic responses that could obscure deeper issues. In order to understand better the ethical decisions that Helen and Alicia face, one might attempt to enter the case, at least imaginatively, through the subculture of the urban housing project in which the Edwards live and through their personal perspectives. In this case conditions of poverty are far more relevant than issues of race.

CHARACTERS: THE PERSONAL DILEMMA

Alicia

"Getting away from it all" may be a temptation for Alicia as well as Helen. Alicia is experiencing pressure from several directions. She is faced with the persistent love of a mother trying to protect her at a stage in life when independence is particularly important. She also cares for a baby sister and has responsibility for meal preparation for two brothers, which began when she was only ten. These tasks are made more burdensome since the baby, Jackie, is the favorite of Alicia's stepfather, while Alicia is rejected. When Jim is drunk, he alternately ignores and yells at her. Alicia may have had no time or way to grieve after the death of her own father.

Alicia is probably also experiencing the physical withdrawal of affection by her mother. Traditionally, when children reach adolescence and parents become aware of their sexuality, there is an unconscious withdrawal of parental touch. Though Alicia hears her mother express concern, she experiences her as demanding and, because of Helen's work schedule in a distant suburb, as absent.

If this is a typical low-income urban area, then school provides more pressure. Alicia's mother wants performance in an urban school system which probably is predominately segregated and likely has high dropout rates and overburdened teachers. Alicia knows the score and so does Helen: There are no jobs, even if one finishes school. The big money is in drugs.

Alicia knows from experience how hard it is to get advice and help. She recalls how embarrassing it was to have her mother drive her to the teen clinic. The counselors were so busy they could only spend a few minutes with her, and nobody is that quick with good advice. Then when Alicia was both scared and happy she might be pregnant, she had to go to Mrs. Anderson's doctor. Alicia may resent the Andersons as the cause of her mother's absence and react with anger to their privileges and access to a private physician in contrast to the public clinic. It would not be surprising that Alicia finds neither dignity nor meaning at home or in school.

Through her sexuality, Alicia finds the intimacy, affection, and attention she craves, as well as a possible means of getting away from the trapped feeling of the project. The normal hormonal changes in her body and increasing sexual energy offer a viable outlet for her frustration. Her boyfriend wants a baby, and Alicia wants to please the only person in her life who makes her feel special. Alicia knows her mother was pregnant at fifteen. Perhaps she and her boyfriend could make it too on Aid for Dependent Children (AFDC). Then she could be free and on her own. However, Alicia realizes that some of the women who have been in the project for two or three generations, like Mae's mother, weren't all that happy. Husbands who last more than two years are in short supply. Alicia must wonder whether she has any real choice or any real hope.

Alicia is a remarkable young woman. She has homemaking and survival skills at age fifteen that would surpass most of her peers in the affluent suburbs. Refusing to be dominated by her mother or her aunt, she appears determined to make her own decisions and create some kind of a meaningful future.

Helen

As the mother of a teenage daughter on the verge of perpetuating the cycle of children bearing children, Helen recalls swearing at Alicia's birth that this would not happen to her daughter. She may feel terrible guilt that she is unable to control the situation. Helen is offered a way, at least temporarily, of getting away from it all. Would a trip to the ocean that she had so longed to see be the break she needs? She knows the Andersons gain the most by her going. They are good people, even if paternalistic. Helen tries not to think about the power they have to shape her situation. Helen must be angry and lonely with Daniel, her first husband, dead and Jim now gone. But if she goes away at this critical time, is this surrender to a system that will swallow up her daughter as well? They will both be victims when that boy disappears and leaves her with a daughter and a grandchild to care for.

Helen also may wonder whether it really makes any difference if she goes or stays. Although the unfolding story seems already out of her hands, she still feels responsible. Helen may dream of the child care certificate and the independence it promises. However, the price is high in precious time, money, and energy with the possibility of only disappointment at the end.

Helen Edwards is a woman of loving instincts with an extraordinary capacity to care for others while still sustaining her own family. She is resourceful with medical options for Alicia, vocational possibilities for herself, and in seeking housing alternatives for the family. Helen is a woman of determination and commitment.

Jim Edwards

For many middle-class readers Jim may be the most difficult of the characters to understand. There are four women to every marriageable man in many poor ethnic communities. Many males in poor urban communities have been killed or disabled through gang or neighborhood clashes and police confrontations. Others are in prison or institutionalized for drug or alcohol abuse. They are caught in a system where inner city unemployment is ten times higher than in most suburban communities. Unemployed men are viewed by the dominant society as redundant or disposable. There must be some place to show your manhood, and fathering children has an honored tradition. Alcohol and drugs are a means of getting away from it all that few would condone, but certainly most who are knowledgeable would also understand.

Jim has the right to seek a loving relationship, including the pleasure of a baby in his house. However, if he is unable to find work, Jim's very presence in the household reduces the social welfare benefits the family would be eligible to receive. He may be taking, in his judgment, the most responsible, caring, and painful decision as he distances himself from the family. Whether his absence is a sign of abandonment or commitment may be a question of perspective.

The Andersons

Helen's employers are clearly middle-class or upper-middle-class, whether they are white, black, or Hispanic. As concerned employers, they have granted maternity leave, offered medical assistance, and encouraged Helen's vocational advancement. Yet the schedule of evenings and overnights does not suggest the job is designed with the need of a parent employee in mind. Whether adequate salary and vacation with pay are part of the package for Helen, we do not know. However, these benefits would be contrary to the accepted pattern for most domestic workers. The decision not to withhold social security payments from Helen's salary, which also eliminates payment of a matching employer contribution, is illegal. Though Helen states she needs the extra cash now, this decision may not be to her benefit in the long run.

The Andersons should be asking themselves several personal and moral questions. How can the welfare of their children be compared to the welfare of Helen's children? Does their access to wealth, at least compared to the Edwards, provide rights of time and attention not equally owed to Alicia, Jackie, and their brothers? The case gives no details about Helen's employee benefits such as medical care or retirement. However, traditionally benefits are rare for domestic help and child care providers, despite the value of these services if measured by their impact on the quality of an employer's family life.

The Andersons appear genuinely concerned about Helen and her family in terms of immediate personal problems. They have provided understanding, some work flexibility, and special resources such as access to their family physician. A major question which arises concerns the degree of the Andersons' responsibility for or even acknowledgment of the structural injustices which burden families such as the Edwards. The gap between poverty and privilege widens when social injustice is reduced to a private concern for a single individual.

Questions of structural justice may be more complicated than the personal issues. What responsibility do the Andersons, or any member of a privileged segment of society, have for the inadequate housing, education, employment, and medical facilities for the poor? Where are the limits of responsibility for the welfare of employees, who are also children of God, with special needs for their families? A critical moral issue in this case may be what the famous twelfth-century rabbi Maimonides called the eighth and most meritorious step of charity—"to anticipate charity, by preventing poverty."

THE SITUATION: A NATIONAL TRAGEDY

A double-edged national tragedy that this case reveals is the growing level of poverty concentrated among children and youth and the higher levels of teenage pregnancy which are a consequence of and contributor to that poverty. The United States is progressively being divided into two nations or two worlds. The communities are as distinct as the separation of First and Third Worlds at the global level. The gap runs along lines of race, economics, and sex.

Senator Daniel Patrick Moynihan in his response to the President's 1988 State of the Union address declared, "there are more poor Americans today than a quarter of a century ago, and . . . the poorest group in our population are children." For the citizens of the wealthiest nation in the world the newest census figures should be profoundly shocking. In the United States: one child in four is born into poverty. One child in five lives through adolescence in poverty. For black and Hispanic families the reality is even harsher. One in two black children is poor as are two of five Hispanic children. One of the most disturbing indices of poverty in the United States is a higher infant mortality rate than in eleven other nations in the industrialized world. This national tragedy challenges our self-perception as a humane, prosperous, and progressive people.

Poverty hits children and young mothers hardest. From 1975 to 1985 female-headed, single-parent households such as the Edwards increased from 2.4 million to 3.4 million, with 40 percent of those households living in poverty even with the mother employed. The United States has the highest adolescent birthrate of any industrialized nation. It is the Alicias of our society who become children bearing children. A 1987 report from the Education Commission of the States notes that at least 15 percent of all Americans between the ages of sixteen and nineteen are unlikely to become productive adults because they are already "disconnected" from society as a result of drug abuse, delinquency, pregnancy, unemployment, and/or dropping out of school — all signs of "alienation and disconnection." The report acknowledges an unconscionably disproportionate representation of poor, black, and Hispanic teens in the statistics.

Over one million teens become pregnant each year. These pregnancies will result in: staggering rates of infant mortality; increased dropout rates; drug, alcohol, and child abuse; divorce; unemployment; and even suicide. Teenage pregnancy of this magnitude is a national as well as a personal tragedy. Yet funding and commitment for prevention-focused education and social programs to address the causes of this moral and systemic problem are at best inadequate. Most authorities on sexuality and health judge current efforts to be paltry.

An extremely high percentage of teenage parents' own mothers conceived in their teens, as did Helen Edwards. The disproportionate number of these who are poor, black, and Hispanic exposes the deep roots of gender, race, and class patterns in our culture. The greatest pressure on those who are extremely poor is often not for stronger ethical norms but simply for survival. The Christian norm for sexual relations within marriage presupposes a loving relationship. Yet the realities of poverty easily threaten the fulfillment of a sustained, loving relationship between sexual partners. The ethical crisis in this case is not simply Helen's parental decision for more supervision or Alicia's decision about childbearing. It is, in many ways, a class-action case that challenges the morality of a society which perpetuates the dehumanizing conditions in which some people live and fails to address the causes of teenage pregnancy.

RELATIONAL NORMS

At the heart of the Christian tradition is a relational norm, the love of God and neighbor. The Christian is called first to love God — "with all your heart, and with all your soul, and with all your mind," and, second, to "love your neighbor as yourself" (Mark 12:30–31). Theologian H. Richard Niebuhr described the principal purpose of the community of faith called the church to be "the increase of the love of God and neighbor." He also suggested that the basic guideline for making an ethical choice is to ask, "What is the loving thing to do?" The biblical standard is a quality of relationship called love that nurtures both freedom and responsibility. This is the freedom for human beings to realize their full potential and for individuals and societies to care for one another. Christians are called to a loving relationship with God, neighbors, and even with enemies. This is the basis for the concept of justice.

Christians consider sexual relationships from the context of the norm of love. Genesis shows God creating partners to be the closest neighbors in this relational norm of love. The New Testament adds to this image, declaring that as God "from the beginning made them male and female . . . a man shall leave his father and mother and be joined to his wife, and the two shall become one" (Matt. 19:4–5). This relationship is sometimes described as a great mystery and compared to the relationship between God and Israel or Christ and the church. Marriage has become so cherished by some Christian churches that it is understood as a sacrament.

It is within this special relational norm of love and marriage that Christianity has traditionally seen the gift of sexuality. Though sexual union produces children, the function of the gift was seldom seen as procreation alone, but was also to enhance the relationship, that quality of loving between the partners. Related to the original biblical accounts, a series of guidelines have emerged from the Christian church, most of which have restricted sexual relations to married partners. Different religious communities at various points in history have employed different standards, but sexual relations within marriage have become normative. These religious traditions have usually been recognized and sanctioned by the secular community as well.

It must be confessed that guidelines for understanding sexual behavior have at times been manipulated, misinterpreted, and used in an oppressive and nonloving manner. Boundaries have been erected by both religious and secular communities with the claim of safeguarding the family or the community. Many who crossed those boundaries were and are treated in ways that violate the very heart of the basic norm of love itself. This is especially true for women who are treated as property not partners, as well as for persons who cross those boundaries in adultery or promiscuity. Those of other sexual preferences are condemned and often ostracized for challenging the interpretation of the norm of married partners and for expressing an alternative understanding of sexuality.

SOME RESPONSES: A SYSTEMATIC AND PERSONAL APPROACH

Having the basic necessities of life to maintain human dignity and a sense of security seem to be essential to sustain loving relationships. Perhaps all the members of the human community must own some responsibility when the support systems for basic needs do not exist or cease to function. In exploring the problems of the ethics of societal structures as well as personal sexual ethics, we should consider which conditions promote and sustain the love of partner, God, and neighbor. Three categories emerge for consideration: education, economics, and emancipation.

Education

While a majority of Americans consider teenage pregnancy a serious national problem, major studies reveal that Americans are also seriously misinformed about the nature and roots of the problem. Better information is especially important for those persons who effect legislation, school policy, and the stated priorities of religious and private institutions. Public forums and seminars must draw on areas of agreement about the data and point to avenues of support and participation.

Myths and stereotypes about teenage pregnancy need to be challenged by comprehensive comparative studies such as those of the Allan Guttmacher Institute. One of the institute's studies compared U.S. statistics with those of six other countries with similar cultural and economic backgrounds, including England and Canada. The results indicate that the United States leads every developed nation in numbers of teenage pregnancies, childbearing adolescents, and in abortion rates. America is the only country in the study where teenage pregnancies have been *increasing*. Teenage mothers are disproportionately high among poor black and Hispanic families. However, it is misleading to conclude that high U.S. figures are simply a result of an ethnic population that lives in a degree of poverty unknown in most of Western Europe. The rate of teenage pregnancy in the United States for white non-poor adolescents also exceeds that of other countries in the study. Another relevant statistic is that American teenagers are not apt to begin sexual activity earlier or be more sexually active. Finally, welfare does not appear to be the determining incentive for out-of-wedlock births; U.S. welfare benefits are *less* generous than in other countries in the study.

Developing an approach to teenage pregnancy requires raising awareness of the high cost of failing to invest in solving the problem. The dislocation created by teenage pregnancy takes an incredible emotional, physical, and economic toll on the lives of teenagers, their families, and finally, on society as a whole. The pregnant teenager is "at risk" in terms of being dramatically less likely to complete high school and secure or maintain a job. The same adolescent is significantly more likely to abuse drugs and alcohol, to give birth to a child with physical and mental handicaps, to have children who become teenage parents, to live in poverty, and to attempt suicide. The direct costs to the society in terms of welfare, medicine, and human suffering are staggering.

The key causal factors of teenage pregnancy identified by scientific studies include: (1) lack of available courses on family life; (2) lack of access to birth control information and resources; (3) the depiction of sex by the media; and (4) the breakdown of the family and the loss of support structures for a meaningful future. The first three will be discussed in this section; the last issue will be taken up in the following section on economics.

In regard to sex education the Guttmacher Institute study draws an important overall conclusion. It is not that American culture is sex-obsessed as might be concluded by a sampling of the media, especially television. Rather, the institute concludes that American culture as a whole is prudish and intolerant of premarital sexual activity. These attitudes stem in part from a fear of sexuality which causes many parents not only to be unable to deal openly with sexual activity but to withdraw physical affection from their adolescent children. The church is cited as a factor in this view of sex that also results in a frequent polarization in discussions about mandatory or even voluntary "family life and sex education," to say nothing about the establishment of school-based health clinics which offer contraceptive information. The institute study concludes, "it is likely that the United States has the lowest level of contraceptive practice among teenagers" of all the industrialized countries studied. Therefore, a critical arena for education is not teenagers but adult Americans who ultimately determine public policy and influence moral values.

Several studies suggest one basic step is to introduce mandatory family and life education courses from kindergarten to grade twelve in as many public and private schools as possible. The fear that such courses will cause earlier or more frequent sexual activity and thus higher pregnancy levels is disputed by most reliable research on the subject. Sex education has been compulsory in Sweden since the 1950s; that country has significantly lower levels of pregnancy and abortion than the United States.

School-based health clinics that are accessible and confidential could also be an important factor in the solution. Some church traditions, however, oppose contraception and abortion on ethical grounds and challenge the use of public tax dollars to support facilities which may dispense information contrary to their teachings. However, in some states pilot school-based clinics have been supported by both prolife and prochoice groups since they have a common interest in preventing teenage pregnancy. Some of these clinics are supervised by parent boards and have restrictions concerning dispensing contraceptives or offering advice on termination of pregnancy. As in Alicia's case, many clinics, even when available, are not near the schools and are often underfunded and understaffed. Given the current polarized climate, enacting necessary legislation for courses and clinics will be a public struggle.

The standard media approach to sex should be countered. Education about responsible attitudes toward sexual behavior must occur in locations where parents and teenagers can be reached effectively. So far the media's impact on people's attitude toward sex has been overwhelmingly negative. Glamorous indiscriminate sexual encounters, usually without a focus on a sustained or loving relationship between partners, are used to sell products and promote ratings. As Planned Parenthood declared in an advertising campaign, "They did it 9,000 times on television last year. How come nobody got pregnant?" A few TV series cautiously discuss contraceptives and condoms, but these are rare. Even fewer series raise the option of abstinence. Fear of AIDS may provide the opportunity to re-evaluate approaches to sexual behavior in the media as well as sex education in the schools.

TV appears to be the most influential media for teenagers and parents. In addition to continuing to pressure the television networks for more responsible broadcasting, concerned citizens need to explore new programs which counter the media's prevailing mode. The most effective programs have focused on community organizations, schools, churches, and clubs. They have employed open and engaging formats such as case studies, videos, and community forums which allow honest discussion of sex and loving relationships. Teenage heroes who speak candidly and confessionally about sex as well as drugs also appear to be getting a hearing.

New educational networks and coalitions are emerging which are taking important steps. Public/private partnership projects are combining the state resources of education, health, and social services with those of corporations, foundations, churches, and civic organizations. One example is The Hartford Action Plan on Infant Health initiated by Connecticut Mutual Life Insurance Company in its concern for a community-integrated project to reduce infant mortality and teen pregnancy in the country's third poorest city. Illinois and Michigan have comprehensive programs, such as Illinois Parents Too Soon, that address the problem through coalitions of the public and private sector. These examples of simultaneous education of policy makers, teens, and parents provide pilot programs for other communities to examine and adapt to their own special circumstances.

Economics

Causal factors of family disintegration and the resulting loss of hope for a meaningful future for both teenagers and parents may be the most critical and also the most complex to address. Without a sense of worth and dignity it is difficult for an individual to utilize the resources made available in schools, clinics, churches, or community organizations. The breakdown of family life in all classes and races, but especially in minority communities, has been linked to economic pressures and the inability to control or even participate in the shaping of one's future in a meaningful way. This breakdown is in part due to racism and the failure of the wider community to provide adequate employment opportunities. Teenage pregnancy is an issue of social justice.

The Census Bureau predicts that 61 percent of the children born in the United States today will live for some time with only one biological parent, usually the mother. Ninety-six percent of all children whose families receive Aid for Dependent Children (AFDC) are from homes with a single head of household; the majority are from minority ethnic groups. Members of the American Public Welfare Association, who often administer such programs, suggest that public aid produces dependency and robs those dependents of dignity. Such programs have produced an "institutional bias against minority children," declares Senator Moynihan. It is revealing that surveys of mothers with dependent children taken prior to the enactment of the program—which was a part of the original 1935 Social Security Act— showed that these mothers opposed the program. These women preferred programs of child care, health insurance, and job training to cope with their economic problems, not welfare payments. A proposal for welfare reform by The National Council of State Human Services Administrators entitled "One in Four" evokes the challenge of children in poverty. It calls for programs to enhance self-support and self-sufficiency for poor families through income security, education, and employment and thus returns to themes articulated by poor mothers in 1935. The report has a special section of recommendations of strategies to help prevent adolescent pregnancy.

There is scant evidence that any nation has significantly addressed the problem of unwanted pregnancies without providing a degree of economic security and hope for a more meaningful life. On a global scale those countries that have combined a guarantee of basic necessities for a life with dignity and reasonable security for senior citizens have achieved significant population reduction. This is true in Western Europe and middle-class North America. This reduction has not occurred in the United States among the "Third World" urban and rural poor who often have little security or hope.

It may startle many North Americans to learn that the Third World is in their midst. U.S. inner city housing projects and rural poverty areas often have a huge number of people who are unemployed and a significant number of temporary workers or migrant laborers. They constitute the so-called Third World or South within a First World or Northern context. A majority of residents in these communities have inadequate resources and virtually no hope that the cycle of poverty will really change. Unless the systemic issues of poverty—unemployment, scarcity of affordable housing, inadequate education, lack of day care, no health insurance, and limited medical services—are dealt with, the educational strategies to reduce teenage pregnancy will reap minimal results.

The biblical mandate for justice makes it ethically necessary that Christians support systemic changes that assure a basic standard of living for all. In this case study the Andersons as the First World component and the Edwards as the Third World component both have responsibilities in moving toward this goal. Power within the system rests more with the Andersons. They could respond with adequate salary and health/pension benefits for Helen as well as become advocates in their schools, church, and community on strategies for the prevention of teenage pregnancy. Helen and Alicia have obligations to demand and help develop child care programs, job enhancement opportunities, and a school-based health clinic. Though it will challenge family patterns, Helen's sons need to assume their share of child care and meal preparation. System modification for the sake of justice is a responsibility of all, though what one can do is often in part determined by one's resources.

Emancipation

Freedom and the ability to participate in decisions and structures that shape our lives are what distinguish us as human beings. The shaping of individual and communal ways of being is essential to morality. The idea of being emancipated or liberated from the attitudes or structures that limit one's human potential is central to this volume. Brazilian educator Paulo Friere notes that cultural forms give meaning to the way human beings think, talk, dress, and act. He calls for people to distinguish between the present as given and the present as containing emancipatory possibilities. Emancipation or freedom is as important to the issue of teenage pregnancy as education and economics.

Morality concerns not only what one does but also who one is. The relational norm of love, rooted in the biblical and theological tradition, has to do with a way of being and the formation of character. Ethical issues link together what persons can be as individuals with what they can become as communities. Individuals are shaped by communities and in turn they shape their communities. Emancipation involves freedom and participation. For Alicia, Helen, and the Andersons to be free to live in different ways means the communities in which they function and the structures of society must change. Alicia needs the experience of being loved and affirmed for who she is as a person with a choice about the sexual and parental obligations she wants to assume and at what stage of her life. These value choices are determined to a degree by what Alicia, her family, and her peers believe are real options for the future. Those caught in a life of poverty are seriously limited in the options available to them. Without some trust that the cycle of poverty and dependency can be broken, there is little motivation to risk new ways of being or relating.

While there is a disproportionately high percentage of adolescent mothers who are women of color, the largest numbers are white and from suburban and rural areas. Though the economic issues are more immediate in the urban project and in areas of rural poverty, concerns for meaningfulness and hope are alive and pressing in every part of American culture. Non-poor adolescents from suburbia drift into drugs and loveless sexual experimentation because, they claim, life is "boring" and unfulfilling. The pressing problems in this case are pregnancy and parenting. But the root issue is whether or not individuals can become free enough from the present to live out the possibilities of loving and just relationships.

The symptoms of drug abuse, self-endangering sexual activity, community-alienating behavior, and increasing teenage suicide point to deep problems of motivation. Teams of students and parents, coalitions from the public and private sectors, and studies by religious and secular institutes consistently recommend a renewed concentration on relationships and ethics. More attention, imagination, and funds need to be devoted to "getting with it" rather than "getting away from it all."

ADDITIONAL RESOURCES

Adolescent Pregnancy Prevention: School Community Cooperation. Springfield, Il.: Charles C. Thomas, 1981.

Cotter, Jessie. *The Touch Film.* Available from many university film libraries as well as from the distributor, Sterling Films.

Dickmen, Irving. *Winning the Battle for Sex Education.* New York: SIECUS, 1982.

Education Commission of the States. "At Risk Youth" project, 1987. Available from the commission at 300 Lincoln Tower, 1860 Lincoln Street, Denver, CO 80295.

Garfinkel, Irwin, and Sara S. McLanahan. *Single Mothers and Their Children: A New American Dilemma.* Washington, D.C.: Urban Institute Press, 1986.

Kanerman, Shiela, and Alfred Kahn. *Mothers Alone: Strategies for a Time of Change.* Dover, Mass.: Auburn House, 1987.

Moynihan, Daniel Patrick. "Our Poorest Citizens—Children." In the *Congressional Record*, 100th Congress, 2nd Session, vol. 134, no. 4 (January 28, 1988), S308.

Rodgers, Harrell, Jr. *Poor Women, Poor Families: The Economic Plight of America's Female Households.* Armonk, N.Y.: N. E. Sharpe, 1986.

Welfare Reform and Poverty. A special issue of *Focus,* vol. 11, no. 1 (spring 1988). University of Wisconsin—Madison, Institute for Research on Poverty.

Wilson, William Julius. *The Truly Disadvantaged.* Chicago: University of Chicago Press, 1987.

A number of helpful resources are available from the Allan Guttmacher Institute, 11 Fifth Avenue, New York, NY 10003.

Case

More Light

Don Chandler read again the resolution presented by the Social Involvement Committee: "Shepherd Presbyterian Church will not exclude any active member from election or ordination to office on the basis of race, class, gender, marital status, or sexual orientation." He examined the faces of the other members of the church session (governing body) and heard the pastor, Elaine Campbell, saying, "You understand that passing this resolution will declare us to be a 'More Light' congregation, and that is the intent of the motion. Is there any discussion?"

Don thought back to where it all began. Shepherd Presbyterian was a small church of 130 mostly young, well-educated members, with a fair record of social ministry in Tucson. Two years earlier the congregation had elected Morris Wilson, who made no secret of his homosexuality, to an unexpired term on the nine-member session. It had been a contested election. Morris had been nominated from the floor, the election was postponed, and the session and pastor had led the congregation in six weeks of prayer and study on the issue of homosexuality and ordination. A 1978 decision of the denomination's general assembly (national governing body) offered "definitive guidance" that "self-affirmed, practicing homosexual persons" should not be ordained. That complicated the matter, but when it came to a vote at Shepherd Presbyterian, Morris was elected by a two-to-one margin. The pastor, therefore, ordained and installed him on the session. Shepherd's session informed the presbytery (the regional governing body) of their action, and there had been no adverse response.

The debate on Morris's election had been intense, but things seemed to settle down after his ordination. Don remembered how uncomfortable he had felt with the whole subject, opposed at first even to discussing it. But after working with Morris for two years, things had changed. Morris had

This case was prepared by J. Shannon Webster. Copyright © The Case Study Institute. The names of all persons and places are disguised to protect the privacy of the persons involved in this situation.

become a real Christian brother and a partner in the session's ministry. Don still felt uncomfortable about Morris's sexuality, but in talking with the pastor and others he had decided God did not want him to ground his actions in fear and prejudice.

During the second year of Morris's term, a few gay and lesbian people started to come to Shepherd Church, their numbers eventually reaching nine or ten. Three of them went through the New Member Class and joined the church. Don had been concerned, but later discovered when talking with them that several did not know Morris at all. He remembered one comment in particular: "We heard that this was a safe place to worship God."

It seemed to Don that the pastor felt a particular calling to care for the homosexuals attending Shepherd. He remembered a few sermons where Elaine mentioned gays and lesbians specifically as people who needed to be welcomed into the family of faith. The session began to discuss the possibility of declaring Shepherd a "More Light" congregation. In collecting information and ideas, they wrote to all the "More Light" churches in the denomination, receiving answers from most. Two representatives from the session of a Colorado church paid them a personal visit.

Don learned that "More Light" congregations were those which had in some way voted to include homosexuals as members eligible for election and ordination as church leaders, thereby ignoring the denomination's "guidance." During this time the Permanent Judicial Commission of the denomination ruled that the assembly's guidance was binding, and "More Light" decisions were unconstitutional. The ruling had heightened the discomfort and confusion on the part of the Shepherd session. Don learned that the ruling had been a particularly hurtful decision to the gays and lesbians in the congregation. One person in particular, Jake Owens, had been threatened by the ruling. Jake was an intelligent young architect who had come to the point that he would openly share his hurt and loneliness with members of the congregation. Now he shared his fears with Don. Jake had felt attacked and wounded by churches in the past and to Don he seemed vulnerable. A friendship had developed; Don felt paternal toward Jake. Some of Jake's pain had touched Don. He recalled Jake saying to him, "I'd hoped to become a full member of this church, but I've been here before. I'm afraid Campbell has led me out on the dance floor only to leave me there. How much control does the denomination have over our congregation?"

Then the lid blew off. It had come as a surprise to Don. The church had seemed stable until several people suddenly left. The pastor began to look weary, and over lunch one day she shared with Don that she had been making calls every night. The focus was the gay issue. "I know what the people opposed to the gay and lesbian members want," Elaine said, "but I want them to love each other and make room."

Don had received several phone calls from upset church members in recent weeks. Don was an official with the Red Cross and had credibility in the community and frequent contact with members of the church. He was a long-time member of Shepherd Presbyterian and was serving his fourth year on the session. People in the congregation, as well as other members of the session, seemed to give weight to his opinion and often sought him out to talk.

Peter Chapson had called him. "What's going to be next? The church is attacking everything I believe in. First, we can't call God 'Father' anymore. Then I find out that Elaine is harboring illegal aliens and advocating breaking the law with this 'sanctuary' thing. Now we're getting this gay business forced on us constantly. When they get up and use those words—gay and lesbian—they're describing sexual acts right in the worship service. How much am I supposed to put up with?"

Patty Becker had called to say she was concerned about her children. "This is not good modeling. The Bible calls homosexuality a sin. I have young children, and I don't want to teach them that it isn't. Look how unhappy those people are. We used to be a family-oriented church. But there's very little emphasis on children or family relationships anymore. Whatever happened to the Ten Commandments: Isn't there anything right or wrong anymore? Have we reached the point where anything you want to do is acceptable?"

Jane Weller told Don how upset she was because her husband was leaving the church. "I don't mind if the gay folks are there," she said. "We've always said we were an inclusive and pluralistic church. I don't want us to turn away anyone who loves Jesus. It's okay if they're there, if they just wouldn't be so vocal. When they become so visible, when you put labels on people like 'gay' and 'lesbian,' all it does is separate us into categories. If we hadn't made such an issue of it, we wouldn't have a problem, and John wouldn't be leaving the church."

Don considered the phone calls as the session turned to the "More Light" resolution. Then he thought about Jake Owens, at home anxious and concerned over the outcome of tonight's meeting. The discussion began in earnest. Morris Wilson sat as restrained and calm as usual.

Alberto Tarver, with occasional nervous glances at Morris, attacked the resolution at once. "We can't condone or accept homosexual activity in any way without flying in the face of biblical anthropology. The model in Genesis for full humanness is a partnership—male and female. In the New Testament the church is the Bride of Christ—same model. Paul classifies homosexuality with idolatry. Will we condone idolatry just to be nice?"

"Why take a position?" said Alice Royal. "Maybe there's another way. I can't agree with Alberto, but we've got a good thing going. Why mess it up by taking a formal vote and making public proclamations? This resolution won't affect our local ministry, and it will only split our congregation. We've reached out to the gay community and fully included them in our church life. The congregation will come around eventually. Meanwhile, we can always take 'no action' on this resolution."

Joan Wall, one of the session's newer members, spoke. "I might favor this," she said, "but first I would need to know how the gays in our congregation feel themselves. May I ask Morris a question? Is this resolution important to the gays? Will they understand it as a sign of care and support, or will it further set them apart and single them out? If we don't pass it, how hurt will they be? Will we lose them?"

Morris sat forward in his chair. "Everyone's different, of course. Yes, it would be affirming, a sign of solidarity. And passing this motion would serve to keep the sexuality issue from coming up every time there is an election. But I doubt anyone would leave if we fail to pass the resolution. Most gays and lesbians are accustomed to rejection and oppression and tend to accept them. In that event I would say most of us would be quite disappointed but not surprised."

"We ought to do the right thing," said Dennis Bench, "whatever the cost. I'm uncomfortable when the denomination asks us to exclude from ordained office one, and only one, group of people. It makes them second-class church members. And the apostle said a lot of different things. In his best moment, he said, 'We are all one in Christ Jesus and heirs of the promise.' Jesus called all kinds of different people to his side and empowered them to serve. If there is any idolatry here, it is thinking sexuality is so all-fired important it could make you unfit for ordination. We've said we are a pluralistic church and we are the Body of Christ. Who is outside God's call? Whom shall we exclude from full participation in Christ's Body?"

"We don't have that choice," Millie Stewart replied. "The General Assembly acted, and our highest court ruled on it. We're still a Presbyterian congregation. We are part of a connectional church. If you disagree with a law, you work to change it. You don't break it. You can always overturn the General Assembly. It's the only thing you can do."

Don felt Elaine Campbell's eyes fall on him. "You've been unusually quiet tonight, Don. Where do you think we should go on this?"

Commentary

More Light

The issue before Don and Shepherd Presbyterian involves choices on three distinct matters. Deciding how to respond to the More Light resolution will require prior decisions about biblically and theologically based moral assessments of homosexuality, about the purpose and shape of Christian ministry, and about the binding character of denominational guidelines. Before taking up each of those issues, it may be helpful first to explore briefly some new information on and perspectives toward homosexuality.

NEW LIGHT

Today most Christian denominations are divided over the issue of homosexuality, largely because the unequivocal condemnation of homosexuality which once characterized the Christian tradition has been challenged by recent social scientific research, by increased openness on the part of homosexuals, and by the resulting increase in knowledge and experience of homosexuals by heterosexuals. Though the social sciences have not by any means answered all the questions about homosexuality, there is a great deal of new light. One conclusion of research is that there is an important distinction between homosexual orientation and homosexual activity. Homosexual orientation refers to a predominate sexual attraction to persons of the same sex. Homosexual orientation for most homosexuals seems to be set at a very early age. It does not seem to be voluntary, often presenting itself to the individual as a fait accompli before the individual begins to reason. It would seem impossible for a homosexual orientation to be sinful if it is not chosen. Homosexual activity is sexual activity with a person of the same sex. To act sexually on the basis of homosexual orientation is a choice, just as to act sexually on the basis of heterosexual orientation is a choice.

There is a great deal of research data, some of it contradictory, on the mental health of sexually active homosexuals and the adequacy of relationships among them. In 1973 the American Psychiatric Association removed homosexuality from the category of mental disorders. The tentative conclusion of most researchers in the last two decades has been that, while social attitudes make it more difficult for an individual to accept a homosexual orientation than a heterosexual one, homosexuals who have fully accepted their orientation match adjusted heterosexuals in mental health and stability. One explanation for earlier classification of homosexuality as a mental disorder is that social attitudes kept gays and lesbians in the closet, thus ensuring that data on homosexuality would be based almost exclusively on those who required psychiatric help—the dysfunctionals.

There is no one clear cause for homosexuality. Some researchers believe there may be a genetic predisposition to homosexuality, a disposition which may be triggered by fetal or infancy experiences. Others assume that unknown environmental factors during early childhood cause homosexuality. Research on the childhoods of homosexuals and heterosexuals reveals no particular phenomenon as especially consequential for either homosexual or heterosexual development. While male homosexuals sometimes show a slightly higher rate of absent fathers, there is some debate about how significant this is, given that it is not the norm. Homosexuals do not differ from heterosexuals in the frequency of heterosexual dating during high school, though they enjoy it less. Despite widespread assumptions to the contrary, homosexuals are less likely than heterosexuals to have been seduced by older or more experienced partners in their initial sexual encounters.

Most therapists agree that exclusive homosexuality is extremely difficult, if not impossible, to change to fully functional heterosexuality, though bisexuals and persons of heterosexual orientation who turned to homosexual encounters due to sexual problems in heterosexual relationships can more often be brought to function fully as heterosexuals.

There is a great deal of variety in homosexual lifestyles. About half of lesbians and one quarter of gays are involved in primary relationships. About 11 percent of lesbians and 16 percent of gays seem little interested in either sexual activity or committed relationships. In between these extremes there are many patterns, and significant differences between lesbians and gay patterns. Lesbians are far more likely to have few partners (the majority have fewer than ten over a lifetime) and to be involved in exclusive relationships.

BIBLICAL AND THEOLOGICAL ASSESSMENTS
OF HOMOSEXUALITY

In general, the attitude of the Bible toward homosexuality is negative. Though it records no teaching of Jesus on homosexuality, the Bible does refer to homosexuality both directly and indirectly. The Mosaic law and St. Paul condemn homosexual practices. The Bible story most often cited in regard to homosexuality is the Genesis story of Sodom and Gomorrah. This story is not a good source because of its indirectness; it is not clear that the immorality for which God punishes the cities is homosexuality, for the event which precipitates the destruction is not homosexual intercourse per se, but the attempt to homosexually gang-rape strangers who should have been protected by hospitality.

The biblical story of David and Jonathan is often cited as one in which homosexuality is approved. Certainly the story suggests a level of intimacy and romance between two men which in our society might suggest a homosexual relationship. But homosexuality is not explicit in the story.

Many biblical scholars insist that condemnation of homosexuality by biblical writers should be understood within the context of those writers' times. Biblical writers did not recognize the existence of homosexual *orientation* and thus assumed that perpetrators of homosexuality acted out of a heterosexual orientation. Condemnation of homosexuality in Mosaic law probably was based on viewing it in terms of its common practice in pagan temple ritual, and St. Paul's condemnation may have referred to the Greek practice of pederasty, the sexual exploitation of young boys by older men. Since none of the biblical references gives any rationale for its stance on homosexuality, the biblical evidence alone is definitive only for those who view the Bible as a compilation of absolute divine laws.

Those who would not see biblical condemnations of homosexuality as determinative for Christian churches insist that they are not "dismissing the Bible" but merely responding to what they regard as stronger biblical imperatives, especially the command to love one's neighbor. Jesus' own ministry, they maintain, focused special concern on marginalized groups, on persons despised and excluded for aspects of their lives beyond their control.

Further, those who insist homosexuality is not sinful argue that the essence of sin is that it offends God. But this does not mean that the designation of what is sinful and what is not is, or could be, arbitrary on God's part. That which offends God does so because it runs counter to God's intentions for creation, because it destroys or impedes the formation of peaceful, loving, and just relationships within human community. When we forget this, and presume that designations of sin depend totally on the judgments of religious authorities who "represent" God, ignoring the need to test designations of sin by examining their consequences, we allow the concept of sin to be used to exploit.

This was the situation Jesus objected to in his own religious milieu. Priests, scribes, Pharisees, and almost all Jews understood sin as failure to obey the Mosaic law. The common people were understood as sinners by the fact of their ignorance of the law. The Pharisees in particular blamed the poor masses for Israel's status as a conquered, occupied nation; this situation was understood as God's punishment for the masses' failure to obey the many and varied prescriptions of the law.

Jesus strongly objected, and called into question this understanding of sin which characterized his age. He refused to treat those designated as sinners with the prescribed avoidance and disdain. He presented God as loving Father, not as legalistic judge, and lifted concern for persons above concern for law. When he said he had come not for the righteous but for sinners, he was referring to those whom the religious authorities regarded as sinners, those for whom the law offered no hope. Jesus did not prejudicially regard all these persons as unredeemable sinners, as did the purveyors of the law; his chief message to these despised masses was that they should have hope in the saving action of the Father who loved them. The sinful deeds, even of persons such as prostitutes and tax collectors, who were considered the worst of the public sinners, were not the focus of Jesus. For Jesus, the real mark of righteousness was concern for the poorest, weakest, and most despised, and the keynote of sin was turning one's back on those persons and, ultimately, on God. This is what the parable of the Good Samaritan is all about: the good person may be a heretical sinner (a Samaritan), and the priest who obeys every part of the ritual law and worships in the temple may be damned.

Viewed from within this framework, it would seem unreasonable to condemn homosexuality simply on the grounds of proclaiming that "it is sin." We have an obligation to evaluate homosexuality and ask whether and how it separates us from loving, just relationships with God and neighbor. It is not enough to say that "this is sin because St. Paul says so in 1 Corinthians 6:9–10 and 1 Timothy 1:9–10." We must question whether homosexuals per se belong in a list of sinners with idolators, adulterers, drunkards, slanderers, swindlers, and thieves. Certainly some forms of homosexuality belong in such a list—those which include coercion, the molestation of children, or the use of others as objects—as do similar forms of heterosexuality. We must probe deeper than this. When we fail to probe the concrete reality of a behavior, but decide it is sinful because we are told so by authority we respect, we take the risk of imitating those who condemn the poor as sinners for their ignorance, the risk of wrongfully judging others as sinners.

Theological, as opposed to biblical, treatment of homosexuality has traditionally included two major objections to the practice. The following paragraphs will sketch those two major objections and also briefly present some of the questions and counter-positions that are frequently raised to the tradition's arguments. This would seem fair because these questions and counter-positions can help stir discussion and thought on the issue and because many are quick to accept the traditional assumptions on the matter without giving it deeper thought.

The first of the tradition's major objections to homosexuality is that it is nonprocreative. For those who view procreative possibility as a normative aspect of sexual activity, sometimes even as the only factor which legitimates sexual pleasure, homosexuality lacks moral validity. Within the Roman Catholic church, interpretations of natural law based on the causal relation between sexual intercourse and procreation have produced a rejection of any use of sexual faculties which is not open to the possibility of procreation within heterosexual marriage. This argument carries much less force among Protestants because they reject the interpretation of natural law on which the argument rests. Protestants do not understand procreation as a normative purpose of sexuality, as the acceptance of artificial contraception by Protestant churches demonstrates.

Further—as to the criterion of procreation—we can question whether it is really a definitive and *consistent* grounds for condemnation of homosexuality. Those who raise this question point out that Christian tradition has never denied marriage to the sterile, or to women past menopause. Thus it does not demand procreation as a criterion for all sexual acts. Nor does the Presbyterian church, or many other Christian churches, forbid the use of contraceptives. For those churches, then, sexual activity can be licit for heterosexuals even when it does not intend or cannot result in procreation. Working from these bases one can go on to argue that homosexuality should not be condemned on the grounds that it is not open to procreation. A variation on this position is that procreation should be normative only for heterosexuals, those for whom procreation is possible. For those with exclusively homosexual orientation, procreation would not be normative.

The second traditional reason for prohibiting homosexuality is the assumption that gender complementarity is an essential part of creation. The assumption that men and women were made essentially different and intended for each other so that together they become one whole has been prevalent in our history. Today it is much more difficult to make this case than in the past because in recent years it has been demonstrated that the vast majority of traits and roles that once were assumed to be sex-based are in fact learned, rather than inherent. There are very few traits and no roles which seem to be inherent in greater numbers of one sex than the other, and those few traits are exclusive to neither sex. Therefore, it would seem that in terms of traits and roles wholeness is not predicated upon "complementary" relations with a person of the opposite sex. And there are other questions we can raise about the notions that the interplay of complementary traits and behaviors is necessary for wholeness and that we gain access to that complementarity only in relations with persons of the opposite gender. One simple but key question in this regard is: Aren't persons of the same sex often more different from us in personality structure and behavior than members of the other sex? Doesn't such wholeness, then, come from our relations with persons of both genders? In short, if traits and roles are not specific to one gender, then where lies the "natural" complementarity? These and other questions and counter-positions are frequently raised by those who challenge the positions on homosexuality that have been traditionally held in the church, and as further research is done into homosexuality and into the positions of theology and scripture on the matter, the debate enters new levels and is enriched.

In summary, we can say that the morality of homosexuality is not easy to assess in clear-cut and simple terms. For many, it seems reasonable to assume that homosexuals should be bound to the same moral criteria for sexual activity to which heterosexuals are bound. Many others take a stance similar to that expressed in an October 1986 Vatican letter to the U.S. bishops, "On the Pastoral Care of Homosexual Persons," which affirmed the existing ban on homosexual sexual activity, and insisted that while homosexual orientation is not sinful per se, it is a disorder because it precedes and often leads to homosexual behavior. The letter urges bishops to discourage organizations of homosexuals on the grounds that, for persons with homosexual orientation, such organizations constitute situations of temptation, called "near occasions of sin."

Clearly, at this time much of the difficulty of assessing homosexuality swirls around the distinctions between homosexual orientation and activity. Until we can separate what is essential to homosexuality from the dysfunctional aspects which attach to it because of social rejection and stigmatization, it will be difficult to judge. Such a separation can occur only where there are no social sanctions against homosexuality.

CHRISTIAN MINISTRY

The three options presented to the session at Shepherd Presbyterian seem to represent different conceptions of what Christian ministry means. Comments of members about concern for family life, and the development of sexual orientation in their children, indicate that these people see ministers as role models, persons who represent to the community the shape of authentic Christian life. It is of course true that ministers do serve as role models. Yet both sociologically and theologically, there are limits to this modeling. Ministers are not the only models children have of leaders, of respected men and women, or even of religious men and women. In addition most children will be exposed to more than one minister, and will therefore not need to choose any one person as a model. Theologically, no single person or group can ever represent the fullness of Jesus Christ. We have only a sketch of three years in the life of the historical Jesus; our imitating Jesus in new times and circumstances will produce myriad models.

Those strongly opposed to the More Light resolution protest that homosexuals are a threat to family life, and we can assume that that protest is largely based on the belief that homosexuals are dangerous models that subvert normative family structure and the orientation of children. However, we know today that modeling is not a cause of homosexuality. Children raised by homosexuals are no more likely to become homosexual than those raised by heterosexuals. The real issue thus is not modeling, but rather it has to do with our definition of the normative family. Most pleas to protect family life today refer to the endangered two-parent nuclear family where the father works and the wife keeps house. However, this type of family accounts for less than 20 percent of the families in the United States. Thus the norm is a decided minority, and we can expect that in the future the vast majority of families will continue to diverge from the traditional norm regarding families.

Should the church retain this norm that implies that most North American families are somehow defective? Where did the norm originate? The Christian church was originally structured as a family precisely to *substitute* for the natural family, since the majority of the early members were estranged from their families by the fact of their Christianity. The early church was founded on those who were outside the predominating model of family; it is ironic that it is today proposed that those who are marginalized from the predominating model of family should be excluded from the church in order to protect nuclear families.

This leads to a final issue regarding Christian ministry, one already raised above. It is simply this: homosexuals are marginalized; a major feature of Jesus' project was solidarity with the marginalized. Thus it is important to consider what kind of church we are modeling when we work to exclude the marginalized from membership or ministry.

DENOMINATIONAL GUIDELINES

Beyond these issues that revolve around the models and roles of ministry and the purpose of ministry itself, the function of denominational guidelines in ministry is in question. Alice Royal's "No Action" proposal seems to presume that the purpose of ministry is to unify persons in an inclusive community and avoid conflicts that could disrupt that community. She argues that Morris's election despite the General Assembly's guidance to the contrary proved that Shepherd was inclusive, and that passing the More Light resolution would only create unnecessary dissension.

Those against the More Light resolution appear to invoke a vision of ministry which is based on witness to Christian law. The guidance of the General Assembly is understood by this group to set clear limits on local congregations' ministry. In addition, many of those opposed understand scripture as a legal source, and read its references to homosexuality as final. The role of the local congregation is to abide by the judgment of scripture and the governing body. Ministry in the local congregation then takes the shape of witnessing to these judgments.

Supporters of the More Light resolution insist there is a Christian obligation to demonstrate inclusiveness of gays and lesbians because they have been despised and excluded in church and community. This group seems to understand ministry in terms of personal and communal outreach to the marginalized.

It is probable that there are other motives animating some members of these groups, motives which are questionable from an ethical perspective. Individuals who oppose the resolution may be acting out of homophobia, an unreasoning fear and hatred of homosexuality. Homophobia is common in our society, and often prevents rational approaches to this issue. On the other hand, those supporting the resolution may be denying that sexuality is a moral concern; they may understand it as private, a matter of individual preference. Neither of these perspectives is acceptable. The first is prejudice; the second fails to understand that all aspects of our lives have moral dimensions and are subject to the gospel.

The No Action supporters may be seeking to avoid conflict at any cost, out of an understanding of unity based on conflict avoidance. But there is no love without a willingness to risk conflict. Real unity arises from resolving conflicts, not from avoiding them after they are present. We have obligations both to reach out in love to those outside the community, and to protect the common life of the community. There is often a real tension between these two obligations, a tension which does not resolve itself without conflict.

One way to think about this issue is to try to reach an "original position" regarding what rules should be binding. If we all sat down to construct the rules for a society and were ignorant of what roles we would play in that society, we might see other sides of the issue. For example, if we did not know whether we would be male or female, straight or gay, white or black, president or migrant worker, we might be forced to stretch our imaginations when seeking to structure a just society. If we suddenly discovered a homosexual orientation in ourselves, would it change our stance?

Another way to approach the issue of who should minister would be to look to crisis situations. What would happen if this community at Shepherd were hit with a devastating tragedy? What if a number of the teenage children of the speakers at the session were killed or seriously injured together in an accident or in some other type of tragedy? The next weeks and months would be filled with desperate needs for comforting the grieving, and supplying emotional, material, and spiritual help to the families who had suffered the tragedy. The community would need to grapple with its faith in the light of this suffering of the innocent. If Morris were to demonstrate his ministerial gifts, and his fellow gays their Christian neighborliness in such a time, would that affect the situation? Would the crisis shed any light on the purpose and meaning of Christian ministry?

Finally, one of the problems with the guidelines from the General Assembly is that they only bar from election and ordination self-affirmed and practicing homosexuals. Covert homosexuals can still be elected and ordained, though research shows that these are the homosexuals most likely to have adjustment problems and relational dysfunctions. To the extent that such a guideline encourages homosexuals who desire service roles in the church to remain covert, it seems both to encourage dysfunction among homosexuals and to perpetuate homophobia through ignorance about homosexuals. The guideline penalizes homosexuals for honesty.

ENCOURAGING GROWTH

In conclusion, we can say that in regard to the morality of homosexuality, both Catholic and Protestant churches are torn by divisions both among theologians and between church teaching and beliefs of vocal members. Adopting the the Catholic rejection of all sexual pleasure and activity outside those heterosexual marriages open to procreation would mandate that no Christian church could ordain anyone who identified himself or herself as an active homosexual. The decision would then be to reject the More Light resolution.

However, for those who accept either artificial contraception or sexual activity outside of marriage and who believe that "complementarity" can occur outside of heterosexual relations, it is entirely possible to reach some sort of provisional acceptance of forms of homosexuality which meet moral criteria for responsible sexual relationships, given the inconclusive nature of biblical and theological reflection on homosexuality, and the lack of definitively negative social science data. Whether the best method of moving in this direction is to pass the More Light resolution, or to take No Action while planning informational programs for Shepherd, is open to debate. No Action alone, without some clear attempt to create support for inclusion of homosexuals who desire to minister, seems a too easy way out. It could be understood as the choice for unity over justice and hard-won community.

Given the debate stirred over this issue at Shepherd Presbyterian and in our society and churches in general, it is clear that the issue is going to command and demand much more reflection and dialogue in the coming years.

ADDITIONAL RESOURCES

Bayer, R. *Homosexuality and American Psychiatry.* New York: Basic Books, 1981.

Boswell, John. *Christianity, Social Tolerance, and Homosexuality.* Chicago: University of Chicago Press, 1980.

Genovesi, Vincent J. *In Pursuit of Love: Catholic Morality and Human Sexuality.* Wilmington, Del.: Michael Glazier, 1987.

Grammick, Jeannine, and Pat Furey. *The Vatican and Homosexuality: Reactions to the "Letter to the Bishops of the Catholic Church on the Pastoral Care of Homosexual Persons."*

McNeill, John J. *The Church and the Homosexual.* Kansas City: Sheed and Ward, 1976.

————. *Taking a Chance on God: Liberating Theology for Gays, Lesbians, and Their Lovers, Friends, and Families.* Boston: Beacon, 1988.

Nelson, James B. *Embodiment: An Approach to Sexuality and Christian Theology.* Minneapolis: Augsburg, 1978.

————. *Between Two Gardens: Reflections on Sexuality and Religious Experience.* New York: Pilgrim, 1983.

————. *The Intimate Connection: Male Sexuality, Male Spirituality.* Philadelphia: Westminster, 1988.

Spong, John Selby. *Living in Sin? A Bishop Rethinks Human Sexuality.* San Francisco: Harper and Row, 1988.

PART VIII

LIFE AND DEATH

Case

Mary Gardner's Fourth Pregnancy

Tom and Mary Gardner had planned their trip to Spain for more years than they could remember. They felt that at last their children, now twelve, eleven, and six, were old enough for them to be away for the four weeks. The children were all in school and Mary's mother, who had always been very close to the family, had flown up to "hold down the fort," as she put it. Westminster Church, where Tom had been pastor for the past ten years, supported the leave with a potluck supper and a monetary gift which made the trip possible.

As both Mary and Tom affirmed, the first week of the vacation was glorious. Thus when Mary began to experience nausea, she was especially annoyed. Her chagrin turned to stunned confusion when she suddenly suspected she was pregnant. Several days later Mary shared her anxiety with Tom, stressing that there was no definite confirmation of her pregnancy.

Tom almost immediately raised the possibility of an abortion. He then tried to clarify his reaction, stating that through his counseling of others and personal reflection he had come to believe that in some circumstances abortion could be a responsible action. Mary felt her feelings of trust and mutuality turning to anger. She stated that she was confused, even deeply disappointed, but added that she did not feel she could ever consider an abortion. Mary then added that they should wait until she had seen a doctor before they discussed it again.

After Mary and Tom left the large hospital in Barcelona with the "positive" medical report in their possession, she cried for nearly an hour. Tom comforted her and assured her that if she decided to have the baby they would surely be able to manage and would love this child as deeply as the

This case was prepared by Robert A. and Alice Frazer Evans. Copyright © The Case Study Institute. All names have been disguised to protect the privacy of the individuals involved.

others. He stressed that his primary concern was for her.

During the next week Mary became increasingly preoccupied with worrying about what she ought to do. She deeply respected Tom's judgment and tried to deal with his suggestion of an abortion. She remembered her pregnancy with Sara, who was much younger than the other children, and the real difficulty she had adjusting to Sara's arrival. Now with three children she felt that the quality of individual attention she considered essential for each child was already threatened by being spread too thin. And to be blatantly practical, Tom's salary covered the family needs only with careful budgeting. Another consideration was college education for three children, the first only a few years away. Furthermore, Mary had always wanted to support a child in a Third World country through the church agency. She was sure this was a responsible use of family funds. Mary tried to pray about the decision, but found little help in prayer and reflection. Suddenly Mary declared to Tom that she would have an abortion while they were still in Spain, and it would all be over, with no one at home ever knowing.

Tom refused to consider this as an option, saying that they would be home in another week with a doctor they knew and trusted and that she might feel differently in her own home environment.

When the Gardners returned home, Mary immediately made an appointment with her doctor. Tom went with her to the office. Dr. Weiss also confirmed the pregnancy, then clearly outlined the pregnancy termination procedure at what he felt was the best clinic in the area. When Mary began to discuss the abortion, however, she was unable to control her crying and expressed the great doubts she really had about the decision.

She had discussed with Dr. Weiss the possibility of sterilization following Sara's birth, but at the last moment did not request it. Dr. Weiss told Mary that if she decided to have this baby, he would deliver it only on the condition that he perform a tubal ligation following the delivery. Upon Mary's insistence, he made an appointment for her at the clinic the next week and filled out the necessary papers, but told her that she could always call him if she changed her mind.

Mary had consciously avoided her close friends after returning from the trip. Her depression deepened. Although she and Tom were able to discuss the decision to some extent, they both decided they needed the help of an uninvolved party. Mary called Carl Jenkins, an experienced family counselor and good friend. He agreed to see them immediately.

In the counseling situation Mary was asked to express the uneasiness she was feeling. "Well," she said, "Tom asked me way back in Barcelona if I had the choice, would I want to be pregnant. I definitely would not. We tried to prevent that from happening as best we could. But now is the issue really what I want? How could God bless my consciously deciding to kill this new possibility of life growing in me? How could I believe that our other three children are beautiful, joyous gifts of God and that this one is just an accident?"

After a pause, she continued. "I guess another thing that is bothering me terribly is that I know my family, certain friends, and surely some members of the church could never understand my having an abortion. The idea of sharing this with our children is absolutely unthinkable. I just could never tell any of them. As a child, any time I felt I had something to hide from my family, I always knew I was doing something wrong. And now I feel really abandoned. Tom wants this to be my decision, but I don't see how I can make it. I see so many valid reasons for not having this child, but I'm unable to affirm that choice."

Carl Jenkins encouraged Tom to respond openly. "I'm pretty sensitive to the fact that Mary will sometimes look to me for answers," he replied. "If I make this decision for her, then it becomes fully my responsibility. I am very concerned about her choosing to have the abortion and then regretting it for the rest of her life. So I want to offer her love and support but not make the decision for her."

"But," prodded Carl, "isn't this your decision too? Does love and support for Mary not demand that you tell her how you feel about the abortion?"

Tom was slow to respond. "Well, if I really speak on the gut level, I want Mary to have the abortion, and that, of course, is what I blurted out when I learned about the pregnancy in Barcelona. We married right after college, and our first son was born a little less than a year later. For so many years she has been bound by her role in the home. I see a good part of this stemming from Mary's perception of herself as a responsible mother. In the past couple of years, though, as Sara has become more independent, I have been elated to watch Mary begin to find out who she really is, to start some projects for herself, and — this is admittedly selfish on my part — to have more time for me. All that had begun to happen in the years before Sara's birth, and I felt at that time Mary's return to the full-time mother role was a real sacrifice for her and in many ways was destructive to her personal growth. I love her too much to want that to happen again."

With Carl's encouragement Mary and Tom talked well into the evening about whether or not to have the child. When they rose to leave, Carl expressed his concern and love for them both and asked Mary, if she were willing, if she would call in a week to let him know what she had decided.

Commentary

Mary Gardner's Fourth Pregnancy

Mary Gardner, with her husband Tom, faces an agonizing decision: whether to terminate with medical assistance an unwanted pregnancy in its early stages. With her decision Mary enters fierce public debates over the definition of human life, the meaning of motherhood, the issue of who should control the abortion decision, and the role of sacrifice in Christian life. If this were not enough, she must also work through a crisis in her relationship with Tom.

In facing this decision Mary needs to investigate the facts about abortion in her society; the resources of scripture and Christian tradition regarding abortion, definitions of human life, and parenting roles; and the choices and roles open to her and other women in contemporary society.

FACTS ABOUT ABORTION IN THE UNITED STATES

Mary's option to elect to have a legal abortion is provided in the United States under that landmark 1973 Supreme Court decision, Roe v. Wade, which ruled that in the early stages of pregnancy prior to the viability of the fetus, the decision to have an abortion must be left to a woman and her doctor. Only after viability may the state prohibit abortion and then not when the woman's life is in danger. This ruling threw out the laws of most states enacted in the second half of the nineteenth century prohibiting abortion unless a physician could claim compelling medical indications. Slightly over 1.5 million legal abortions are performed in the United States each year. This number has risen from about 650,000 (200,000 legal and a best-guess 450,000 illegal) in 1970. The years immediately after the Supreme Court's Roe v. Wade decision saw a sharp increase in abortions, but the numbers have remained fairly constant since the early 1980s. Approximately one in three pregnancies ends in legal abortion, with over 90 percent of these being in the first trimester. Another 15 to 30 percent end in spontaneous abortion (miscarriage). For 35 percent of the women who obtain abortions, it is not their first.

Seventy-four percent of women who get abortions are unmarried. Over 26 percent are teenagers. Of the 1.1 million or so teens who get pregnant each year, 400,000, or about 36 percent, get abortions. The rate is much higher for teens from affluent families than it is for those from poor families, and among all women, the rate is higher for whites than for blacks. Another 15 percent of teens experience spontaneous abortions. Of the roughly 50 percent of teens who give birth an overwhelming number (more than 95 percent) keep their children.

Abortions are relatively safe for the woman involved. Only one woman in one hundred forty experiences complications. The maternal death rate due to abortion-related causes is 1.6 per 100,000. The figure for live births is 14 per 100,000.

Women seek abortions for many reasons. Contraceptive failure may have been a factor in this case, as Mary states that she and Tom "tried to prevent the pregnancy as best we could." Contraceptive failure is often cited by women seeking abortions.

In the United States, opinion polls indicate substantial acceptance of abortion in cases of rape, incest, danger to the mother's life and mental health, or a deformed fetus. Most polls indicate majority approval of the Roe v. Wade decision, although a few polls indicate a fairly even split. Disapproval of abortion is greatest when it is viewed as a form of family planning. Studies also indicate that for most women the decision to abort is an agonizing one that is often followed by feelings of guilt and sometimes regret.

SCRIPTURE AND TRADITION

At the outset of this exploration into Christian scripture and tradition on the issue, it might be good to stress here something that is obvious in the case: Mary and Tom are Protestants. Given the name of their church, it is quite likely that they are Presbyterians, or at least members of a church of the Reformed tradition. Most Reformed churches, in particular the Presbyterian Church (U.S.A.), do not dismiss abortion as an option. In what follows a number of positions are discussed, but in the end the perspective of Tom and Mary's religious community must be appreciated, for it is from within that perspective that Mary and Tom struggle with their decision.

It also might be helpful to point out at this point that as one surveys the Christian tradition, scripture, and the contemporary views and roles of women, five central issues keep rising to the fore. These are: the goodness of life, natural law, self-sacrifice, freedom, and the well-being of women. In the rest of this commentary these issues will come up again and again in varying combinations, and will be viewed from various perspectives. Students and instructors may find it helpful to keep these views in mind as a way of focusing dialogue and thought as they reflect upon the case.

Survey of the Tradition in General

Historically, abortion has not been a major issue in the Christian tradition. For centuries it was unsafe, children were considered an economic benefit, and underpopulation, not overpopulation, was the more common problem. The Bible itself has nothing directly to say about the morality of abortion. Although the Bible does not legislate about abortion, the Old Testament does indirectly provide some insight. Within the Mosaic law, fetal life was held to have value. Anyone who caused the loss of fetal life was held guilty and subject to sanctions. But the loss of fetal life was not of equal weight with the death of the already born. Responsibility for loss of fetal life was not considered murder, but a lesser crime for which payment in coin was to be made in restitution. It is perhaps most accurate to say that the Mosaic law regarded fetal life as potential human life and therefore of value. The New Testament does not directly deal with abortion or the value of fetal life.

The Christian theological tradition has been rather consistently against abortion since the early church. Some describe this as continuity within the tradition, but others make two points which undermine the value of the tradition's consistency. It may be useful at this point briefly to discuss those two points, for that discussion will help to bring the key issues in the debate into focus.

The first point is that although "abortion" has been denounced within the theological tradition of the church, until relatively recently the term was understood to describe the deliberate termination of pregnancy after the infusion of the soul (ensoulment), which was generally held to occur anywhere from six weeks to four months after conception. Thomas Aquinas, the Scholastic thinker whose philosophy and theology were made normative for the Catholic Church in 1878, adapted Aristotle's teaching and held that God infused the soul into the fetus at forty days after conception for males, and eighty days after conception for females. In fact, popular folk practice for over a thousand years in Christian Europe until after the Reformation was to regard quickening (first fetal movement) as the definitive evidence of ensoulment, which was understood to be the cause of animation. Quickening usually occurs about the beginning of the fifth month. Until that time midwives regularly practiced various methods of terminating pregnancy, most of them dangerous.

Tradition carries great weight in theological and moral thought, especially when it has been consistent. This is appropriate because of the recognition that the Holy Spirit not only enlightens the present generation, but has also enlightened past Christian communities who passed this tradition on. But if all Christian communities condemned "abortion" but permitted termination of pregnancy for some time after conception, does this really constitute a consistent tradition for banning all termination of pregnancy?

A second issue raised concerning the critical views of the Christian tradition on abortion is the fact that at least some of the tradition's opposition to abortion rested upon false understandings about the nature of conception and the natures of men and women. Many of these beliefs are no longer accepted by Christians. In the past there was widespread agreement in the theological tradition that the primary purpose of marriage was pro- creation; that the only purpose of sexuality was procreation; that women as a sex had been created by God solely for motherhood (although they could renounce sexuality through religious vows of celibacy); and that a woman's sole contribution to the process of procreation was acceptance in her body of the self-contained seed of her husband, which it was her role to shelter and nourish. Christian churches have modified or abandoned all these beliefs.

Today Roman Catholics and almost all Protestant churches agree that procreation is but one purpose of marriage, and that the covenant love between the spouses is equally or more important. There is similar agree- ment that sexuality is not an evil or near-evil tolerated for the sake of children, and that sexual pleasure is itself legitimate and valuable for its role in bonding the spouses to each other in love. All Christian churches accept the findings of biological science regarding the equal genetic con- tribution of parents in conception. All Christian churches recognize the equality of women at least in theory, although there are tremendous divi- sions among and within denominations over whether women's nature is ordained for motherhood or is open to other roles which women might choose.

Those who support the ban on abortion are quick to point out that raising the above issues within a centuries-old tradition is not sufficient reason to reverse the ban. The heart of the issue is the preservation of human life. This is why much of the discussion within and outside the churches is about when in the process of gestation fetal life becomes human and should be protected by the law and about how much to emphasize the life of the fetus in relation to the life of the mother and others affected by a birth.

Finally, as regards the tradition as a whole, there is the matter of con- science. All churches, including the Catholic Church, which takes a definite and rigorous stance on abortion, have long-standing teaching regarding the moral necessity of developing and following individual conscience. There are very complex relations among one's individual conscience, the teachings of one's church, and the values of the society in which one lives, but all churches agree that the conscience is a lynchpin of the process of making important decisions.

This would mean that Mary should not make her decision based on the fact that the majority believe that abortion can be moral, or that those who approve abortion tend to be more educated and middle-class. Nor should she make her decision based solely on the teaching of her religious tradition or authority. She must consult all sources and judge for herself. Religious traditions can furnish arguments that Mary finds ultimately convincing. Sociological data about the opposing sides in the abortion debate can il- luminate the reasons individuals are more influenced by some reasons than others. But it is never legitimate to shortcut the formation of personal conscience and blindly accept the conclusions of others.

Groundings of Catholic and Protestant Positions

In the ethical treatment of abortion in Christianity today there is great division that appears at a number of ethical levels. As was touched upon above, a primary division occurs over the definition and value given to fetal life.

The Roman Catholic Church has defined all fetal life as full human life, while most Protestant churches are unwilling to define any specific point at which the fetus is fully human. Pope Pius IX in 1869 stipulated excommunication for abortion and fixed conception as the moment when the fetus, in technical terms at this stage a zygote, becomes a person, and, religiously speaking, ensoulment occurs. In so doing he closed the door on the hitherto prevailing view that distinguished between an animate and an inanimate fetus, that fixed the moment of ensoulment at quickening, and that by implication permitted abortion before quickening. Protestants in the United States, influenced like Catholics by more than a century of opposition to abortion by physicians attempting to take over the birthing process from "unscientific" and "untrained" female midwives, generally followed suit with the pope. From the 1870s to the 1960s the matter was settled and debate virtually closed.

Today the Catholic Church's strong opposition to the practice of abortion as well as to allowing women the legal option of abortion is based primarily on two moral principles. The first is that according to natural law tradition, God's will is embedded in the patterns of creation and can be apprehended by the human mind. According to the Catholic interpretation of this tradition, a rational investigation of sexuality reveals that its innate purpose is twofold: procreation and mutual love. Therefore every sexual act must be open to the possibility of conception and should express love. Anything which interferes with either thwarts God's intent. This perspective has been the backbone of Roman Catholic proscription of both abortion and artificial contraception. It is for this reason that abortion is understood as a sexual sin, as well as a form of murder.

The second moral principle used by the Catholic Church in its rejection of abortion is one which absolutely forbids the direct taking of innocent life. This is not a prohibition against all taking of life. Not all life is innocent. It is not forbidden for the state to take the life of the guilty in capital punishment, or for soldiers to kill other soldiers who are presumed to be trying to kill them, or for anyone to kill in defense of self or others under attack. Further, under this principle it is possible that one would not be held responsible for killing an innocent, if that killing is indirect. For example, indirect abortions can be permitted under this principle. If a pregnant woman has a cancerous uterus, a hysterectomy to remove the cancerous uterus is permitted if the delay until delivery poses a threat to her life. The purpose of the hysterectomy is to remove the diseased body part that threatens the woman's life. The loss of the life of the fetus is indirect and not intended, for the hysterectomy would have been performed had she been pregnant or not.

Most Protestants are not convinced by these Catholic arguments because they do not share Catholic biological interpretations of natural law or Catholic assumptions about full human life existing from conception. While virtually all Protestants accept the ban on direct taking of innocent life, many deny that fetal life is fully human and therefore protected by the ban. Nor have Protestants relied on natural law as a moral grounding because historically Protestant churches have understood the Fall to have corrupted human reason to such an extent that humans are without any natural capacity to comprehend God's will, and are instead dependent on God's grace for understanding.

Today natural law is receiving more Protestant attention than in the past largely because of its role in civil morality. But the biologically based model of natural law used by the Catholic Church is rejected in favor of models which draw upon other human capacities as well. For example, one might find that a number of types of actions and goals—preservation of human life by avoiding overpopulation or the use of abortion when family income is already minimal or a mother's health is in danger—rest on equally compelling interpretations of natural law, in that God gave human beings the desire to preserve the species with dignity.

A further problem for Mary in this perspective is the finiteness of human rationality. God's will can be intentionally or unintentionally misread and is always discovered through the eyes of a specific culture. What in one culture or historical period seems "natural" or clear does not in others. There is no way to decide what is natural short of imposing authority. Mary is caught in this dilemma as she struggles between the perceptions that "our children are beautiful, joyous gifts of God" and "this one is just an accident."

CONTEMPORARY ATTITUDES
TOWARD WOMEN AND MOTHERHOOD

Other religious arguments which favor or condemn abortion depend heavily upon the two issues discussed above—whether the fetus is fully human life and whether God's will can be determined through investigation of biological processes. The way in which these two issues are interpreted not only shapes much of the basis for the way in which abortion is viewed, but also affects our view of motherhood and the role of women in our society. As stated above, in Christianity much debate around the issue of abortion focuses upon nuances and inconsistencies in the Christian tradition's position on the nature of fetal life. Those positions and debates have been spelled out in the previous sections because they form part of the backdrop of and resources for Mary and Tom's decision. Without losing sight of those issues, this section will shift the focus more to the varying conceptions of women and motherhood that are powerful aspects of Mary's context as she strives to reach a decision about her pregnancy. A cornerstone in the debate about motherhood and women's roles is the norm of well-being, with its attendant norms of self-sacrifice and self-development, freedom, and justice and equality. The emphasis in this section is upon the perspective that stresses freedom, justice, self-development, and equality for women. The reasons for emphasizing this perspective are that it has been a key catalyst for the current debates about abortion and is a major element in the strains in Tom and Mary's relationship.

Well-being

At the heart of the clash over abortion and what constitutes the well-being of women are two quite different views of motherhood and the role of women in society. Mary Gardner is caught between these views, and her struggle runs much deeper than the decision of whether or not to abort. It involves how she understands herself as a woman, wife, and mother. There is, of course, a great variety of views on the issues of women's role and what constitutes their well-being. Without doing too much injustice to these views and for the sake of clarity and discussion, these many views will be arranged under two opposing headings, the "traditional view" and what is called a "new conception."

The traditional view stresses that a woman's well-being is fulfilled through her service to her children and husband. Such service is what truly frees. This traditional view is held by many of the most ardent opponents of legalized abortion. In part rooted in the natural law position discussed above, their view is that there are intrinsic differences between men and women, differences which lead to dissimilar roles. Men work in paid jobs and provide for women whose primary role is child bearing and rearing. Male leadership, exercised in a benevolent way, is considered normal and right. Freedom for women to work outside the home or to abort is of little practical importance and may even be a threat since it appears to upset the natural pattern and downgrade traditional roles. In sum, at one end of the spectrum on the views of what constitutes women's well-being is the position which stresses service to children and husband, and self-sacrifice. The structure of Mary and Tom's marriage seems to reflect this traditional view, which held sway until quite recently.

Opposed to the above position is a view which, in essence, holds that women's well-being is fostered through equality with men and through the freedom to make choices about a host of issues — from careers to motherhood to the structure of relationships between men and women. Those who advocate this position hold that the context of women's lives today is radically different from the context in which the traditional view of women's roles developed. They point out that, for instance, dramatic changes are now occurring in the relation between men and women, changes partially indicated by the great increase of women in the work force. In 1960, women were 30 percent of the work force. In 1981, 43 percent, with many seeking career patterns. This is not a mere change in numbers. This shift reflects a new self-conception of women as free and equal partners in society capable of doing what men do, and having the right to pursue nontraditional roles.

This new conception of women, the dominant one among those who advocate women having a choice about abortion, sees men and women as substantially equal. Traditional roles are seen as reflecting not the order of nature but the ideology of a male-dominated society. The combination of male domination and oppressive ideology inhibits the full development and well-being of women. Being a mother is important, and many will elect it, but it is not the only role for women. In this view women must have choices about service and sacrifice, two central Christian affirmations it would do well to explore in greater depth before moving on to the central issues of choice and equality.

Self-sacrifice

Within the Christian tradition there are various views of self-sacrifice, all largely stemming from interpretations of the words and actions of Jesus. One powerful image that is frequently raised here is that of Jesus on the cross and the implied mandate to sacrifice the self on behalf of others. In very broad terms, we can say that many who stress this interpretation of Jesus urge a woman such as Mary to choose against having an abortion and to opt for sacrifice for others—her family, husband, and the fetus she carries. But here the discussion returns to a key question raised above—Is the fetus fully human? Does it constitute one of the "others" that Mary is called to sacrifice for?

There are also questions about the understanding of self-sacrifice. Counter to the more traditional position is one that stresses a different interpretation of Jesus' sacrifice on the cross. In this interpretation Jesus did not go to the cross for the sake of self-sacrifice, but in order to bring others a full and new life in the realm he announced. Self-sacrifice was a means, not an end, the end being entrance into the realm of God. Thus what is normative is bringing others to this realm. Still, self-sacrifice, or, in less extreme terms, service to others, is often a good means to this end, so much so that in certain circumstances it is legitimately normative. The legitimacy of self-sacrifice depends on whether there is an integrated self to sacrifice or give in service freely. The integrated self is a gift given by God through Jesus Christ and received in mutual love and community. It cannot be commanded or exhorted from individuals who are in a state of disintegration due to oppressive forces and repressive ideologies. These individuals literally have no self to give. This is crucial. Calling for self-sacrifice from someone without an integrated self—for example a slave or an abused and passive woman—is not a call to new life but to further slavery and oppression because it does not produce but in fact impedes the mutual love and community to which the realm of God calls us.

These cross-currents over self-sacrifice are affecting Mary and the decision she faces. Mary must carefully evaluate her personal situation. She must try to understand what kind of relationship she and the child will have and whether it ultimately will be one that will support the mutual growth of each. She must, in short, try to come to conclusions about the relative values of fetal life, her life and personal choices and development, and the life within the communities of which she is a part.

Freedom of Choice and Equality for Women

As has been discussed, the decisions Mary faces are in large measure left to her conscience. Hers is the freedom to exercise conscience, although the responsible use of conscience means consulting the wisdom available from the larger community, including her husband, her religious tradition, and her society. Mary must decide whether the use of her freedom to abort in this situation is a legitimate exercise of her power to control her own body or a misuse of her power to control her body by denying life to the fetus she carries.

Freedom is part of the biblically-based understanding of justice which has evolved in Western thought. In the United States the legal system provides for individual freedom unless democratically determined laws are broken. The norm of freedom places the burden of proof on those who would restrict the control that Mary and other women have over their bodies. Opponents of legalized abortion are convinced they have satisfied this burden. They argue that just as society rightly denies freedom to a murderer, so it should deny a woman the right to abort a fetus, which in their view has full rights as a person. Proponents of legalized abortion counter by denying full legal status to fetal life in the early stages of pregnancy and point to the injustice of the state or any other body compelling Mary to bear a child. They argue that women should have the freedom to control conception in order to control their bodies and their lives. At issue is whether the power to control conception includes the right to abort a fetus, and whether this power to control fertility is essential to women's well-being.

Obviously, this notion of the right to control one's own body is a key element in the position that sees abortion as an option. Those who hold this position argue that in order for women to take control of their lives and to construct a meaningful life plan, they must have the capacity to break the link between sex and procreation. Otherwise their bodies, or

whoever controls their bodies, will control them, and pregnancy will inter-
rupt all possible plans except mothering. Statistically effective contraceptives and safe, affordable abortions make breaking the link possible for the
first time in history. Tom seems to be working out of an acceptance of this
view, one he hopes Mary will share.

For many who support choice, the right to choose is more than just a
symbol of the new-found freedom and equality of women. For those who
hold this view the freedom to choose is fundamental to all other justice-
claims of women. They argue that without the right to choose contraception
and ultimately abortion—the last resort in contraception—women will be
discriminated against. Employers, for example, will be reluctant to train
women for or employ them in significant positions because those employers
will anticipate that women will be in and out of the work force. There can
be no equality in the work place when women and men function under the
assumption that a woman's occupation will be subordinated to each and
every pregnancy.

Those who hold this view project that if the abortion choice is eliminated,
women's vocational options will narrow as women will have no certain
method of controlling fertility. In effect the traditional view of motherhood
will be forced on women. This would be an injustice to women, an injustice
compounded by the male domination of legislatures and the medical profession. Men would make the decisions and women would suffer the consequences. In the case study there is a taste of this in the arrogance of the
doctor who demands sterilization.

In essence, then, those who stand for women's choice in abortion argue
that for women the capacity to choose is the capacity to gain equality, new
identities, and new avenues for vocation. The very well-being of women is
at stake and society has a moral obligation to further this well-being.

Finally, part of the well-being of women will include openness to the
growth possibilities inherent in child rearing and housekeeping. If women
are to be free to choose how to pursue their lives, then obviously they must
be free to choose child rearing and homemaking as focal points of their
lives. It does no one good to draw the options as being between passive,
dull housewives and active, responsible career women. There are many
paths between the stereotypes.

Like many women, Mary seems caught between her socialization, which
led her to understand herself as first wife and mother and then secondarily
a person who could plan a life for herself, and the contemporary message
to women—sketched in the preceding paragraphs—that they are to evaluate themselves based on their own growth and achievements and not on
their fulfillment of ascribed roles. But society gives little help to women
caught between the demands of both views of women and their accompanying roles. For Mary this is not merely a choice between self and child,
but a forced choice between two conflicting selves that she would like to
integrate, but cannot.

THE CHOICE

The Mosaic view that regarded fetal life as potentially human and therefore of value, the norm of the goodness of life, and considerations of legitimate self-sacrifice would lead Mary Gardner in the direction of preserving the fetus. The norm of freedom makes her morally responsible for the decision. She must also consider the well-being of her family, her own circumstances, her new-found freedom, and who she is as a mother and a woman in society. While the family finances are strained, they are not impossible, and the child would enter a loving family.

Although Tom sees Mary's freedom from the restrictions of motherhood as a movement toward growth, Mary may not. Her identity may be so bound to the traditional role of motherhood that an abortion, indeed the view which allows choice in abortion, may be read by Mary as "pro-self." The sense of selfishness may so violate her identity as a care giver that it seems a denial of the invitation to fulfillment in the role of mother.

Mary speaks of a child, not a fetus. Since she sees her three children as "gifts of God," abortion might mean for her the destruction of God's good creation. Mary keeps her pregnancy a secret from almost everyone in her life. Her action implies that an abortion would be something "wrong," at least for her, and leave her with an immense burden of guilt. Her depression and emotional instability suggest she already feels this burden.

If abortion may be read as too "pro-self," then in contrast the decision to go to term and reject abortion may seem to her too "pro-birth." The norm of self-giving and self-sacrifice may be perceived as an alien demand forcing her to negate herself endlessly for child bearing and rearing.

In light of this, Tom favors an abortion. But in the early going he was not of much help to Mary. His insensitive announcement of his preference while still in Spain shocked Mary and is partially responsible for the alienation they both feel. In counseling, however, Tom expresses much greater sensitivity for Mary's growth as a person, which he feels will be enhanced if she does not have another child. Still, he offers her only the abortion option to achieve personal growth. The case does not reveal everything about Tom and Mary's discussion of the matter, but based on the information in the case it is clear that Tom does not appear ready to sacrifice and take on more child care if Mary decides to have the child. This apparent unwillingness to sacrifice suggests he wants what is best for Mary, but only if there is no cost for him.

For her part, Mary expresses concern for the quality of life of her three children already born, as well as for needy children in her global community. The suffering of children worldwide makes its claim even on the Gardners' meager resources.

Beyond these considerations there are apparently strong internal pressures for Mary to be a loving wife who pleases her husband. Tom is rightly concerned that these pressures could lead Mary to a decision based on what he wants and eventually increase the alienation between them.

Rather than facing alone an impossible choice between the potential life within her and her own and her family's needs, Mary may be freed by considering her interdependence with other persons. She might ask how her decision would enhance not only her well-being and that of her immediate family, but the well-being of those in the wider community. Mary's freedom may come in how she and Tom make the decision. She has an opportunity to help others understand the dilemma of an unwanted pregnancy and simultaneously to draw on the considerable resources of a community in making decisions and mediating care.

Opening to the community has its costs, however, and while participation in community is essential to wholeness, so is a place apart. Somehow Tom and Mary will have to balance these needs and come to a decision which mends their relationship and, above all else, makes available God's love and new life.

Whatever the decision, Mary's present depression and the seeming choice between guilt over a decision to abort and resentful surrender to having another child must be faced. Presumably both Tom and Mary "know" the healing power of forgiveness which comes through faith in Jesus Christ. The task will be to unite head and heart so that this power can do its work.

ADDITIONAL RESOURCES

Burtchaell, James Tunstead, ed. *Abortion Parley*. Kansas City: Andrews and McNeel, 1980.

Frochock, Fred M. *Abortion*. Westport, Conn.: Greenwood Press, 1983.

Gilligan, Carol. *In a Different Voice: Psychological Theory and Women's Development*. Cambridge, Mass.: Harvard, 1982.

Harrison, Beverly Wildung. *Our Right to Choose*. Boston: Beacon Press, 1983.

Jung, Patricia Beattie, and Thomas A. Shannon, eds. *Abortion and Catholicism: The American Debate*. New York: Crossroad, 1988.

Luker, Kristin. *Abortion and the Politics of Motherhood*. Berkeley: University of California Press, 1984.

Rubin, Eva R. *Abortion, Politics, and the Courts: Roe v. Wade and Its Aftermath*. Westport, Conn.: Greenwood Press, 1982.

Case

Witnessing to Life

Mary and John Haven were in a state of shock as they sat in their living room trying to grasp the significance of this new decision they had to make in the life of their comatose son and waiting for words of counsel from Father Charles Wilbur.

Tom had been eighteen years old and in perfect health. He was tall, handsome, and active in sports in high school. During the summer two years ago he had been helping his father on the family farm. He had also volunteered to be on the local ambulance squad as a way of serving his community. He was planning on medicine as a career. Responding to a call from a person suffering from a heart attack, the ambulance collided with a car which had run through a stop sign. Tom sustained massive head injuries.

Unconscious, he was rushed to the hospital where doctors performed a tracheotomy which improved his respiration. Tom never regained consciousness. The concussion entailed damage to the entire brain. After one month in a comatose state, he was transferred to a nursing home, where he received skilled care. Although his heart rate, blood pressure, and respiration continued with youthful vigor, he was immobile and helpless. Feeding was accomplished through a tube. Each day he was bathed and changed before his parents came to visit.

As the weeks and months passed, Tom's parents watched for signs that he was coming out of his coma. Sometimes they would be encouraged by a seeming glimmer in his eye or a twitch of his muscles. They would begin to hope. But nothing developed.

The most sophisticated neurological tests indicated that brain activity was minimal. Although Tom was not entirely brain dead, the doctors

This case was prepared by James B. Hofrenning. Copyright © The Case Study Institute. The names of all persons have been disguised to protect the privacy of those involved in this situation.

doubted that he would ever come out of the coma. Still, Mary and John continued to hope and pray.

Dr. Karen Cook, their family doctor, discussed with them the possibility of halting nourishment. She stressed that because Tom showed no signs of life in the sense of being aware and interacting with human beings, it would be the humane thing to permit him to die peacefully. Christians, she insisted, do not consider the mere functioning of the body to be of ultimate significance, but rather the life of a person lived in community. She said she had come to the conclusion that feeding through tubes was a form of extraordinary medical treatment—merely a way of keeping a mindless body alive—and therefore not morally required.

John's uncle, Bill Thompson, who was visiting from Texas at the time and was present in the doctor's office, was aghast at the doctor's comments. His big frame stiffened as he quoted the commandment, "Thou shalt not kill." He seemed ready to pound the table as he declared that terminating nourishment would be a form of killing. More calmly, he added that killing destroys relations in a community as much as it destroys individuals. Then he got up, ready to leave the office, and concluded, "God alone has the right to take life away, because he is the one who authors it in the first place."

John looked sadly at Uncle Bill and asked, "How can you kill a person who is already dead?" He didn't wait for an answer. He knew what Bill would say. Rather, he asked another question, this time the words barely audible. "Could keeping him alive also destroy community?"

Mary turned to John and replied, rather softly, "I could never agree to the termination of nourishment. I nourished him as a child before he could talk, before he could walk, and now, though he is not conscious, he is a human being, my son. Giving nourishment is the most basic, most humane form of care." Then looking at the doctor, she concluded more vigorously, "Fate has dealt Tom a tragic blow. But I refuse to accept an act which would deliberately end his life. Do we really wish his death?"

As time passed, little by little, Mary and John lost hope. Tom's younger brother Andrew, an outstanding student who also wanted to go into medicine, was ready to enter college in the fall, but there were no longer funds available for his education. The family savings, including the equity in the home and farm, were exhausted as were insurance funds. They refused to go on welfare. Tom's fifteen-year-old sister, Grace, was often left alone while her parents visited Tom. A change seemed to take place in her personality. She started hanging around with "a different crowd." Her school work and extracurricular activities suffered drastically. Meanwhile, her parents became increasingly depressed and irritable. The use of sleeping pills, tranquilizers, and alcohol became part of the routine of their lives.

One November evening during the supper hour, Mary suggested that maybe this year they should have Thanksgiving dinner with Tom at the nursing home. Grace quickly responded by saying that she had other plans and excused herself from the dinner table. Andrew said nothing but also slipped away. Mary, with tears in her eyes, turned to her husband and said, "I feel I have lost not only Tom but Grace and Andrew." John replied, "And sometimes I feel that I am losing you." Then he added, with some desperation as he put his arm around his wife, "There must be some better way of dealing with a tragedy like this."

In December Tom contracted a severe chest cold which turned into pneumonia. After Dr. Cook made the diagnosis, she called John and Mary. She asked them if she should prescribe penicillin and aggressively treat the pneumonia. Without the medicine, she said, Tom would live only three or four days and die quite peacefully.

Father Charles Wilbur, the priest at Tom and Mary's church, was informed of the situation and called on Mary and Tom after supper that evening. Andrew and Grace were also home. For two hours pent-up grief and anger, resentment and guilt were expressed. The priest was about to bring the visit to an end with some words of counsel and prayer when Uncle Bill called. He asked about Tom. After hearing their uncertainty about what to do, he urged them to be unrelenting in their treatment of the pneumonia. "Life is sacred," he said. "We should do all in our power to preserve it."

John hung up the phone and turned to Father Wilbur with a confused look on his face. "How can life in such a state be called sacred?" he asked him.

Commentary

Witnessing to Life

John and Mary Haven had decided that halting nourishment to their son Tom, who had been comatose for months, was not an acceptable option. Since that decision, Tom had remained in his coma. The question many months later is whether they should choose to treat his pneumonia or not. Since Tom's accident the dimensions of the situation have shifted from an initial focus on Tom's right to life and the obligations of family and medical staff to nourish that life. Now Mary and John feel forced to consider the effects of their decisions about Tom on the rest of the family, effects which they feel are destructive.

THE MOURNING PROCESS

Long-term coma patients present great difficulties for the spiritual and mental health of families and friends, because the onset of the coma initiates in them a process of mourning. The continuation of the coma lengthens the mourning process, which can be ended only by recovery or death of the patient.

The diagnosis of any terminal illness precipitates the beginning of mourning in friends and relatives. It raises the threat of loss of the patient, fear of death itself, and anger both at mortality and its arbitrariness. Many people initially experience denial, a refusal to admit the reality of the situation.

For many mourners the period preceding death is one of sorting out and facing up to these conflicting emotions. Death itself is usually the moment when we begin the final stages of integrating and accepting the various parts of the mourning process, in order to reconcile ourselves with the death and to take up our lives with some sense of peace, despite our loss. When patients are conscious, meeting their needs, being present for them, mutually reviewing their lives and relationships with us, expressing the feelings for them previously unexpressed, can all help the mourner as well as the terminal patient by providing direction and structure for this daunting time.

But when the patient is comatose for long periods of time, especially when the coma has come on abruptly without previous signals of impending death, the mourning process is more difficult. For there is no gradual sinking toward death that allows the mourners to prepare. There is also no possible interaction with the patient to structure the mourning process. Relatives and friends stand by helplessly, useless to the patient, suddenly left to struggle through separation, loss, and fear of death. When death is interminably postponed, when there is no closure in sight, it becomes difficult to go on with one's life. In many ways one is stuck in the past.

Some people face this dilemma by trying to create closure through deciding that the patient is dead and life must go on. But their decision is supported by none of the social rituals created to help people make this transition from focusing on life, to death, and back to life. Wakes, funerals and burials, and the customs surrounding them are normally ways that a society recognizes the fact of death and then calls mourners nevertheless to transfer attention back to the living. Andrew and Grace seem to have taken this route. They may be suffering from the lack of social support for their decision that Tom is dead and they are alive. Their decision is probably therefore surrounded by feelings of guilt over their possible abandonment of Tom, feelings which serve to alienate them from others, especially from their parents who have insisted that Tom is still a part of the family. There is probably also some resentment both of their parents' preoccupation with Tom, and of their apparent willingness to sacrifice the other children's futures to keep Tom in his present state.

Mary seems to have chosen a different option, to see Tom as still living despite the long coma. She therefore wanted to celebrate Thanksgiving at the nursing home, and refused to make distinctions between Tom's condition now and that of the infant she nourished. John refers to Tom as already dead, but it is very unclear whether he has been emotionally ready to give Tom up, as evidenced by his continuing visits. He seems aware that as long as Tom continues as he is, the family will not be able to come together or plan their future.

There are, of course, other hardships involved. The loss of economic security, of Andrew's college fund, and of the equity in the home and farm are difficult to bear. In addition it often happens that long vigils at the side of dying relatives isolate us from friends and acquaintances both because so much time is spent at the hospital or nursing home, and because our preoccupation with the patient either forces friends to take on our mourning as their own, or severely lessens the degree of common interests we have with them.

RESPECT FOR LIFE

There have been various approaches taken in Christian ethics to situations such as this. Uncle Bill represents one, the understanding that God is the author of life, and only God has the right to end life. The biblical tradition tells us that life is a gift of God to be valued and respected. The

Old Testament depicts the value of life not in terms of enduring biological functions, but in terms of participation within a human community. To this end individuals who constituted a threat to the community were executed (murderers) or exiled from the community (lepers) under the Mosaic law. In Genesis, the punishment of Cain for his brother's murder was exile. He was forced to wander the face of the earth, and his punishment was considered in Israel to be increased, not ameliorated, by God's vow that no one would kill him to end his exile. Individual physical life is not absolutely valuable; for the Old Testament, the welfare of the human community comes first. But the Old Testament gives no warrant for taking innocent individual life in the interest of community well-being.

The New Testament contains no warrants for taking life at all, but only for sacrificing one's own life in the interests of others. The miracles that Jesus performed as signs of the kingdom he announced were intended to restore community. The significance of the healing miracles was not merely the alleviation of physical ails, but the restoration of the sick to the community. The lepers and the woman with the discharge were unclean, and excluded from community. Those possessed by demons, the paralytics – the chronically ill in general – were excluded from participation in the life of the community until healed by Jesus.

CRITERIA FOR DECIDING

Scripture does not answer for us the question that John puts to Uncle Bill: whether Tom should be understood as living. One piece of information which would be helpful to know in deciding this question is whether or not the low level of brain activity Tom demonstrates is irreversible. The doctors doubt that the coma will end, but this is not to say that there are not some minority of cases in which the patient recovers. Could this coma end without death, and what kind of life could Tom have if he were to emerge from the coma? If we knew whether coma patients with his level of brain activity and his length of coma have ever recovered, and how often, we could better make a decision. If the doctors base their doubt on the absence of *any* instances of recovery, on the other hand, then a case for Tom's right to life becomes weaker, since those things which make life valuable are and will be absent.

Yet sanctity of life arguments are not premised solely on the rights of the patient. An important part of the distinction between active and passive euthanasia is based in the need to respect life in such a way that the life of the wider society is enhanced. We all need to feel that our own lives are valuable and respected; when persons take active roles in ending the life of another, the living feel less secure in their own lives. In addition, active roles in ending even lingering deaths can cause acute feelings of doubt and paralyzing guilt in the actors. The more passive the role in ending life, the less likely are such recriminations. In general, then, even when patients are both clearly comatose and irreversibly dying and there seems to be no purpose to continuing life, the more passive means toward death are preferable. Passive here would refer not only to low levels of involvement, but also to the amount of pain the patient seems to suffer. Sometimes it is difficult to decide the least painful withdrawal. The untreated comatose pneumonia patient may gasp for breath and rattle for hours, perhaps a few days; the unfed coma patient is silent, but may fade to nothingness over a period of days to weeks.

The Catholic church's distinction between ordinary and extraordinary means of preserving life which Dr. Cook invokes is not very helpful in this case. Although food *is* clearly an ordinary means of preserving life not to be morally withdrawn, *intravenous* feeding is often considered extraordinary, and Tom's tubal feeding lies somewhere between these. Tubal feeding would be extraordinary care were Tom to be confined to the care of his family. Even within the hospital, tubal feeding could be extraordinary care if the comatose patient cannot retain food, if feeding and retching are constant, or if the tubal feeding causes other medical problems, as is sometimes the case. Similarly, it is unclear whether antibiotics for Tom's pneumonia fall under ordinary care or not, though they are standard treatment for pneumonia. Pope Pius XII, who first used the ordinary/extraordinary distinction, once defined extraordinary means of preserving life as "means that do not involve any grave burden for self or others." This definition can cover many treatments, and would seem by itself to support Dr. Cook's stance. Catholic medical ethics has clearly taken the position, supported by bishops and clergy (some of whom have testified in court cases), that irreversible comatose patients need not be artificially kept alive by mechanical means; those means may be disconnected. But Tom is not maintained by respirators, mechanical hearts, or other such mechanisms.

WHO SHOULD DECIDE?

In cases where euthanasia is a possibility, an important issue is who should decide. When the patient is competent, the decision is his or hers, and a decision to die is usually accepted by the medical staff so long as the patient is clearly terminal and the means acceptable. With comatose patients the decision is left to close relatives and doctors. The doctors make the initial decision as to whether considering euthanasia is appropriate in a given case. If there is some reasonable hope of recovering some quality of life, doctors do not raise the issue of euthanasia. When it is raised, usually by doctors, the final decision is left to the family, as it is in this case. For fear of wrongful death suits, doctors and hospitals will seldom agree to even the most passive euthanasia decisions if there is any member of the immediate family opposed to that decision. The presumption is for extending life. This is as it should be in a society which can afford such approaches. If keeping Tom breathing occurred at the cost not of home and farm equity and college funds, but of feeding the family and providing basic shelter, respect for life could appropriately lead to discontinuing support at more basic levels, as Pius XII made clear.

CARE FOR ONESELF

One of the reasons that life support decisions for comatose patients are so difficult for close relatives in our society is that Christianity is most often understood to demand that we suffer out of love for others. Many theological understandings of agape, Christian love, revolve around agape as self-sacrificing love. Such an understanding in this case would encourage all the members of the family to accept the suffering placed on them by Tom's situation, and to understand as illegitimate any attempt to balance their personal needs against Tom's. Such an approach would not mean that only Tom's interests count; John, for example, could balance Tom's needs against those of Grace, Andrew, and Mary. But understanding agape as self-sacrificing love would preclude John from considering his own needs and desires as having any weight in this case.

Sometimes we attempt to avoid religiously based guilt feelings by not only excluding our own needs from the decision making, but by discounting as well those whose needs are closest to our own. In this case, perhaps both John and Mary have given more weight to Tom's right to life and less to those of family members who share their need for closure, for economic security, and for a return to normal family life.

Many would respond that a right to life has inherent priority over these other rights and needs. But it is not clear that what life Tom retains has this same priority. This is the issue here. Many theologians reject the view of agape as self-sacrificing love, and understand self-sacrifice as having only instrumental value. It is a part of love only when it contributes to ultimate mutual good. Such a view is based on an insistence that Jesus Christ did not come to earth to suffer and die for humankind. Rather, he loved humanity so well that he devoted himself to the furthering of the reign of God, which he understood as the inclusion of his followers into the rewarding but demanding relationship of mutual love which he shared with God. In committing himself to this reign, he took a serious risk of suffering and death. Love demands a willingness to suffer for and with loved ones, but that suffering is not the essence of love, rather only an expression of it. This implies that not all suffering is good, but only that aimed at mutual good, only that which furthers the reign of God. In this view, we have to ask how keeping Tom breathing furthers the reign of God.

APPLYING THE PREFERENTIAL OPTION FOR THE POOR

When Christian theologians today insist on a preferential option for the poor as central to Jesus' teaching, they, like Jesus, understand the "poor" to include all those in need, those who are marginalized from participation in social decision making. This would include the comatose, who are totally dependent. But it may be simplistic to understand a preferential option for the poor as requiring a decision to keep Tom alive. The rationale for the preferential option for the poor is that God hears the cries of the poor and oppressed, and takes their need as the divine cause. God's abhorrence of human suffering thus causes God to accompany the poor in a struggle for wholeness and justice. Our preference for the poor is predicated on God's, and God's is based on a commitment to rectify the situation of the oppressed by empowering their struggle.

In our case, we have more than one person in need. If, to use classic theological language, Tom's soul already rests with God, then his situation is not reversible, and the impetus of the preferential option will call for a decision to aid those needy who *can* be helped. On the other hand, if Tom's coma is still reversible, then he is needy, and his needs should weigh heavily against competing needs. Once we abandon a definition of life as pure biological existence, almost any moral principles to which we have recourse will make a final decision hinge on social analytic calculus of need.

CALCULATING NEED

In making such a calculation, John and Mary would need data about other coma patients. What percentage of coma patients recover consciousness? How many of those have brain activity as low as Tom's? Have any of these recovered after more than a year in a coma? If the answer is no, that there are no recoveries in cases similar to Tom's or in cases in any way comparable, the decision becomes in some ways easier. John and Mary could then apply scriptural insights about life being communal and participative, and decide that the needs of the rest of the family take precedence here.

It would then be appropriate for Dr. Cook to sit down with the family and determine what should be done. If Tom is in a final and irreversible stage of movement toward death, then therapeutic (curing) procedures are no longer in order, but other kinds of care are still appropriate. They might decide not to give antibiotics; they might call upon their Catholic tradition in deciding to use antibiotics but to draw the line at mechanical respiration or aspiration. The family must choose the decision which they feel is best for the common good.

The family should involve the nursing staff in their decision. No one, doctors or family, should make decisions about ending life without consulting those who must carry out such decisions. Many nurses, like many doctors, choose their careers out of a commitment to healing, allied with a call to nurture. To have to care for patients—to change sheets, feed patients, bathe them—day in and day out, and be unable to provide the oxygen for which a patient gasps, or the antibiotics that would relieve a high fever, is painful and often experienced as coerced betrayal. Not only would the nursing staff have valuable insights about implementing let-die decisions, but they have a right to participate in decisions that fall to them to implement.

Finally, if it is certain that Tom's condition is going to result in his death, then at the time the decision to let-die is made, Father Wilbur should call the family together for Tom's final reception of the Anointing of the Sick. Tom has undoubtedly already received this sacrament, since it is given to the sick as well as the dying, but the grace of the sacrament is not limited to the recipient. The family should participate in a service of farewell at Tom's bedside. This would bring them all together at the same point in the mourning process and allow them to be with others who loved Tom; it would give them a ceremony through which to bless Tom, to celebrate his life, and to recognize that his life has ended.

FAITHFULNESS IN SUFFERING

If, on the other hand, Tom still has some chance of recovery, the decision will be more complicated because less clear. Does it make a difference whether he has one chance in a hundred, or one chance in ten thousand of emerging from the coma? Are the Havens obliged to do everything to keep Tom's body functioning even if it results in further estrangement from their other children and a deterioration of their health and their financial security? Perhaps they are. For if Tom were conscious, but suffering from severe organ and bone damage, the family could still be divided over the parents' preoccupation with Tom, their financial security would still be gone, and the parents might still be reliant on drugs and alcohol. But were Tom conscious, however damaged, they could not morally decide for his death. If he were conscious but dying, the choice would be his alone. If he were conscious but stable, euthanasia would not be appropriate, for the term "euthanasia" means "good death," and is about choosing to hasten a death that is already imminent in the interests of making that death more humane.

Sometimes the Christian ethic calls us to suffer in our love. There is sometimes no way to avoid the deepening paths of suffering. The promise of Christianity is that God will be with us as we suffer, and that if we open ourselves up to God's presence, God will not let us be destroyed by suffering.

This does not mean that if full care for Tom is to be continued, then John and Mary must allow the patterns of alienation to continue in their family. They would need to find counseling help for the children, perhaps through Father Wilbur or the hospital. John and Mary need to seek help for their chemical dependency before it becomes too deeply habitual. Perhaps they could locate persons or groups of persons who had faced similar protracted deaths of loved ones, perhaps through their parish bereavement group. They need to focus some attention on Grace and Andrew, and demonstrate that the primary focus of their lives is not inert in the nursing home, but is their family, of which Tom is only one part.

Mary and John should also look into welfare. Tom is eighteen; in most states he is a legal adult. He is totally dependent; he should be eligible for some level of public assistance. If the level of public money available is not sufficient for the care he now receives, his parents must decide whether to supplement it, worsening their financial situation, or move Tom to a less expensive facility with perhaps a lower level of care. The damage inflicted on the rest of the family by the grave economic consequences are too great for the Havens to be exonerated for refusing welfare on grounds of pride alone. However, if welfare would make demands which further endanger their economic well-being, such as sale of the farm and home, they would not be obliged to apply.

Mary and John also need to seek out other relatives and friends who could take on some of their burden. This could not only lessen the time demands on them, but might provide a real sense of support and community for them and for Grace and Andrew. Such support could help the Havens feel that there is some *social* recognition of and support for Tom's life. Perhaps Uncle Bill and other relatives could be invited to help with the costs, and to spend vacations sitting with Tom. All those who value life should be a part of supporting it in the difficult cases; one who feels as strongly as Uncle Bill would surely respond positively to such an invitation.

The Havens have sacrificed a great deal. Now they need to press for more information about comas, and then choose a path of action. Both avenues call for further pain: either to accept a terrifying responsibility for ending their son's life, or to continue to live loyal to and mourning for a child who cannot respond, despite the familial and financial problems this entails.

ADDITIONAL RESOURCES

Jonas, Hans. "The Right to Die." In Thomas Shannon, ed., *Bioethics,* rev. ed. New York: Paulist, 1981.

McCormick, Richard A. "To Save or Let Die." In Shannon, ed., *Bioethics.*

Maguire, Daniel. "The Freedom to Die." In Shannon, ed., *Bioethics.*

Nelson, James. *Human Medicine: Ethical Perspectives on New Medical Issues.* Minneapolis: Augsburg, 1973.

Shannon, Thomas. "The Withdrawal of Treatment: The Cost and Benefits of Guidelines." In Shannon, ed., *Bioethics.*

Shannon, Thomas, and Charles N. Fazo. *Let Them Go Free: A Ritual and Guidelines for the Withdrawal of Life Support.* Kansas City: Sheed and Ward, 1987.

Appendix

Teaching Ethics
by the Case Method

The authors' use of the case method to teach Christian ethics is conscious and deliberate. The educational philosophy behind the authors' use of the method is Paulo Freire's notion of "education as liberation" from his now classic *Pedagogy of the Oppressed*. In that volume Freire distinguishes between liberating education and the "banking" approach to education. "Liberating education," he says, "consists in acts of cognition, not transference of information." In contrast the banking approach views education as a matter of possession — the teacher "deposits" information in a student who, as an "empty vessel, receives, memorizes, and repeats." A "withdrawal" is made at exam time with the hope that some "interest" has accrued.

Besides involving acts of cognition, liberating education also involves genuine dialogue between student and teacher with the realization that they are partners educating one another. The goal in this "problem-posing" approach is the development of "critical consciousness" and "creative power" leading to the transformation of one's world rather than passive adaptation to it. The authors of this book hope that the cases contained in it will engage students and teachers in a dialogue that will free them to apply new insights and learnings to their own unique experiences.

The contrast between liberating and banking approaches can be drawn too sharply, of course. By stressing education as liberation the authors do not imply that facts, theories, and knowledge of situations and contexts are unimportant. These are critical to informed ethical decisions. They are just not the essence, which should always be the individual in a community sustained by a critical consciousness and the creative work of the Holy Spirit.

The difference between making necessary background information available to students for purposes of empowerment and the banking approach is not always easy to discern. Ideally, with liberating education there are no pat answers. Dialogic forms of education stressing experience are preferred whenever possible. Questions are asked first and problems posed. Then the provision of information responds to a need and opens up alternatives. Students are encouraged to develop and share resources with other members of the learning community. Both critical and constructive tasks are taken seriously. Decision and action are important outcomes.

But problem-posing education is not just a matter of form. The spirit is different. Teachers and students are both seen as learners with something to offer. The community of learners is central, and the dynamism of community endeavor provides the spirit which pushes and pulls individuals to their best insights and makes them active participants rather than passive recipients.

Although the case approach is not without limitations, the authors have found that it has great potential for both liberating education and the teaching of Christian ethics. The approach is dialogic by its very nature. As participants in the discussion of a problem, students teach others in the process of learning themselves. Cases are written so as to transfer the point of decision to the student. The commentaries and even some of the cases provide background and alternatives for the development of a critical consciousness, a key stage on the path of liberation. The potential for creative teachers to enliven the classroom experience is virtually unlimited.

As for the teaching of Christian ethics, the case method as used in this volume opens a number of doors. First, it introduces students to contemporary ethical issues. This is the reason the cases have been arranged under specific problem areas and why the commentaries focus primarily on the central issues. The authors would contend that thorough knowledge of issues is one of the first steps in a liberating education.

Second, cases are a way of entry into Christian tradition. At some point both teachers and students need to ask how the Bible, theology, and the church inform issues. The case on euthanasia, for example, raises questions about the nature of God and the purposes of human life. The case on homosexuality challenges accepted perspectives on sin. The cases on violence lead to an investigation of the church's historical stances. Thus at the same time students are addressing issues and making decisions, they are in a position to learn the content of the tradition and how to apply it.

Knowledge of the tradition is liberating if it helps students detect selective and self-serving attempts to manipulate authority for the purpose of supporting conclusions arrived at on other grounds. Tradition provides an alternative perspective to understand and challenge cultural myopia. It provides the wisdom of experience, lends authority, offers general guidance, sets limits, and designates where the burden of proof lies—all helpful in finding ways through the maze of experience and conflicting opinion and on to good moral choices.

Third, repeated use of the method encourages students to economize in the way they approach ethical problems. That is to say, cases teach ethical method. The more cases are used and the more explicit method is made, the more indelible a pattern for making choices becomes. However little students retain of the content of a given issue or the theology which informs it, the authors are convinced they should leave a course in ethics knowing how to address ethical problems and liberated from the confusion of too many options and conflicting guidelines.

The authors also believe that an essential component of any pattern of learning is drawing on the insights of others, which the case approach encourages. Discovery of the limitations of individuals acting alone and of the liberation in learning to trust others in community is an important benefit of the dialogic approach. The case setting calls on participants to listen to one another, to challenge their own and others' perceptions, and to build on one another's insights and experiences.

Fourth and last, the case approach is an experience-based form of education. As one veteran case teacher put it, "Cases are experience at a fraction of the cost." The cases in this volume represent the experience of others which students can make their own without going through all the turmoil. The cases encourage students to express and apply their own experience. Finally, the cases push students to "practice" resolving complex dilemmas of parenting, personal responsibility, individual and community rights, etc., and thus to add to their own experience.

CASES FOR GROUP DISCUSSION

As stated in the Introduction, there are numerous types of cases used in contemporary education. These range from a hypothetical problem, to a one-page "critical incident" or "verbatim" which reports a specific actual incident, to a four-hundred-page case history describing an event or situation. The type of case employed in this volume is modeled after those used by the Harvard Law and Business Schools and the Association for Case Teaching: that is, each case consists of selected information from an actual situation and raises specific issues or problems that require a response or decision on the part of one or more persons in the case. The problem should be substantive enough and so balanced in its approach that reasonable people would disagree about the most effective or appropriate response. As a pedagogical tool the case calls for a response not only from the case characters but from those studying the case.

Although cases can be extremely useful for inducing reflection by an individual reader, they are specifically designed for group discussion. They might be used in classrooms, retreat settings, community gatherings, or with any group seeking to gain new perspectives.

As this is a distinctive educational approach, the authors feel it is important to offer suggestions for guiding a case discussion. To begin with, while it is possible to hand out copies of shorter cases, for example, "Mary Gardner's Fourth Pregnancy" or "Rigor and Responsibility," and ask participants to read them immediately prior to discussion, the quality of discussion is heightened by careful advance reading. The case leader might suggest that participants: (1) read through a case at least twice; (2) identify the principal case characters; (3) in cases like "Eye of the Needle" develop a "time line" to indicate significant dates or events; (4) list the issues which appear to surface; and (5) think through a number of creative alternatives to the dilemma posed. Small groups meeting to prepare ideas about a case prior to a larger group discussion can also be extremely beneficial to the total learning experience. This type of detailed and structured analysis of a case is equally valuable for the individual reader. A structured process for entering each case provides a base that may be challenged, expanded, or affirmed by the commentary which follows each case.

The primary functions of a case leader are catalyst, probe, and referee. A good case leader highlights insights and assists in summarizing the learnings from the discussion. As a facilitator, the case leader is responsible for clear goals and objectives for each discussion session and for guiding the quality and rhythm of the discussion. Many who have worked with cases suggest that the most crucial factor for a rewarding case experience is the leader's style. Openness, affirmation, and sensitivity to the group create the climate in which genuine dialogue can occur. Second in importance is that the case leader thoroughly master the case facts and develop a discussion plan or teaching note.

It is important to keep in mind that there is no single way to approach a case. The Introduction to this volume highlights in general terms what the authors find significant in the cases, and the commentaries offer the authors' analysis of more specific issues. Neither the Introduction nor the commentaries should constrain teachers or students from taking different entry points or addressing different topics or issues.

Whatever approach is taken should draw participants into dialogue, uncover what is needed to make an informed ethical decision, and push students to a critical consciousness and finally to a decision which will help them when they encounter similar situations in their own lives.

There are no "right" answers to the dilemmas presented in this volume. This means that the problems posed are open to a number of creative alternatives. This approach stands in contrast to a closed, problem-solving approach in which the right answer or solution known only by the teacher can be found in the back of the book. In a banking approach students are receptive objects of the teacher's wisdom and insight. In contrast, the case approach calls for participants to become active subjects in the learning process, to consider various responses, and to analyze the norms which inform their decisions.

Experienced case leaders report that recording the essence of participants' contributions on newsprint or a chalkboard gives order and direction to the discussion. A skilled instructor is able to help participants show the relation among contributions. The leader should be willing to probe respondents for additional clarification of points.

Honest conflict of opinion is often characteristic of these dialogues and can be quite constructive in a case discussion. The case leader may need to assume the role of referee and urge participants to listen to one another and to interpret the reasoning behind their conclusions. It is often helpful to put debating participants in direct dialogue by asking, for example, "Laura, given your earlier position, how would you respond to Mark's view?" The leader's role as mediator is also significant, especially as a discussion nears conclusion. It is helpful to encourage a group to build on one another's suggestions. One constructive process for closing a case discussion is to ask participants to share their insights from the discussion.

Two additional techniques are often employed by case leaders. A discussion may be focused and intensified by calling participants to vote on a controversial issue. For example, in a discussion of the case "More Light" one might ask, "If you were a member of the church governing board, would you vote for or against the motion to become a 'More Light' church?" The dynamics of case teaching reveal that once persons have taken a stand, they frequently assume greater ownership of the decision and are eager to defend or interpret their choice. Voting provides an impetus for participants to offer the implicit reasons and assumptions that stand behind a given decision. It can also be a test of the group's response, especially if one or two outspoken participants have taken a strong stand on one particular side of an issue. If a vote is taken, it is important to give participants an opportunity to interpret the reasons behind their decision.

Another way to heighten existential involvement in a case is to ask participants to assume the roles of persons in the case for a brief specified period of the discussion. When individuals are requested to assume roles before a group, experienced case teachers have found that rather than making assignments prior to class or asking for volunteers, it is better to invite participants who give evidence during the case discussion that they can identify with the characters and understand the issues. It is often most helpful for individuals in a role play to move into chairs visible to the entire group. The personal integrity of those who assume individual roles can be guarded by giving them an opportunity to "de-role." This is done by asking them, for example, how they felt during the conversation and by asking them to return to their original seats. Then the group can be called on to share learnings from the experience.

Notwithstanding the preceding suggestions for case teaching, the authors wish to acknowledge that a good case discussion is not ultimately dependent on a trained professional teacher or a learned group of participants. A gifted leader is one who listens well, encourages participants to do the same, and genuinely trusts the wisdom, insights, and personal experiences of the group. To benefit significantly from the cases a reader needs to be willing to wrestle honestly with the issues in the cases and to evaluate with an open mind the insights of the commentaries.

Most case teachers prepare in advance a "teaching note" with suggestions for the general direction of the discussion as well as clear, transitional questions to move from one topic to the next. The following note is intended as an illustration of how the first case in this volume, "Rigor and Responsibility," might be taught in a short session.

A. Read the case if not preassigned. (ten minutes)

B. Have the class sketch a biography of each character. (ten to fifteen minutes)

C. Identify the basic question: How is a family to live? Alternatively, should an affluent family follow the rigorous "holy poverty" of Jesus or another option which might be called "responsible consumption," stressing right use and good stewardship. (one to two minutes)

D. Identify alternative issues. (five minutes) (This category could be eliminated if the basic question is the focus. Or, one of the following issues could become the main issue.)
  1. Stewarding an inheritance.
  2. Living in an impoverished and malnourished world.
  3. Discovering the biblical and theological witness on justice, wealth, poverty, possessions, and consumption.
  4. Overworking in modern society.
  5. Making a family decision.
  6. Dealing with guilt.
  7. Acting as an individual in a world dominated by mass culture.
  8. Distributing income and wealth.
  9. Raising children.

E. Ask each student to identify with one of the following: (ten minutes)

  1. Nancy or Clea.
  2. Nathan.
  3. Al Messer.
  4. The children.

F. Adjourn to four separate groups. (twenty minutes)

  1. Discuss what is and what should be the normative position of the character selected. Point to:
    a. Biblical and theological views of justice, wealth, poverty, and consumption.
    b. The two normative positions identified in the title of the case.
    c. The norms of justice and sustainable sufficiency.
                        OR
  2. Discuss the family relationships and how they should be worked through to arrive at a decision. Point to:
    a. The involvement of the Trapp family in a number of issues, the extent of its giving, and the crisis of the family in the United States.

     b. Cultural attitudes in the local community.
     c. Poverty and malnutrition in the world community.
     d. Traditional patriarchal family patterns.
OR

  3. Discuss the method question. How is a Christian family to decide?
     a. Point to the normative approach and the situational approach.
     b. Apply each to the case and note the differences.
OR

  4. Discuss the character question. What are the characteristics of a person who responds well to the main problem. Point to:
     a. Basic character orientation, loyalties, and worldviews.
     b. How this situation can build character.
  5. Select one person for a role play.
G. Conduct a role play of the four group representatives. Add David as an option. (ten to fifteen minutes)
  1. Role players discuss what the Trapps should do and how it relates to the main issue and to the alternative issues selected in "D" above.
H. Debrief and generate discussion. (ten minutes)
  1. De-role.
  2. Ask students to identify learnings.
  3. Open to a general class discussion of the main issue.

If more than a short period of time is available, the case leader has the opportunity to provide background in lectures, readings, films, small study groups, etc. The more background, the more the small group discussions can be open-ended.

CASES AND COURSE DESIGN

How might cases be used in a course in Christian ethics? For starters the authors recommend using cases in conjunction with other methods. Cases can be overworked and the freshness they bring lost.

In terms of overall design the teacher might select one of the cases with high student interest and open with it the first day of class. Cases are good discussion starters, and early use can introduce students to the method, to the use of critical consciousness, and to the goal of liberating education.

Following this, several general sessions on ethics would be appropriate including something on the nature and task of ethics, the use of the tradition, and the nature of situations, contexts, relationships, method, and decision making. Use of a case or two to illustrate specific aspects of the ethical discipline would also be appropriate.

The remainder of the course could be devoted to the specific issues categorized in this volume. Using all of the cases in a single semester might be ill-advised. Selectivity on the basis of student interest and teacher expertise would be more suitable.

The authors also recommend that students write "briefs," which are three- to four-page analyses of a case. This process accomplishes several things. First, it brings writing into a course. Second, particularly if graded, briefs heighten interest by increasing the stakes. Discussion is more intense because preparation is more thorough. Third, briefs offer less vocal students another avenue of expression. Fourth, briefs are a vehicle for method, since method is implicit in any act of organization. Methodological awareness is more pronounced if the teacher either requires a certain approach, or better, if the teacher insists that students be cognizant of the approach they are taking. Finally, the brief may serve as the first stage of a multiple draft term paper.

If briefs are used, students must be selective in what they cover. Three or four pages simply are not sufficient to analyze fully any case in this volume. In the briefs the students should to some extent present the facts in the case, perhaps by inserting short introductory summaries of the situation and a summation of pertinent facts or theories. Somewhere in the brief the "problem" should be clearly stated. The larger part of the brief should be devoted to the ethics of the issue, that is, to the derivation of norms, to the relating of norms to situations, and to the relationships involved in the case. Briefs may be expository and present the various sides, or they may be persuasive and argue one side in depth. While the commentaries in this volume avoid arguing for a particular side of an issue, the teacher may want students to make a decision and defend it.

For the workshop setting lack of time makes selectivity a cardinal virtue. The typical one-hour adult class is long enough for a good discussion of a single case, especially if it has been read prior to the session. Needless to say, the teacher should have a very clear idea of what he or she wants to accomplish and try to keep the class on task. An alert teacher, picking up on points in the discussion, can even insert background material through minilectures or asking students to elaborate. Small groups and role plays are especially helpful in stimulating discussion and breaking complex cases down into manageable units.

When more time is available, the two cases in each chapter are both available. One way to use both cases would be to lead off with one, then provide as much background as time permits, then finish the unit with the other. Alternatively, the teacher could utilize cases from different chapters to address the connecting themes, such as liberation and racism, listed in the Introduction.

LIMITATIONS OF THE CASE APPROACH

The case approach is not without limitations. First, case material must go through the personal filter of a writer. The situation is seen through the eyes of a single character with all the limitations of perspective. Seldom is enough information provided to satisfy participants. Crucial signals can be misread or misunderstood.

A second drawback is that the success of this form of education and presentation of material is dependent on the participation of readers and those discussing the cases. This can be quite disconcerting, even threatening, for those who are accustomed to a process in which they are handed a complete analysis from the lectern. For most learners tutored in an educational system which fosters, even if unintentionally, uncritical acceptance of the teacher's wisdom and authority, passive reception of information is the comfortable norm. This is, however, also the pattern of uncritical acceptance of the world as it is and helps lead to the loss of a vision of the world as it could be. Case leaders need to develop a mode of open rather than closed questions to induce genuine dialogue.

Third, case discussion can consume much more time and emotional energy than the direct communication of information. Intelligence is imperfectly correlated with the propensity to speak. Some participants are bent on dominating the discussion rather than learning from others. Tangents can carry the discussion into deadends. These limitations call for "referee" skills from the case leader.

Fourth, the forest can be lost for the trees, the macro for the micro, and the social for the individual by focusing on the particulars of a given situation to the exclusion of the context. For example, to reduce "Mary Gardner's Fourth Pregnancy" to a discussion of her moral decision is to lose sight of the critical social question about who should control the decision. The cases and in particular the commentaries have been written to help avoid this problem, but it is well to keep it in mind.

Finally, relative to other methods the case approach is limited in its capacity to convey large blocks of factual information. This drawback does not mean teachers need to revert automatically to the banking style of education. There are alternatives to "depositing" information, and even the lecture style can be approached with a different spirit. Many case teachers, for example, use "minilectures" in case discussion to introduce relevant material when it is needed.

The case approach is no panacea and must be seen as only one of many effective educational instruments. The authors have attempted to respond to the limitations of the approach. They have not removed them. They trust, however, that the cases in this volume and the approach can lead to constructive, liberating engagement with what they think are critical contemporary issues. Their trust is based on many years of experience with the approach. They are convinced that the approach is not only a valuable and liberating pedagogical instrument, but also a way to build community in the classroom.

List of Authors
and Contributors

AUTHORS

Alice Frazer Evans is director of writing and research, Plowshares Institute, Simsbury, Connecticut. She was educated at Agnes Scott College, the University of Wisconsin, and the University of Edinburgh. She is the co-author of numerous books, including *Casebook for Christian Living*; *Introduction to Christianity*; and *Pedagogies for the Non-Poor*.

Robert A. Evans is the executive director of Plowshares Institute, Simsbury, Connecticut. He studied at Yale University, at universities in Edinburgh, Berlin, and Basel, and received his doctorate from Union Theological Seminary, New York. He is the author and editor of several books, including *The Future of Philosophical Theology*; *Christian Theology: A Case Method Approach*; and *Human Rights: A Dialogue between the First and Third Worlds*.

Christine E. Gudorf is professor of theology at Xavier University in Cincinnati where she teaches ethics with special attention to liberation theology and feminism. Her publications address feminism and liberation theology and their impact on the Catholic Church.

Robert L. Stivers is a professor of Christian ethics at Pacific Lutheran University, in Tacoma, Washington. He holds a Ph.D. in social ethics from Union Theological Seminar and Columbia University, New York. His publications include *The Sustainable Society* and *Hunger, Technology & Limits to Growth*.

CONTRIBUTORS

William P. Bristol is a physician in private practice and the former dean of Mercer University Medical School, Macon, Georgia.

Nat B. Frazer is an assistant professor in the biology department, Mercer University, Macon, Georgia. Educated at Sagamon State University, the University of the South, and the University of Georgia, he has served as a research fellow at Woods Hole Oceanographic Institution. He is currently the editor of *Marine Turtle Newsletter* and has published extensively in journals of medical education, marine science, and herpetology.

James B. Hofrenning is a professor of religion at Concordia College, Moorhead, Minnesota. He was educated at Concordia College, Luther-Northwestern Theological Seminar in St. Paul, Union Theological Seminary, New York, and New York University. He has done postdoctoral work at Yale Divinity School and Duke University. His publications include *His Hand on Me* and (as editor) *Continuing Quest—Opportunities, Resources and Programs in Post Seminary Education.*

Janet M. Viktora teaches pastoral theology and is the coordinator of the Teaching Parish Program at Saint Paul Seminary School of Divinity of the School of Saint Thomas, St. Paul, Minnesota. She holds a Master of Arts degree in theology and is completing work on a graduate degree in pastoral studies with a focus on church administration.

J. Shannon Webster is the Executive Presbyter of the Sierra Blanca Presbytery, Roswell, N.M. He is a member of the task force on AIDS of the New Mexico Conference of Churches. He was educated at San Juan College, the University of New Mexico, and McCormick Theological Seminary, Chicago.

Elizabeth Wieman is a Presbyterian minister currently serving as associate pastor of Grace Congregational United Church of Christ in Framingham, Massachusetts. She is a member of the Strategic Action Committee of the Massachusetts Council of Churches. While serving as the Program Coordinator of Plowshares Institute, Simsbury, Connecticut, she traveled to South Africa, Kenya, Mexico, Nicaragua, and the People's Republic of China. She was educated at Williams College and Yale Divinity School.